The German Aesthetic Trad

This is the only available systematic critical overview of German aesthetics from 1750 to the present. The book begins with the work of Baumgarten and covers all the major writers on German aesthetics that follow, including Kant, Schiller, Schelling, Hegel, and Nietzsche up to Heidegger, Gadamer, and Adorno. The book offers a clear and nontechnical exposition of ideas, placing these in a wider philosophical context where necessary.

Such is the importance of German aesthetics that the market for this book will extend far beyond the domain of philosophy to such fields as literary studies, fine art, and music.

Kai Hammermeister teaches in the Department of Germanic Languages and Literature at The Ohio State University.

The German Aesthetic Tradition

KAI HAMMERMEISTER
The Ohio State University

PUBLISHED BY THE PRESS SYNDICATE OF THE UNIVERSITY OF CAMBRIDGE
The Pitt Building, Trumpington Street, Cambridge, United Kingdom

CAMBRIDGE UNIVERSITY PRESS
The Edinburgh Building, Cambridge CB2 2RU, UK
40 West 20th Street, New York, NY 10011-4211, USA
477 Williamstown Road, Port Melbourne, VIC 3207, Australia
Ruiz de Alarcón 13, 28014 Madrid, Spain
Dock House, The Waterfront, Cape Town 8001, South Africa

http://www.cambridge.org

First published 2002

Printed in the United Kingdom at the University Press, Cambridge

Typeface ITC New Baskerville 10/13.5 pt. *System* LaTeX 2ε [TB]

A catalog record for this book is available from the British Library.

Library of Congress Cataloging in Publication data available

ISBN 0 521 78065 9 hardback
ISBN 0 521 78554 5 paperback

For Matthew Crosby

Contents

Preface

The questions regarding art and beauty are as old as philosophy itself, or older, considering that Homer, Hesiod, and Pindar already reflect on the role and particular gifts of the poet. Yet for the longest time, art and beauty have been treated separately for the most part. The two notions were generally discussed in the context of other philosophical issues in which art and beauty played only a subordinate role. Philosophically, beauty more often than not was treated in the context of metaphysics, be it for Plato, Plotinus, or Thomas Aquinas. The concept of art, on the other hand, underwent a long series of permutations that have by no means reached an end. The tendency was for the concept of art to become narrower and to exclude more and more activities and products. Crafts, trades, and skills were originally all included in the concept of art, understood as τἑχνη and *ars*; the equation of art with the fine arts was a very late development.

No art, whether as practical know-how or as a member of the fine arts family, was ever considered autonomous before Kant. Art was imbedded in a social, pedagogical, theological, or merely economic program that regulated its production. Not until the eighteenth century were the questions regarding art's epistemological and practical value, and about the nature of the work of art and of beauty, integrated into a systematic, independent philosophical discipline that then became known as aesthetics. Before this time, the term "aesthetics," derived from the Greek *aisthesis,* meaning perception, had referred to the philosophical theory of sense perception. Baumgarten and Kant both still use it in this sense, although Kant adopts the new meaning of the term between the first and the third *Critique,* that is, between 1781 and 1790. Taking up some British and French ideas from Hutcheson, Shaftesbury, Burke, Dubos, and others, as well as from rationalist metaphysics, a unique philosophical discipline emerged in Germany around the middle of the eighteenth century. This book tells the story of the emergence and the subsequent development of aesthetic philosophy in Germany.

Philosophical aesthetics was not only born in Germany; the development of this discipline is also a predominantly Germanic affair for two specific reasons. First, the German aesthetic tradition is resistant to outside influences to an unusually high degree. The writers who belong to this tradition respond to one another without introducing ideas adopted from contemporary discussions in other languages, the standard references to antiquity notwithstanding. Second, while the German tradition of philosophical aesthetics is self-sufficient, philosophers outside this discourse respond to German concepts without themselves having a significant influence in shaping the tradition. Thus, Dewey, Sartre, Croce, Satayana, Danto, Langer, and Ricoeur, to select a random few, all take up concepts developed within the German context of aesthetics. Philosophy of art in the nineteenth and twentieth centuries written in Britain, France, Italy, the United States, and elsewhere constantly has recourse to the German tradition. In short, philosophical aesthetics as a discipline is thoroughly grounded in German thought and, hence, cannot be understood without a detailed knowledge of this tradition.

This book is true to its title insofar as it tells the story of the German aesthetic tradition. Yet, its title is not entirely true to its subject. Properly, the book would have had to be called *The German*ic *Aesthetic Tradition.* As a glance at the table of contents will make evident, not all of the authors discussed herein are German. In fact, some have not even written in German. In three cases, the extension from German to Germanic is especially in order. First, Søren Kierkegaard is a Danish philosopher who wrote his books in Danish. Even though Danish is a Germanic language, other characteristics of his work not only justify his inclusion but make it a necessity. Kierkegaard developed his thought in opposition to the tradition of German idealism, primarily the objective idealism of G. W. F. Hegel. Much of what Kierkegaard writes is directed against the systematic philosophy of the eminent Berlin thinker. This holds true as well for his aesthetics: Kierkegaard's conception of this philosophical discipline is a direct challenge to Hegel's position. Without Kierkegaard's specific contribution to aesthetics that later becomes important to Heidegger, Adorno, and Lukács, the narrative of the German aesthetic tradition would be incomplete.

The second case concerns Georg Lukács, who was a Hungarian citizen and wrote both in German and in Hungarian. Although his early essays on aesthetic questions were written in Hungarian, Lukács was educated in Germany, lived there, and took classical German philosophy as his frame of reference.

Since I read neither Danish nor Hungarian, I rely on existing translations of the works of Kierkegaard and Lukács into English. All other translations from all other languages are mine; in the case of Baumgarten's writings, I translated from the Latin into English, consulting a German edition where appropriate.

The third case concerns both Ernst Cassirer and Herbert Marcuse, both of whom were German expatriates. Marcuse became an American citizen and published a good number of his books and essays in English. Still, his work is connected to the Frankfurt School and takes up the traditions of German idealism, Marxism, and Freudian psychoanalysis. Where his texts have first appeared in English, I naturally quote these editions. Where Marcuse himself or his wife translated (and often edited) from original German publications into English, I take this to be the authorized translation and quote from it. Cassirer happened to write down most of his aesthetic philosophy late in life during his years in exile. Hence, some of his most important pronouncements on this subject were written in English, either in the context of an introduction of his philosophy to an English-speaking readership or as classroom lectures.

This book on the German aesthetic tradition serves several purposes. First, it introduces the major positions in German philosophical aesthetics and elucidates their interdependence and their attempts at overcoming and renewing previous positions. Second, the book introduces the important figures of this tradition, not merely as a collection of isolated portraits but in the context of a historical narrative. Hence, the grouping of the individual thinkers under the rubrics of The Age of Paradigms, Challenging the Paradigms, and Renewing the

Paradigms indicates their belonging to larger historical movements. Third, the book gives expression to the conviction that the history of philosophy cannot be separated from systematic philosophy. History only comes into view when questions of problems, concerns, and philosophical interests are raised, and these interests must naturally be those of our own age. This hermeneutic principle forbids the claim that our narrative exhausts the historical material. No single narrative can ever accomplish such a feat. On the other hand, the same hermeneutic grounding demands that our engagement with historical philosophical texts be motivated by questions that concern us today. What is of merely historical interest is of no interest at all.

This book also argues that there is an internal logic to the narrative that unfolds. The examined positions in philosophical aesthetics do not simply follow one another; they adhere to a larger pattern that becomes clear in retrospect. In short, the thesis of this book is that paradigmatic positions in aesthetic philosophy were established during the period of German idealism and romanticism, that these paradigmatic positions were subsequently challenged by writers in the nineteenth century, and that in the twentieth century all the positions were renewed precisely in the order in which they first emerged. This last fact, and I take it to be a fact, still allows for a number of possible conclusions to be drawn. These can be aligned along a spectrum of which the two extreme positions would be the following. On the one side, the weakest version of this stance argues for a simple coincidence in the historical pattern by claiming that the positions of idealism and romanticism are so rich and varied that they attract new interest after a period of challenges and attempts to dismantle them. Nevertheless, the renewal of the paradigmatic positions could have started as well with Hegel, then moved to Kant and progressed to Schelling from there. That the original order – Kant–Schiller–Schelling–Hegel – held up in the twentieth-century revival is seen as more or less a convenient pattern for organizational purposes, but hardly an essential feature. On the other side of the spectrum, though, we find a strong stance that might be called hard-core Hegelianism. In this view, the idealist positions are challenged, only to be amended and elevated later to a higher level. True to the dialectical model, this view does not regard the historical pattern as a coincidence but, rather, as the display of logic and hence of necessity in history.

Both positions are plausible, and good arguments can be advanced against both of them as well. It is less important to subscribe to either than to acknowledge a historical pattern in the first place. To attempt an explanation of this pattern would bring us into the field of the philosophy of history and, hence, further away from our subject than we might like. It is not our aim to venture into this other philosophical discipline, let alone the *prima philosophia,* namely metaphysics, which is very likely to enter into this discussion as well. But to write intellectual history means to narrate a story and, hence, to believe in a beginning, a middle, and an end. The assembling of facts or the portrayal of a number of individual thinkers is not yet historiography, but merely the preparation for it. To stop at this point means to have failed as a historian of philosophy.

In the present context, it is unnecessary to abstract from the material at hand, that is, the aesthetic discourse, in order to examine overarching patterns of the movement of thought. Instead, the material must speak for itself. I did not write this study with a theory of history in mind to which the material was meant to conform. Rather, a pattern emerged as I read and reread the texts in a historical sequence. All I ask of the reader for now is to pay some attention to the striking historical parallels and the repetition of questions and approaches in different ages. And while my thesis of the patterned progression of Germanic aesthetics might not be in sync with the spirit of our times – in fact, it probably runs against its current – the book can be read without subscribing to any such narrative. Before I establish historical influences and similarities, I take each thinker on his own terms. Most of the space in every chapter is devoted to the detailed discussion of the aesthetic theory of one or more philosophers. Hence, all chapters can be read independently, in reverse order, or selectively. But to say it again: What makes this study a book, rather than a collection of portraits, is its narrative.

It could be argued against our narrative of an inner logic in the history of German aesthetic thought that it is achieved at the cost of eliminating those contributions to aesthetics that do not fit the scheme. I do not believe, however, that this charge can be substantiated. Certainly there are omissions: Little if any reference is made to the writings of Marx and Engels, Freud, and the artists' aesthetics of J. W. Goethe, Jean Paul, R. Wagner, W. Kandinsky, and P. Klee, to name only some. Still, I hold that an inclusion of these writers would not have changed the historical pattern significantly. They were omitted not because their writings would disturb or overturn the presented narrative but for two very different reasons. The first is that these writers themselves did not situate themselves within the tradition of German philosophical aesthetics. Generally speaking, one joins a philosophical discourse – at least in the continental tradition – when one responds to problems previously unsolved or inadequately solved by referring to writings of other philosophers and by continuing or challenging a certain vocabulary. In respect to philosophical aesthetics, this gesture of joining the discourse is hardly present in any of the omitted writers. The second reason for the omission of these thinkers is that their writings on art generally do not advance a position that answers to the basic questions and concerns of the aesthetic tradition. Rather, one aspect from which to view art is singled out and made the sole focus of the writer's contribution. This is not to say that these texts can be neglected in our philosophical inquiry into questions of art, beauty, ugliness, and so on. Quite the contrary is true, since much originality can be found in these books and essays. And still, all of them fail to respond to some concerns that are central to philosophical aesthetics, for example, the arguments for or against a practical and epistemic value of art, the inclusion or exclusion of nature in philosophical aesthetics, and the relation of aesthetics to other philosophical disciplines. In the end, the omissions were not mine. The tradition of philosophical aesthetics itself selects those who belong. In this process, the votes of those who opt out of that tradition count most.

To facilitate the comparisons among the many different writers in the German aesthetic tradition, we will consider their contributions under three specific aspects, although our discussion will nowhere be limited to these moments. The first is the philosopher's ontological discussion of art, the second the epistemic role attributed to art and beauty, and the third the practical function the writer locates in artworks. While many other aspects of aesthetics will demand our attention in addition to these factors, they nevertheless serve well as principles of comparison. To be sure, the selection of these criteria does not imply that all aesthetic philosophy must answer these questions. Rather, I isolated only those issues in the history of the philosophy of art and beauty that were addressed by thinkers time and again. Not all philosophers were interested in all of them, and the fact that all of them were discussed by one thinker or another does not make for a better or more complete aesthetic philosophy at all. Yet the comparison of many varied approaches to the same discipline becomes much easier if we focus on a few characteristic features. This procedure might have a certain artificiality, but I hope that it will facilitate the comprehension of aesthetics as a historical process in which similar questions find similar or radically different answers, or in which certain questions are dismissed, ignored, or forgotten. Historiography depends on comparability, and comparability rests on the identification of elements that are neither unchangeable nor radically unstable.

Many friends and colleagues took time to read the manuscript or parts of it. All of them offered helpful comments, although I could not incorporate every single one. Among those with whom I discussed the manuscript in its entirety or in parts, I would like to thank especially Bernd Fischer, John Davidson, and Paul Reitter. My student Benjamin Beebe helped greatly with the editing process of the last draft of the book. An anonymous reader for Cambridge University Press offered helpful suggestions. As always, my first reader was Matt Crosby. His presence is the most important reminder for me that art, despite its inexhaustible richness, cannot fill a life. To him this book is dedicated.

This study was written in Columbus, Ohio, the Black Forest, and New York City. To dwell in these places while working with the great texts from the German aesthetic tradition brought home once more the relevance of philosophical aesthetics to the understanding of both the beauty of art and nature and the ugliness that is thrust to the foreground in modernist art and the cityscape of Manhattan. The advantage of life in a metropolis, however, is that our large cities allow for multiple encounters with a wide spectrum of great art that force philosophical aesthetics into the background and remind us that it is of secondary status only. What comes first and foremost are the works of art themselves.

February 2002

The German Aesthetic Tradition

PART I

THE AGE OF PARADIGMS

1

Baumgarten, Mendelssohn

Alexander Baumgarten

Immanuel Kant's (1724–1804) towering presence at the end of the eighteenth century tends to throw a shadow backward in history, eclipsing many of the less forceful and original thinkers. The situation is no different in philosophical aesthetics. Although Kant's 1790 *Critique of Judgment* – unlike the 1781 *Critique of Pure Reason* that received little friendly attention until Reinhold's *Briefe über die Kantische Philosophie* (Letters on the Kantian philosophy) of 1786–7[1] – created a fanfare on the philosophical scene (some slight delay in reception notwithstanding), it did not emerge from out of the blue. Kant had already reacted against previous, albeit more modest attempts to ground a philosophical aesthetics – attempts, however, that ultimately failed to establish an aesthetic paradigm to serve as a starting point for productive elaborations or dissent for future generations.

The pre-Kantian philosophical aesthetics were not meant to be a break with the dominant philosophical system, namely, that of Leibniz and Wolff. Instead, they should be considered elaborations of it that *nolens, volens* helped to undermine the foundations that they labored to strengthen.[2] When Alexander Baumgarten (1714–1762) introduced the plan for aesthetics as a new philosophical discipline with its own name, he did so in order to prop up the traditional rationalist metaphysics by making it more encompassing. Yet Baumgarten's attempt to consolidate rationalism turned, under his hands, into a critical endeavor. Aesthetics, intended to be an extension of a rationalist worldview, became more and more independent, until finally the rationalist metaphysics were discredited and aesthetics remained behind as a survivor. Therefore, in order to understand Baumgarten's and Mendelssohn's projects, it is necessary to briefly outline that philosophical system that they adhered to and planned to amend by their writings on aesthetics.

In 1735, the young Alexander Baumgarten published his *Meditationes philosophicae de nonullis ad poema pertinentibus* (Philosophical meditations on some requirements of the poem), which appeared in Latin, as did almost all of his writings, and in which he identified a theory of sensibility labeled aesthetics as a desideratum. Here we find for the first time in the history of philosophy the notion of aesthetics as an independent philosophical discipline. Yet the meaning of the term is far from our understanding of aesthetics as a philosophical investigation of art and a theory of beauty and ugliness. Baumgarten's aesthetics refers to a theory of sensibility as a gnoseological faculty, that is, a faculty that produces a certain type of knowledge. Aesthetics is taken very literally as a defense of the relevance of sensual perception. Philosophical aesthetics originated as advocacy of sensibility, not as a theory of art. Yet without a positive valuation of the senses and their objects, art could not have achieved philosophical dignity but would have remained with the lesser ontological status that traditional metaphysics had assigned to it, compared to rationality.

The aesthetics of Baumgarten and Mendelssohn can be considered an undertaking to claim epistemological relevance for sensual perception. This was no small task, since Descartes (1596–1650) had just renewed the Platonic devaluation of the objects of the senses in favor of a rationality cleansed of sensibility.[3] The Cartesian mathematization and rationalization of cognition entailed a certain impoverishment of reality by excluding the evidence of sensual perception that could not be elevated to a general principle. Descartes had explained his rejection of aesthetic cognition by claiming that it consists of value judgments that are not methodical but merely subjective. Sensibility's epistemic force was considered weak after Descartes, although Leibniz (1646–1716) took the first step away from purely mathematical cognition. Moreover, that part of the Christian tradition that insisted on the mortification of the flesh was still largely unchallenged and received new vigor in the eighteenth century in the form of Protestant Pietism.

Leibniz rested his philosophical system on a theological basis, namely, the assumption of the world as *creatio Dei,* a creation of God. Therefore, the world can be nothing but a well-ordered unity in which the structures of reality are identical with the laws of rationality, as they are predominantly expressed in logic, physics, and mathematics. This logico-ontological equivalence, as it is sometimes called, is not a simple mirroring of reality in cognition. Instead, Leibniz assumes a hierarchy of cognitive levels that range from largely unconscious perceptions to complete comprehension. He develops this system of cognitive differentiation in several of his writings that provide the foil for the aesthetic attempts of Baumgarten and Mendelssohn.[4] Leibniz distinguishes on a first level between cognitions that are obscure and those that are clear. Obscure cognitions are such that do not become fully conscious and of which we therefore have no concept. They are so-called *petites perceptions,* too obscure to allow for the recognition of their object. Leibniz mentions the noise of the ocean as an example, since we cannot attribute the overall noise to the breaking of the individual waves. Clear cognition, however, is conscious and allows for the recognition of the object. But clear cognition subsumes under it a whole spectrum of cognitive achievements that become ever more complete. The lowest level of clear cognition divides itself into confused and distinct cognitive insight. We call a cognition clear and confused if the object possesses a multitude of (sensible) features, but we cannot list them separately. We do know they exist, but we would fail in an attempt to list them one by one. In opposition to this level, a clear and distinct cognition is able to enumerate all features of the object and give a complete definition of it. Leibniz splits the distinct cognition again into adequate and inadequate, as well as into symbolic and intuitive. Somewhat simplified, we can take him to say that these higher levels of cognition are purely rational, most of them are rare achievements for human beings, and the very highest level, adequate and intuitive knowledge, is reserved for God who possesses a complete and instantaneous knowledge of all features of the object.

What concerns us in the present context is the level of clear and confused cognition. If this sounds paradoxical, it is important to remember that a clear cognition achieves only the recognition of an object, but that it does not exhaust its elements in an analytic procedure. We are aware of the complexity of the object, although we cannot separate and enumerate its elements. This cognition is rich, multifaceted, lively, even emotionally charged. It involves responses of like and dislike, and Leibniz locates both art and beauty on this level of cognition. But aesthetic judgments necessarily have to remain unjustifiable statements of emotional response. In a famous pronouncement on art, Leibniz states: "We sometimes comprehend in a clear manner without any doubt whether a poem or a picture is well made or not, because there is an I-don't-know-what (*je ne sais quoi*) that satisfies or repels us."[5] It is not only that a vague *je ne sais quoi* – a phrase that was to become very important in British eighteenth-century aesthetics, as can be found for example in William Hogarth's *The Analysis of Beauty* in which several references are listed[6] – is responsible for our liking or disliking of works or art; beauty in general exists solely for the incomplete human cognition. It is a precondition for our valuation of an object as beautiful to have a merely confused idea of it and to be unable to transform it into a distinct idea. Beauty therefore is a by-product of flawed human cognition; in God's mind beauty is absent. God's cognition is instantaneous, that is, without sensible elements and, thus, devoid of the category of beauty. This is the point where Baumgarten's reevaluation sets in. His aim is to convince us that confusion of perception is not exclusively negative and privative but, rather, a unique mode of cognition that carries its own richness, complexity, and necessity.

As we have seen, Baumgarten is the philosopher who in the middle of the eighteenth century begins to advocate aesthetics as a new philosophical discipline and who coins the name that soon was to designate it as an independent field of inquiry. After Baumgarten concluded his treatise on the philosophical requirements of the poem with the call for aesthetics, he continued to lay the groundwork for his publications on aesthetics of the 1750s. In his book on metaphysics of 1739, he devotes a noticeable amount of attention to what he calls sensual or aesthetic cognition, and he also takes up this cause in a series of letters published as a kind of philosophical journal under the title *Aletheophilus* (Friend of the truth). In 1742, Baumgarten became the first philosophical teacher ever to lecture on aesthetics, and out of these academic courses grew his two-volume *Aesthetica* of 1750 and 1758. Partly because these publications were written in somewhat forbidding Latin, his direct influence on contemporary philosophy and literary theory remained limited. Indirectly, however, his ideas soon acquired a certain influence. This was due to a publication of Baumgarten's student G. F. Meier, who in 1748 printed his German treatise *Anfangsgründe aller schönen Wissenschaften* (Foundations of all liberal arts) that was based largely on his teacher's lectures and quickly popularized Baumgarten's ideas.

Alexander Baumgarten defines aesthetics in the first paragraph of his *Aesthetica* as follows: "Aesthetics (as the theory of the liberal arts, as inferior cognition, as the art of beautiful thinking and as the art of thinking analogous to reason) is the science of sensual cognition."[7] Baumgarten packages quite a few things into this definition, and he basically spends the rest of the *Aesthetica* elaborating on the different elements of this opening statement. The most important thing to be noted is that his aesthetics is the combination of a twofold approach to the subject. Aesthetics is considered to be a science of sensual cognition, as well as a theory of art. The general aim for Baumgarten is to establish the latter by means of the former, although the relation of the two moments is not always as clear as Baumgarten thinks it might be. It should also be mentioned that both in respect to terminology and in terms of structure, the *Aesthetica* is committed to the traditional rhetorical system that it frequently challenges but that is nevertheless taken to be the common horizon of author and readers. That is to say that Baumgarten's elaboration on the stages and elements of aesthetic truth is modeled on the production stages of a public speech (*inventio, dispositio, elocutio*) as taught by rhetorical treatises. And yet in Baumgarten's view, the rhetorical model, as was recently renewed by the Swiss literary critics Bodmer, Breitinger, and others, stands in need of expansion since it is limited to the linguistic arts and can provide no direct assistance for composers and painters.[8]

Despite its emphasis on the senses and their cognitive value, Baumgarten's aesthetics must not be regarded as an intentional break with, or even an intentional critique of, the rationalist metaphysics of Leibniz and Wolff. Its primary interest seems to be the strengthening of the rationalist system by including neglected elements that should ultimately serve to further the cause of rational cognition. Baumgarten argues that sensual cognition is essential for rational cognition: "The major inferior faculties of cognition, namely the naturally developed ones, are required for beautiful thinking. They are not only simultaneously possible with the higher natural ones, but they are required for them as a precondition (*sine qua non*)" (*Aesthetica*, §41). In anonymously published lecture notes, a student reports Baumgarten stating that in order to improve reason, aesthetics must aid logic.[9] With

Leibniz, Baumgarten assumes that some of our cognition is obscure while some is distinct; that is, cognition at one end of the spectrum is entirely without concepts and thus without rational justification, while at the other end it rests on complete conceptual knowledge. Between these two extreme forms of cognition some mediation must be found, for there is no direct way from the obscurity of the unconscious *petites perceptions* to rational cognition. The connecting link between the two Baumgarten claims to have found in the confused cognition of sensuality:

> [It is said that] confusion is the mother of error. My answer to this is: it is a necessary condition for the discovery of truth, because nature does not make leaps from obscure to distinct thought [*ubi natura non facit saltum ex obscuritate in distinctionem*]. Out of the night dawn leads to daylight. We must concern ourselves with confused cognition so as to avoid errors in large numbers and to a large extent that befall those who ignore it. We do not commend confusion, but rather the emendation of cognition insofar as a necessary moment of confused cognition is mixed into it. (*Aesthetica,* §7)

It is the primary aim of the science of sensual cognition to aid the faculties of logical cognition. In order to do so, the unique modes of sensual cognition need to be investigated. But to claim relevance for sensual perception as an unavoidable element of all cognitive procedures was not an easy task. Not only did Baumgarten have to struggle against the devaluation of sensuality that runs through the history of Western philosophy from Plato onward and is a dominant motive in the rationalist metaphysics of Leibniz, but he was also moving against the headwind of religion. Protestant Pietism gained more and more influence during Baumgarten's lifetime and argued for a break with the Catholic medieval tradition according to which the glory of God shines forth from the splendor of the world. For Pietism, one's relation to God was to be purely inward and nonsensual. Yet Baumgarten's new science of sensual cognition was determined not to regard sense data merely as stimuli for higher and more advanced processes of cognition but, rather, to consider it an independent form of cognition itself.

In fact, the logician who neglected sensory moments was considered a philosopher manqué, an incompletely developed human being who lacks the fullness of existence. Baumgarten (and even more so his student G. F. Meier) pitched against the dry logician the *felix aestheticus,* the successful aesthetician, who combines attention to and love for the sensory world with the faculty of rational cognition.

Sensual cognition must not be seen as a faulty or incomplete rational cognition but, rather, as an independent faculty. Baumgarten argues that to comprehend an object obscurely, confusedly, or indistinctly is not a failure, and must thus be considered a specific achievement of the soul (*Metaphysica,* §520). If a representation is not distinct, it can only be sensual for Baumgarten. Therefore, the inferior cognition is a sensual mode of cognition (*Metaphysica,* §521). Although it is not rational itself, the fact that it is a faculty of cognition makes it analogous to rational procedures. Baumgarten thus defines aesthetics as the art of thinking analogous to rationality (*ars analogi rationis*). This mode comes to human beings as part of their instinctive heritage, and as such it is something that does not yet set us apart from animals. This so-called natural aesthetics, however, needs practice in order to develop its potential. Properly trained, natural aesthetics can be transformed into the art of beautiful thinking, a term that we shall have to return to (*Aesthetica,* §47). Such training for the *felix aestheticus* depends as much on repeated exercises, as prescribed by the rhetorical system, as on familiarity with aesthetic theory. Baumgarten concludes that practical exercises need to be supplemented by theory, and theory in turn must be brought down to a practical level by means of exercises (*Aesthetica,* §62).

Inferior cognition does entail a lack of rationality, but it does not entail a lack of truth. In a rather bold fashion, Baumgarten states that aesthetic cognition does indeed have its own truth claim. He argues that there are several levels of truth that coincide with the levels of cognition. A metaphysical truth seems the equivalent of an intuitive and adequate cognition, that is, something that is restricted to God. As far as man is concerned, his rational insights produce a truth that Baumgarten labels logical. The third truth is the result of confused cognition, namely, aesthetic truth (*Aesthetica,* §423). Baumgarten elaborates on how he understands aesthetic truth by situating it between falsehood and the certainty we achieve through correct employment of our rational faculties. Aesthetic truth for Baumgarten seems to come rather close to the rhetorical conception of truth, namely, probability. In the rhetorical tradition, an argument was true if it was convincing, probable, or more likely to be true than other contenders for truth, but it did not have to agree with the substance of the object as the philosophical *adaequatio*-theory demanded. An argument would be deemed probable if we hold something to be true without having any logical proof for this belief. The object of aesthetic truth, Baumgarten writes, "is neither certain nor is its truth perceived in full light" (*Aesthetica*, §483). This kind of truth strays a good way from the traditional philosophical conception of truth as correspondence of mind and reality as the system of Leibniz advocates it and to which Baumgarten clearly subscribes at other times.

Although logical truth, and logical truth only, can provide us with certainty, it pays a high price for it. Much like Nietzsche, Baumgarten regards logical truth to be an impoverished abstraction, that is, a movement from concrete instances to a general concept. The multitude of concrete sensual experiences carries with it a sense of fullness, vibrancy, and liveliness that gets lost in abstraction. Therefore, Baumgarten famously concludes: "But what is abstraction if not a loss?" (*Aesthetica*, §560). We are to think of abstract logical truth as somewhat pale and somewhat lifeless in comparison to the probability that the aesthetic faculty provides. Aesthetic truth, in opposition, celebrates "richness, chaos and matter" (*Aesthetica*, §564). The term chaos, however, does not indicate that Baumgarten considers aesthetic truth to be unstructured, devoid of recurring elements or without necessary conditions. Instead, he proposes three criteria according to which the unique perfection of sensual cognition can be judged. The first of these moments is richness of imagination, which means that an aesthetic idea is the more perfect the more individual elements it contains. Complexity of content becomes elevated to a characteristic of aesthetic perfection. In Leibniz, confused cognition had little value attached to it, but in Baumgarten it encompasses a redeeming fullness and complexity that we find pleasurable. An aesthetic idea, though, does not merely have to be complex to be perfect. Baumgarten defines the second characteristic of aesthetic perfection as magnitude of imagination. In this, the mere sensual complexity is linked with the notion of relevance and, thus, to a form of judgment that is no longer purely sensual. Rather traditionally, Baumgarten argues that aesthetic ideas are more satisfying for us if they pertain to more relevant matters, that is, if a narrative tells about the lot of humans instead of that of animals or if pictorial representations depict historical scenes instead of flowers. The third and final element in Baumgarten's list is that of clarity of presentation, which is a traditional rhetorical ideal.

The most interesting of these characteristics is certainly that of richness of imagination. We can understand it to express the fact that aesthetic perception and aesthetic truth consist of an ever-renewed contemplation of the multitude of elements contained in the aesthetic object without our being able or willing to unify them under a concept. But what remains confused also remains rich. Baumgarten, with this elevation of confused richness, obviously points forward toward Kant and his important notion of the aesthetic idea.

As has been pointed out, the aim of an aesthetic theory for Baumgarten is to aid in the perfection of sensual cognition. Perfection of sensual cognition, however, is defined as beauty. Conversely, imperfection of aesthetic cognition is ugliness. Art as the manifestation of the beautiful therefore aims to represent the purposeful unity and harmony of the world. In this, Baumgarten subscribes to the classical *pulchrum* theory that regards the universe as a beautiful creation and every beautiful object as a mirroring instance of the whole. Representation in the form of mirroring is an idea that Baumgarten takes from Leibniz's *Monadology* that rests on the assumption of a coherence of subject and object, that is, the logico-ontological equivalence. Later we will see that the notion of the aesthetic monad also recurs in the writings of Adorno. The aesthetic representation of the larger unity in one beautiful object is what Baumgarten labels "thinking beautifully" (*pulchre cogitare*).

With this definition we have come full circle and find ourselves again at the point where we started the analysis, namely Paragraph One of the *Aesthetica*. Aesthetics, as we recall, was defined not only as the science of sensual cognition but also as the theory of liberal arts, an inferior cognition, the art of thinking beautifully, and the art that is analogous to rationality. Thus, the opening sentence contains, in the form of brief parenthetical definitions, the arguments that the many hundreds of paragraphs that follow elaborate. Some of the definitions, as has become clear, are obliged to the traditional rhetorical system and to the rationalist metaphysics of Leibniz and Wolff, whereas others break away from these traditions and open new paths of inquiry into the unique status of aesthetics as a philosophical project.

As has been demonstrated, Baumgarten's aesthetics takes a double approach to its subject matter, namely, as a theory of sensual perception and as a philosophy of art. Philosophy of art, however, has to be understood in a wider sense than usual so that it can encompass the theory of production of art, that is, those elements that Baumgarten incorporates from poetics and rhetoric. True art, and that means good art, depends on the application of rules that the science of art and beauty is to develop. With this proposition, Baumgarten exerted some influence on the *Regelpoetiken* (regulative poetics) of the eighteenth century that continued the Baroque tradition of M. Opitz and others until they were displaced by the *Geniepoetik* (poetics of genius) that florished with the Storm-and-Stress movement in Germany.

Yet another important factor in Baumgarten's theory of aesthetics is his inclusion of emotional aspects into the process of cognition. His notion of "aesthetic enthusiasm" reunites artistic emotionality and cognitive achievements that had been opposed to each other since Plato's criticism of artistic inspiration (*mania*) as an interference with rationality. One of Baumgarten's arguments implies that the aesthetic effect allows us to tap into memory resources no longer available to voluntary recollection. Without having to stretch this theory too far, we can find its repercussions in Marcel Proust's notion of the *memoire involontaire* that is set in motion by sensual experiences and contains an equally unique mode of cognition.

Turning to our three aspects under which we want to consider the contributions of the individual writers, namely the ontological, the epistemic, and the practical functions attributed to art and beauty, we shall first consider Baumgarten's response to the ontological question. His answer to "What is art?" is nowhere stated explicitly, yet can be inferred easily from the argumentation. An object of art, it can be concluded, is one that, better than other objects, represents the purposeful unity and the beauty of the world. This ontological stance is rather conservative and limits itself to restating the familiar positions of the metaphysical theories of Leibniz. Questioned about the cognitive value of art, Baumgarten repeats the ontological argument in somewhat different form, but he also adds an important new element. Certainly we can learn from a work of art that the world is created beautifully and that harmony prevails in it. Yet this is a rather abstract truth. Aesthetic truth, on the other hand, shelters the immediacy of experience in all its individuality, richness, and complexity. The truth of art can thus be pitched against logical truth – a criticism of rationality that is taken up by romanticism and brought to prominence by aesthetic theories of the twentieth century. The truth of art for Baumgarten is not a mere preparation for logical truth, nor, even more importantly, is it accessible by means of logic. The truth of art remains sensual, unconceptualized, or, as Adorno would later call it, nonidentical.

Closely related to this argument are the statements on the practical value of art. If we ask what exactly art can do, Baumgarten's answer seems rather straightforward, but it undercuts itself. Baumgarten justified the need for an aesthetic theory with the argument that it helps to make the transition from unconscious and obscure cognition to distinct cognition. A theory of confused cognition as a theory of sensuality thus aids rationality. But this answer creates more problems than it solves. If the aesthetic truth is independent from the logical truth, it can also not be reduced to the latter's handmaiden. The practical purpose of art is not to train our aesthetic sensibilities in order to leave them behind for more rational conduct. More likely, the repeated encounters with art help us to become more well-rounded human beings who are able to balance sensuality and rationality, aesthetic immediacy and abstract cognition. Aesthetics might have been meant to be a prop for the perfection of rationality, but it emerged as a lively critic of it. After Baumgarten, however, aesthetics no longer defended its usefulness by reference to its helpfulness for logical modes of thought. Instead, it presented itself both as independent of and even productively opposed to rationality.

With Baumgarten, aesthetics takes a great step toward its independence as a philosophical discipline. While Baumgarten was mainly concerned with the aspect of *cognition,* Moses Mendelssohn contributed essays exploring the unique *pleasure* man derives from the aesthetic object.

Moses Mendelssohn

Whereas Alexander Baumgarten embodies the rationalist side of mid-eighteenth-century aesthetics, Moses Mendelssohn (1729–1786) represents the emotive side. Together these two thinkers sum up the aesthetic tendencies of this century in Germany. Much like Baumgarten, Mendelssohn is an adherent of the rationalist metaphysics of Leibniz and Wolff, and consequently, his aesthetic writings share many features with those of Baumgarten. There is little need to restate these principles of Baroque philosophy since Mendelssohn takes them for granted, possibly to an even larger extent than Baumgarten. He, too, assumes a hierarchy of cognitive achievements in which little cognitive value is attributed to sensuality, whereas rational cognition is considered devoid of sensuality. Arguing in the Platonic tradition, Mendelssohn states that beauty as a sensual phenomenon is part of the realm of change about which ultimate truth statements cannot be made due to its ephemeral character. The volatile nature of beauty thus has to be separated from rational cognition. Our judgment of the beautiful – Kant will later argue this point vehemently – is therefore not a judgment that holds true for everyone by virtue of its adherence to undeniable principles of reason (cf. *Verwandtschaft des Schönen und Guten* – Affinity of the beautiful and the good).[10]

The elevation of sensuality, beauty, and works of art to cognitive respectability, however, is not Mendelssohn's primary concern. Of higher importance to him is the pleasurable sensation that the perfection of art and beauty induces.[11] Mendelssohn's aesthetics constitutes the link between the rationalism of the Leibniz/Wolff system and the aesthetics of classicism as advanced by Goethe, Schiller, W. von Humboldt, and others. Insofar as his writings emphasize human perfectability and art's contribution to the aesthetic education of man leading to the well-rounded human being, they anticipate in several respects classical anthropology and art criticism. Therefore, it appears justified to label Mendelssohn's an aesthetics of perfection, albeit one that changes the focus from the perfect universe of the rationalist metaphysicians to the classicists' teleological improvement of man.

Mendelssohn explicates his ideas on aesthetics in a number of essays, as well as in an exchange of letters with Friedrich Nicolai and Gotthold Ephraim Lessing. His most relevant aesthetic texts are *Briefe über die Empfindungen* (Letters on sensations, 1755) and its sequel *Rhapsodie, oder Zusätze zu den Briefen über die Empfindungen* (Rhapsody, or addenda to the letters on sensations, 1761), *Über die Hauptgrundsätze der schönen Künste und Wissenschaften* (On the main principles of the beaux arts and liberal arts, 1757), and *Über das Erhabene und Naïve in den schönen Wissenschaften* (On the sublime and naïve in the liberal arts, 1758). Most relevant might be the first essay in which Mendelssohn develops his basic ideas, which he later elaborates and modifies only slightly.

The *Letters on Sensations* are modeled in form and diction on Shaftesbury's (1661–1713) *The Moralists or A Philosophical Rhapsody* of 1709. From Shaftesbury Mendelssohn takes the notions of creative genius and the work of art as an organic totality, but largely discards Shaftesbury's moralistic tendencies. Mendelssohn agrees with Baumgarten that the sensation of beauty rests neither on an obscure nor on a distinct cognition, but on a confused one. That said, he leaves epistemological concerns behind to turn toward the psychological ramifications of art and beauty.

Beauty – this is an idea Mendelssohn repeats throughout his writings – depends on an easily comprehensible unity of the manifold in sensual perception. The beautiful object therefore must neither be too small nor too large (originally, this is the Aristotelian notion of ευσΰνοπτον, i.e., that which can be visually grasped at once) because if too great in size, an immediate comprehension of its unity will be impossible, whereas if too minute, the object will lack in variety of elements – a theory that Johann Joachim Winckelmann (1717–1768) in his 1764 *History of Ancient Art* also proposed.[12] This reduction of beautiful objects to a human scale not only comprises a classical thought in itself, but also indicates a clear break with the traditional *pulchrum* theory, according to which the cosmos is a beautiful entity. The universe is much too large to be sensually comprehended, and thus it disqualifies itself as an object of beauty: "This infinite universe is no visibly beautiful object. Nothing deserves this name that does not enter our senses all at once" (*Letters on Sensations*, 51).

Whereas this humanization of the beautiful marks a break with traditional notions of beauty, Mendelssohn's debunking of Gothic architecture that results from the same argumentation is perfectly in keeping with the taste of the age. The eighteenth century at large regarded the Gothic period as inharmonious and tasteless, although this valuation goes back in its essence to Vasari's attempt to establish the superiority of the Renaissance artists by discrediting their precursors.[13] Mendelssohn, too, subscribes to this judgment by arguing that Gothic cathedrals fail as architectural objects because their endless detailing, that is, the manifold, cannot be perceptually unified and thus remains scattered, random, and dissatisfying. Not until Goethe and Herder and the essay *Von deutscher Baukunst* (On German architecture) of 1772 by the former – who made a point of emphasizing the "complete, great impression" consisting of "a thousand harmonizing details" in Gothic architecture[14] – did this derision of the Gothic style come to an end. Ironically, it was soon celebrated by the romantics as a genuine and superior German contribution to art.

Another break with the aesthetic tradition can be detected in Mendelssohn's separation of beauty and perfection. Although he subscribes to Leibniz's theorems that beauty consists in perfection of sensual perception, truth in logical perfection, and the good in man in moral perfection, he no longer equates every expression of perfection with beauty. In fact, there are distinct instances where a perfect form, that is, one that fulfills its *telos,* is outright ugly. Picture the human body suggests Mendelssohn, and he takes up an argument that can already be found in Xenophon and Longinus's treatise *On the Sublime* (42; 5). If it is perfectly formed, we admire its beauty, but such beauty is merely external, because the body as a whole also possesses an inside that repels us:

> The beauty of the human form, the pleasant colors, the curved features that enchant in his face, are only as if molded into the exterior shell. They only last as long as our senses. Underneath the skin terrible forms lie hidden. All vessels are intertwined seemingly without order. The entrails balance each other, but without harmony. Much manifold, but nowhere unity. Much activity, but nowhere ease in activity. How much the creator would have failed if beauty had been his only aim!" (*Letters on Sensations,* 59)

The world at large and man are indeed perfect creations for Mendelssohn, who, like Leibniz, could not envision a more perfect universe. Yet perfection does not express itself any longer as beauty: The universe because of its size and man considered as a biological creature fail to satisfy our sense of beauty, since it does not grant us aesthetic pleasure to ponder the cosmos or man's intestines. Mendelssohn here advances the same argument that Edmund Burke had put forth when he declared that functional perfection ("fitness") is not the cause of beauty, a theory that had originated with Socrates. Burke uses the same example of the inner organs of man as fit, but not beautiful.[15]

Mendelssohn distinguishes three sources of pleasure; the first stems from the unity of the manifold and is called beauty, the second is the unanimity of the manifold called perfection, and the third results from the improvement of our physique and is called sensual pleasure.

Ideally, aesthetic pleasure contains all three elements, but practically, only works of music have achieved this aim for Mendelssohn, who nevertheless hopes for the discovery of new forms of art that will result in the same unified pleasure for the other senses. The sensation of perfection produces a feeling of bodily ease and relaxation, a "pleasant affect" that consists of a harmonious nervous tension and a stimulation without fatigue. In *Rhapsody*, Mendelssohn adds that sensual pleasure not only improves our bodily condition but leads to a harmonious play of all human faculties. While the pleasure of viewing a painting here comes dangerously close to that of eating a cake, Mendelssohn nevertheless advances the fruitful idea of the harmonious play of faculties caused by aesthetic cognition. Moreover, he distinguishes between the perfection of the object and the perfection of its representation in the subject. This important differentiation allows for a beautiful representation of objects that fail to be perfect themselves: "This artistic representation can be sensually perfect even if the object of it would be neither good nor beautiful in nature" (*Main Principles*, 431). Although Mendelssohn insists on the perfection of aesthetic representation as a necessity, the distinction between artistic representation and the referential object to which an independent aesthetic value can be assigned also takes the first cautious step in the direction of representations, both without recognizable object and without beauty.

Mendelssohn was also the first German philosopher to devote significant attention to the concept of sublimity that had already been discussed in Britain and France for a couple of decades. He defines the sublime as the sensual expression of an extraordinary perfection, as well as beauty of such enormous dimensions that it cannot be sensually comprehended all at once. Although it remains unclear how we should judge something to be beautiful first in order to move from there to the realization that we fail to encompass it and consequently have to classify it as sublime, Mendelssohn insists on the beautiful element in the sublime object. Sublimity produces a divergent complex of emotions in us due to the pleasure that results from its beautiful aspect and the frustration caused by our failure to grasp it in its entirety. Unlike Edmund Burke, however, Mendelssohn regards sublimity not as inciting terror but admiration and, thus, associates it with an ultimately positive emotional response. Most future philosophers, however, insofar as they deal with the concept of the sublime, will refer back to Kant's concept of it and disregard the contributions of Mendelssohn. His notion of the naïve, on the other hand, clearly influenced Schiller's definition of naïve art. He defines as naïve the simplistic representation of a beautiful and noble soul. Thus, the naïve is restricted to the representation of man and his actions, although these have to be of relevance. The representation itself will hide more than it reveals, and therefore it conforms to the rhetorical style of *genus humilis,* yet without weightiness of its object, the naïve collapses into the ridiculous (cf. *On the Sublime*).

Another influential feature of Mendelssohn's writings is his attempt to classify the individual forms of art according to a semiotic system, distinguishing the different art forms according to the signs they use. He follows the French philosopher Jean-Baptiste Dubos (1670–1742) by basing painting, sculpture, architecture, music, and dance on natural signs that are determined by their affinity to the represented object, whereas poetry and rhetoric depend on arbitrary signs without any connecting element between sign and signified (except for the rare onomatopoetic instance). This conception was taken up and modified in the writings of both Lessing and Herder and might very well be the first attempt at a semiotic theory of art in German.

Interesting as these ideas may be, Mendelssohn's main importance nevertheless is to be found in his undertaking to secure greater autonomy for art. While Baumgarten labored to gain acceptance for the cognitive aspects of beauty and art, Mendelssohn did the same for art's emotional elements. And whereas Baumgarten's theory led to a strengthening of the *Regelpoetik* (poetics of rules), Mendelssohn emphasized pleasure over regulations. With this, he contributed significantly to the paradigmatic shift from an aesthetics of production to an aesthetics of reception and a general psychological aesthetics that reached its epitome in the writings of Karl Philipp Moritz (1756–1793).

This tendency toward greater autonomy of the aesthetic sphere was aided further by Mendelssohn's concept of *Billigungsvermögen* (faculty of approbation) that must be considered a direct precursor of Kant's notion of "disinterested pleasure."[16] Mendelssohn, who in turn was preceded by Shaftesbury and his notion of aesthetic sensation as "disinterested love," as well as by Dubos's concept of *plaisir pur* (whether he knew of Winckelmann's notion that the reception of art must be "cleansed of all intentions" is hard to assess), distinguished between three faculties of the soul, the faculty of cognition, the appetite, and the faculty of sensation (after 1785 called faculty of approbation). The third faculty handles aesthetic perception that is removed from both rational cognition and appetite as a form of pleasure without desire. Finally, Mendelssohn argues for greater autonomy of art by separating art and morality, to some degree, by allowing for the artistic representation of morally wrong acts because of their emotive potential. These morally reprehensible acts do not serve only as negative examples in art; they are artistically good and valuable elements:

> The stage has its own morality. In life nothing is good that is not grounded in our perfection; on the stage, however, everything is good that has its ground in the most forceful passions. The reason of tragedy is to incite passions. Therefore, suicide is theatrically good. (*Letters on Sensations*, 94)

This is not to say that art does not fulfill ethical purposes for Mendelssohn, since it does so without a doubt. And yet its subject matter is free from regulation; and it is this freedom that allows art to contribute to man's betterment. Mendelssohn's psychological aesthetics of perfection ultimately underwrites an anthropological model that unites the sensual perfection of art with the perfectability of man. As art is no longer the result of successfully applied rules, the original creator, that is, the genius, moves to the forefront of the discussion. Works of art are created by the man of genius, who is characterized for Mendelssohn by his perfection of all faculties and their harmonious interplay (*Main Principles*, 433f.). But art does not only originate in perfection; it also stirs its recipient toward it: "The soul does not only enjoy the contentment of its body as a spectator, as it responds to the perfection of an object with serenity; rather, through sensual pleasure it gains no small degree of perfection by which the pleasurable sensation is enlivened in turn" (*Rhapsody*, 392f.). Art turns into a means of aesthetic education – a notion that plays a significant role in Schiller's *Letters on Aesthetic Education* and in Goethe's bildungsroman *Wilhelm Meister's Apprenticeship*. Mendelssohn has a clear picture of man's perfection: "The perfection of man consists – despite the ridicule of those who despise wisdom – next to the well-being of the body in a cleansed reason, in an upright heart and in a fine and tender sense for true beauty, or in a harmony of the lower and upper faculties of the soul" (*Briefe über Kunst* – Letters on art, 166).

Mendelssohn's main interest with respect to aesthetics does not lie with its epistemological nor with its ontological aspects but, rather, with its psychological element. Therefore, it is hardly surprising if he does not explicitly address the question of what a work of art is in opposition to nonartistic objects. We can nevertheless deduce an ontological definition: A work of art is the perfect (or at least properly idealized) representation of an object that does not have to be beautiful in itself and that causes us pleasure. This definition is somewhat weak and due to the shift in its definition of art from an objective feature to a subjective response – a move that Kant will shortly thereafter radicalize. The problems of this subjectivization will be discussed in the context of Kant's approach that is altogether more sophisticated and well thought out.

Mendelssohn does, however, attribute a practical function to art, namely, its potential to move man toward perfection. With this, art becomes an indispensable tool in all education that has little choice but to become aesthetic.

Epistemologically, Mendelssohn's theory remains weak, since it does not attribute any unique cognitive function to art. It results from a skepticism regarding the cognitive approach to art that tends to eclipse the emotional aspect. Since Mendelssohn considered it his role to emphasize the contentment produced by encounters with aesthetic perfection, the subordination of the epistemological moment is likely to have been the price Mendelssohn had to pay. Between Baumgarten's emphasis on cognition and Mendelssohn's stress on aesthetic psychology and human perfectability, the realm for aesthetic investigation was largely staked out.

Baumgarten and Mendelssohn are a farewell and an annunciation. Their aesthetic theories are committed to the metaphysical rationalism of the eighteenth century, and yet they undermine its foundations involuntarily. But because they adhere to the rationalism of the Leibniz/Wolff system, they do not achieve the autonomy necessary to establish aesthetics as an independent discipline in philosophy. Both thinkers open vistas for the idealists, but they do not advance strong aesthetic paradigms. The age of aesthetic paradigms in philosophy only begins with Kant.

2

Kant

If the single most influential text in the history of philosophical aesthetics were to be chosen, Immanuel Kant's (1724–1804) *Kritik der Urteilskraft* (Critique of judgment) of 1790 might very well turn out to be the one that a majority of philosophers would point to. Despite all the good reasons they can list for their justification, the selection of the third *Critique* is peculiar, because in the history of philosophical aesthetics (that properly only begins with precisely this publication), Kant is probably the one thinker who attributes the least significance to the work of art. And yet Kant must be regarded as the philosopher who at the same time claimed an importance for the aesthetic judgment that is on a par with those of a cognitive and moral nature. Kant, however, does not understand an aesthetic judgment to refer exclusively to art. In fact, for him most aesthetic judgments are not about art, but nature. They are about beauty in natural objects, as well as about our experience of the sublime.

The *Critique of Judgment* was written not as a theory of art and beauty but as an exploration of that faculty that is meant to guarantee the unity of reason, as Kant explains in his introduction. After having written the first two *Critiques*, he encountered the difficulty that the principles of pure reason and of practical reason are not identical and that, therefore, a gap had opened between theory and practice or freedom and nature. The third *Critique* is Kant's attempt to bridge this rift through the advancement of judgment as a faculty that mediates between sensuality and cognition on the one hand and between sensuality and moral action on the other.

Art nevertheless achieves a new dignity in this philosophy that stems from its independence. Art for Kant is seen neither as a faulty cognition nor as a handmaiden of any specific ethical teaching. These insights, however, can by no means be taken for granted. The philosophical tradition had been very skeptical about art's capacity to contribute insights to the workings of our world or any transcendent realm. Plato had argued in the *Republic* (Book X) that art imitates objects that the artist finds in his surroundings, but these objects in themselves are already mimetic approximations to ideas, mere copies of a lost original. These ideas are eternal, without change, and as such they are preconditions for the existence of their material manifestations. Thus, a bed is an object that can only be produced by a craftsman because he knows about the idea of the bed; and yet the individual bed will not achieve the perfection of the idea after which it is modeled. A painted bed, moreover, does not even possess the usefulness of a real bed; it is a mere depiction that shares only a few characteristics with the real bed and even fewer with the bed-idea. Looking at a painted bed, therefore, can teach the viewer disappointingly little about those facts that matter most, namely, the ideas. Although Plato also accounts for the possibility that the artist, like the craftsman, does not imitate material objects but paints his pictures according to his vision of the idea[1] (a notion that will become relevant for Schelling's and Schopenhauer's philosophy of art), the general tendency of Plato's philosophy is to devalue art in its epistemic potential, that is, the possibility to ground any kind of insight.

This suspicious attitude toward art's claim to knowledge persists more or less unbroken until the eighteenth century.[2] Gotthold Ephraim Lessing (1729–1781), for example, states in the influential essay *Laokoon oder über die Grenzen der Malerei und Poesie* (Laokoon or on the limits of painting and poetry, 1766), faintly echoing the aesthetics of the Stoa:

> Truth is necessary for the soul; and it becomes tyranny to exert any force upon it in respect to this vital need. The ultimate end of the arts, however, is pleasure; and pleasure is dispensible.[3]

Even Baumgarten, as we have seen, cannot free himself entirely of this aspect of art theory insofar as he claims a potential for cognitive insight for sensual and artistic perception, but this insight is still of a lower nature than that of reason. For Kant, who valued Baumgarten highly as a metaphysician but not at all as an aesthetician, the attempt to advance principles of reason for the critical judgment of beauty and to claim the status of science for such rules was hopelessly flawed. Kant argues that art will always seem inferior when its potential for cognition is compared to that of reason. Therefore, the status of art can only be raised if the connection between art and cognition is severed: Both must inhabit realms independent of each other. This is the aim of the *Critique of Judgment*, namely, to establish our pronouncements on art and beauty not as an inferior version of our judgments on truth or morality, but as independent of both, albeit related to both and thus able to span their divergence.

Art, however, does pay a price for its new independence as well. Although Kant has a certain interest in showing that art still relates to morality, its relations to our faculties of cognition are much less important to him. To be sure, the aesthetic judgment is not and cannot be devoid of cognitive elements altogether, and yet Kant reduces them drastically by advancing the notion that art has basically no relation to truth.[4] One of the ongoing projects of the aesthetic tradition ever since has been to challenge Kant in this respect and to demonstrate the epistemic relevance of works of art. This project, as we shall see, led to an overcompensation in several cases where exclusive or at least predominant truth-claims were conferred upon art.

There is another reason that Kant's *Critique of Judgment* can be considered a watershed in the history of aesthetics. It is precisely in this text that the term "aesthetics" comes to acquire the meaning we attribute to it today. The term traditionally referred to the theory of sensual perception, and Kant himself uses it with this understanding in the *Critique of Pure Reason* of 1781 in the section on "Transcendental Aesthetics," in which he attempts to demonstrate the transcendental conditions of sensual experience. Less than a decade later, though, the term aesthetics has shifted its meaning for Kant, and now he employs it as a designation of his theory of taste, that is, an inquiry into beauty and art.

Despite this new junction of the term aesthetics with the artistic and beautiful, Kant's exploration of these areas contains hardly any references to concrete works of art. St. Peter's in Rome and the Egyptian pyramids are mentioned as sole examples of works of art, but only in passing and without any attempt at an analysis. Moreover, Kant does not cite them as examples of the beautiful, but in the context of his discussion of sublimity. This almost complete absence of all references to specific works of art has led to the distinction between Kant's aesthetics as formal and that of primarily Hegel as one of content, all the more so since the latter's *Lectures on Aesthetics* are, under one perspective, a veritable world history of art.

The sense in which Kant uses the term "critique" must be distinguished from that which the term came to acquire simultaneously in art criticism. Critique in the context of Kant's philosophy refers to the attempt to investigate the requirements of the possibility of concrete philosophical endeavors. Kant's critical project in the *Critique of Pure Reason* begins with a doubt about the truth of all synthetic a priori sentences in order to then move to the demonstration of their possibility that is in accordance with the conditions of our reason. At the same time, however, the term critique also started to be used for the process of the qualitative evaluation of individual works of art. In this sense, it is employed in Herder's *Kritische Wälder* (Critical forests, 1769) and practised in Lessing's *Hamburgische Dramaturgie* (1767–9).

Apart from the fact that it is not Kant's interest to interpret individual artistic achievements but, rather, to lay the foundations for our ability to judge something as beautiful or artistic, he also did not have a very intimate knowledge of the arts. In fact, Kant's firsthand familiarity with works of art was limited at best. As has been pointed out correctly, Kant did not even take those examples of great art for his model that were available to him, like the Königsberg cathedral, but instead oriented himself toward wallpaper patterns, porcelain, paper cutouts, and the carved handles of walking sticks as prime artistic examples.[5]

The *Critique of Judgment* of 1790 was not Kant's first attempt to deal with the subject of art. In his so-called precritical period, that is, before the year 1770, Kant not only published on philosophy but also wrote treatises on the natural sciences and in other fields. His first text on beauty is his booklet of 1764 *Beobachtungen über das Gefühl des Schönen und Erhabenen* (Observations about the sensation of the beautiful and sublime), which closely follows Edmund Burke's publication of 1757 *Enquiry into the Origin of Our Ideal of the Sublime and Beautiful.* Kant's text, though, is more a study in anthropology and moral psychology than in aesthetics. But he does treat questions of beauty and art in other contexts, namely, in his lectures on logic and anthropology, as well as in a treatise written after the *Critique of Judgment*, the *Anthropology* of 1798. And yet the most influential and original treatment of the newly founded philosophical discipline of aesthetics can certainly be found in the third *Critique* that we shall explore in some detail.[6]

Beauty: The Judgment of Taste

Pre-Kantian philosophers who dealt with questions of art and beauty had kept these two notions more or less strictly separated. Hand in hand with this separation went a decisive difference in valuation. Whereas beauty had always been at least respected, if not highly praised, art, on the other hand – including all the trades that were frowned upon because of the necessary physical labor – oftentimes achieved only a dubious status in the reflections of these philosophers. Plato, for example, placed the idea of beauty together with that of the good on the very top of his hierarchy of ideas. In his view, beauty, understood as a harmonious totality, mirrors the state of the world and the cosmos as created by a demiurge (*Timaeus*). This ideal of the divinely created cosmos that radiates the beauty of its creator continues to determine aesthetic thought from Plotinus to Thomas Aquinus, but the thinkers who subscribe to this ideal generally have rather little to say about the value of art. Kant does not differ from the tradition in this respect all that much. He, too, separates beauty from art and treats both of them under different headings in his *Critique of Judgment* (CJ). In this division, beauty is the much wider category and contains all of the artistic products in addition to all the objects of beauty in nature. This emphasis on natural beauty was soon to disappear from the writings on aesthetics – as we shall see shortly, Hegel deliberately excludes nature from his aesthetic reflections – and did not return to aesthetic investigations until the late twentieth century, most prominently with Adorno.

Kant distinguishes two types of beauty, a distinction that will turn out to be somewhat at odds with several of his valuations in the field of beauty:

There are two types of beauty: free beauty (pulchritudo vaga) or merely adherent beauty (pulrichtudo adherens). The first does not presuppose any concept of what the object is meant to be; the second presupposes such concept and the perfection of the object according to it. The types of the former are called (independently existing) beauties of this or that object; the other, as adherent to a concept, is attributed to objects that are classed under the concept of a particular purpose. (CJ, §16)

As examples of free beauty Kant lists flowers (the purpose of which only the botanist knows), "drawings à la grecque, vine patterns as framework or on wallpaper, ... all music without text." Its opposite category, namely adherent beauty, is purposive. Kant mentions the beauty of a horse, a building, and the human figure as examples; and the judgment regarding them depends as much on a sense of purpose as on a concept of perfection. Whereas the judgment of free beauty is pure, that of adherent beauty is an applied, impure judgment. In order to find an architectural object or the body of man beautiful, we need to connect the object to a concept of its purpose in the world, its telos, and hence a sense of its usefulness. Yet "the connection of the good [in this case the purposive] with beauty does the purity of the latter harm" (CJ, §16). Kant, however, does not want to classify *objects* according to their type of beauty, but only *judgments* regarding these objects. He states that many arguments about beauty result from a confusion of the speakers regarding their point of view, so that the beauty of a flower could be judged by a botanist as purposive while his interlocutor refers to it as an example of free beauty. The dispute can be solved on the level of argument about the object itself, but only through reflection on the type of discourse brought to bear on the object.

As fascinating as this self-reflexive aesthetic turn is, it does not solve all the problems that Kant's distinction of pure and adherent beauty produces. While everything in this paragraph seems to indicate a superiority of the pure aesthetic judgment, all the following discussions surprisingly rank adherent beauty as higher. A certain tension between these views, however, cannot be eliminated. Kant's definition of beauty as purposiveness without purpose does align well with his notion of free beauty, yet in the paragraph following this discussion he argues that the highest form of beauty is the human body, that is, precisely an object that receives its beauty through its manifestation of a purpose.

The reverse effect takes place with music, the only form of art that Kant includes under the category of free beauty. Yet in his discussion of music in §54, Kant ranks music as the lowest of the arts, since "it only plays with sensations," is "more pleasure than culture," and is farthest removed from understanding of all the arts. Furthermore, while the association of the good with the beautiful is presented in §16 as an infringement on pure beauty and, hence, as adverse to the pure aesthetic judgment, we will see that in §59 Kant goes to great lengths in order to establish precisely such a connection between the moral and the aesthetic judgment. Thus, we are left with the impression that the distinction between the two types of beauty is not integrated well into Kant's exploration of the aesthetic.[7]

To be sure, not all that is beautiful has to be art for Kant, but all that is art has to be beautiful. Kant does not allow for the possibility of ugly art, although he concedes – following Aristotle's pronouncement in his *Poetics* – that art can certainly portray ugly subjects in a beautiful manner:

> The Furies, diseases, devastions of war and the like can (as harmful events) be described beautifully, even be depicted in painting; only one type of ugliness cannot be represented according to nature without destroying all aesthetic pleasure and hence aesthetic beauty, namely that which causes disgust. (CJ, §48)

The part of the *Critique of Judgment* in which he analyzes beauty and our judgment of it, namely, the "Analytic of Aesthetic Judgment," is probably the most tightly argued section of the third *Critique*, although there are still enough problematic and puzzling statements left. One of the aspects that might strike us as somewhat confusing is the fact that Kant presents his four definitions of the aesthetic judgment and thus of beauty in the form of four seemingly contradictory theses. To sort out these contradictions is one task of our explication. We should mention in passing that the fourfold structure of the aesthetic judgment is set up according to the criteria established for judgments in the *Critique of Pure Reason* (1781/1787), namely quality, quantity, relation, and modality. By applying these necessary moments of the analytic and synthetic judgments to the aesthetic judgment, Kant emphasizes the cognitive aspect of the latter. Although the aesthetic judgment cannot lay claim to the logical universality, it nevertheless invites, as we shall see, universal consent. In order to evaluate what is beautiful, Kant argues, we need taste, which he defines as "the faculty of estimating the beautiful" (CJ, §1, footnote). Such an estimate must meet four criteria in order to be considered a judgment of taste, and that in turn means that beauty is defined by those very same criteria.

The first and possibly most surprising moment of the judgment of taste is that it does not refer to any qualities of the object, but merely to the feeling of pleasure or displeasure within the subject. The opening sentences of the *Critique of Judgment* are remarkable for their radicality, and they should still elicit a reaction of at least surprise from the reader:

> In order to discern whether something is beautiful or not, we do not submit its representation to (the faculty of) understanding for cognition, rather we relate it by means of the imagination (possibly connected to understanding) to the subject and its feeling of pleasure and displeasure. The judgment of taste is therefore no cognitive judgment, hence not logical, but aesthetic, meaning that whose determining ground can only be subjective. (CJ, §1)

Kant makes it perfectly clear that the aesthetic judgment shares precious little common ground with the rational judgment, and that art therefore has no capacity to teach us anything. Beauty has no relation to insight and cognition.[8]

It is equally important for Kant to separate the aesthetic judgment not only from the rational judgment but also from two forms of pleasure with which it could easily be confused. He distinguishes three kinds of pleasure of which the pleasure in beauty is one. The other two pleasures, though, differ in one very important aspect from this one, because they are interested in the existence of the object. The first of these is the pleasure of the agreeable, which is purely subjective. This type of pleasure accounts for my preference of wine over beer or of soup over salad. As these examples demonstrate, my pleasure in the agreeable has a strong interest in its existence, because I have no intention of leaving the object intact; instead, I want to use it for the gratification of my desires.

The same holds true for the pleasure we feel in encountering the good. This pleasure is precisely the opposite of the agreeable, not in that it is not subjective at all but in that it depends on a concept of the good, and that this concept must hold true, not only for myself but for everyone. The cognition of the good, however, brings in its wake the interest in its existence, because we cannot think of something as good without wanting it to exist. The only kind of pleasure that does not take an interest in the existence of its object is therefore the aesthetic pleasure – a concept that occurs for the first time in the aesthetic writings of Hutcheson and Shaftesbury. Instead of inciting desire, the pleasure of beauty frees us from all such longings and strivings – a thought that will soon emerge at the center of Schopenhauer's aesthetics. Despite beauty's power to "quicken" our faculties, it also calms us. It is at the same time profoundly moving and deeply satisfying, stirring, and quieting. This, as it were, becomes the starting point for Schiller's reception of Kant. Kant, thus, gives the first of his four definitions: "Taste is the faculty of judging an object or a mode of representation based on pleasure or aversion, yet without any interest. The object of such pleasure is called beautiful" (CJ, §5). An anticipation of this position can be found in the aesthetics of Karl Philipp Moritz (1756–1793), who writes in his earliest treatise on the subject in 1785, hence half a decade before the third *Critique:* "But what brings us pleasure without actually being useful we call beautiful. . . . I have to take pleasure in a beautiful object purely for its own sake; to this end the lack of an exterior purpose must be replaced by an inner purpose; the object must be something perfect in itself."[9]

Whereas the pleasure of the agreeable is purely subjective, that of the beautiful is not, because it lays claim to a universal delight. On the other hand, the aesthetic judgment cannot claim that kind of universality that is only possible for rational judgments. Therefore, aesthetic pleasure becomes defined as *subjective universality.*[10] This second contradiction can be explained and solved as follows:

True universality, Kant argues, can only be achieved by means of concepts, that is, something that is validated by its logical necessity and that cannot therefore be disputed without self-contradiction. Aesthetic judgments, however, are not of this kind. In order to see how they differ, we need to understand how we arrive at any kind of perceptual knowledge. For Kant, there are three faculties involved in the type of knowledge that depends on experience, the first being *sensibility* (the passive reception of sensory stimuli), the second *imagination* (the ordering of the sensory manifold into a unity), and the third *understanding* (the provision of a concept under which to subsume the results of imagination's activity). It is the nature of the aesthetic judgment, though, never to move from step two, imagination, to step three, understanding. But since only understanding can provide concepts, and no universality can be reached without conceptualization, the aesthetic judgment has to resort to some other claim that allows it to transcend its subjectivity.[11]

Kant explains this universalizing claim of the aesthetic judgment by recourse to the commonality of the pleasure involved in it. Not to reach conceptualization does not mean to be a frustrated judgment but, rather, the opposite. The nature of the aesthetic pleasure can be found in the constant attempt to move from imagination to understanding without ever arriving there. This free play of the faculties, as Kant calls it, produces a feeling of pleasure that results from a "quickening of faculties." No matter how many concepts understanding offers for that aesthetic unity that imagination passes on to it as a candidate for conceptualization, no concept ever suffices. Yet the attempts at finding an appropriate concept cannot be abandoned. Ever new conceptual suggestions have to be made. This process is, in principle, endless because it can never be brought to a satisfying conclusion. Aesthetic pleasure, therefore, always renews itself. We don't get tired of looking at a familiar painting or listening to the same symphony because we do not come to terms with these sources of aesthetic pleasure by placing them under a concept to which we could then return for future reference.

This thought is expressed in a slightly different fashion in Kant's notion of the *aesthetic idea*. Kant's famous definition reads as follows:

> By an aesthetic idea I mean that representation of imagination that incites much thought, yet without any thought, i.e. concept ever being adequate to it and that can therefore not be reached and rendered comprehensible by any language. (CJ, §49)

Kant describes an aesthetic idea as that procedure by which we attempt to subsume the unity of the manifold under a concept, but fail to do so. In other words, it is never possible for us to say what a work of art is exactly about, although it appears to have advanced into a depth that could not have been reached by other means. We will have to continue to make attempts to express what this depth contains, but no single one can be satisfying and final. We shall always have to return to the beautiful object and puzzle over it again. What we find in this formulation of the aesthetic idea is one of the first attempts of modern aesthetics to explain the ultimate uninterpretability of works of art especially.[12] This idea can be found in many subsequent aesthetics, especially in the romantic contributions, most prominently in Schelling, as well as in Heidegger and Adorno, although none of them share the subjectivist aesthetics of Kant. Ultimate uninterpretability after Kant becomes more a feature of the object than characteristic of the aesthetic pleasure that the subject feels.

It might also be, however, that Kant is less consistent when it comes to the aesthetic idea than it appears at first sight. One critic has argued that the third *Critique* does not only establish a new hermeneutic paradigm in aesthetics, namely, one that rests on the infinite interpretability of the work of art, but also legitimizes a variety of aesthetic forms that resist this paradigm. Both music and nonsense literature are regarded as too far removed from conceptual cognition to be more than merely pleasurable for Kant, yet on the other hand, he argues that these anticognitive aesthetic pleasures are greatly beneficial for man's mental and physical well-being.[13]

It still needs to be explained why the aesthetic judgment can make any claim to universality, because the pleasure of the agreeable certainly cannot. We have seen, however, that the agreeable is tied up with the interest of the subject in its existence, whereas the beautiful had been defined as that which pleases without satisfying any concrete antecedent desire of the subject. Kant claims that I can expect everyone else to agree with my aesthetic judgment exactly because no purely personal like, dislike, or interest is at stake. When we encounter the beautiful, we should all experience the same pleasurable feeling of the free play of faculties. We have no arguments at hand actually to convince others that a given object is beautiful, but we can reasonably expect them to share our judgment nevertheless because as human beings with the same faculties as ours, they should experience the same stimulation of these faculties. Thus, Kant defines: "The *beautiful* is that which, without any concept, pleases universally" (CJ, §9).

Kant's fourth definition of the aesthetic judgment resembles the second one very closely and elaborates on the argument from a different angle; therefore, it is less repetitious to treat it together with the second definition before we advance to the third. For our purposes, it suffices to point out Kant's claim that the aesthetic judgment is necessarily collective: "The beautiful is that which, without any concept, is cognized as an object of a *necessary* pleasure" (CJ, §22).

The third moment advances the famous definition of beauty as purposiveness without purpose. For Kant, the work of art or the beautiful object of nature does not have an end outside itself; it does not serve any purpose and is thus free from all finality. One reason that we can never attribute an end to a beautiful object is that every definition of an end for Kant relies on some idea of perfection, namely, the ultimate purpose of an object. Since beauty, as we have seen, can never be conceptualized, no beautiful object can ever be thought to have a purpose. And yet when we encounter it, it seems that it has been designed as if to fulfill a very particular function, since there is nothing arbitrary about it. One way to solve this seeming contradiction is to think of it as saying that beauty does of course incite pleasure in us and that this is very well a purpose. And yet the beautiful object does not exist on behalf of its viewer; it is truly independent. Beauty seems to exist for our pleasure, yet it is not the aim of any beautiful object to do so. Kant's fourth definition reads: "*Beauty* is the form of purposiveness in an object, insofar as it is perceived without the representation of a purpose" (CJ, §17).

To sum up this discussion of the aesthetic judgment, Kant settles the old dispute whether one can argue about taste or not (*de gustibus non est disputandum*) by stating that it is certainly possible to do so, but the argument can never be settled because neither party could give any universally valid reason for its judgment. Although aesthetic judgments do not provide knowledge, they are still related to the faculty of understanding, and thus they participate in cognition. Since animals lack cognition as based on concepts, their world certainly knows the agreeable, but it is devoid of all beauty.[14]

Sublimity

Kant distinguishes between two manifestations of the sublime: the mathematical sublime and the dynamic sublime. In both cases, the sublime is not a quality of an object but, rather, much like the pleasure that we call beauty, a response of the subject:

> ... the sublime in the strictest sense cannot be contained in any sensual form, but only refers to ideas of reason. (CJ, §23)

Kant defines the sublime as that "which is absolutely great," and which here means "great beyond all comparison" (CJ, §25). It follows that it can therefore not properly be an object of the senses, because imagination will not be able to synthesize the sensual manifold of an absolutely great object into a unity. In other words, there are no sublime objects, but only sublime states of subjectivity brought about by encounters with certain classes of objects.

In the case of the mathematical sublime, it is primarily the idea of infinity that qualifies as sublime. We can never arrive at the concept of infinity, namely as an absolute totality, by means of sensory experience and, thus, by the means of the faculty of imagination. Imagination does not allow us to think a totality because every sum of units of measurements can be further enlarged. We can always add on to any number, large as it may be, and we can always think of any space as expandable. And yet to be able to think the infinite indicates that a faculty exists in man that transcends experience, and this bestows a unique dignity upon man: "To merely be able to think the given infinite without contradictions requires a faculty in the mind that is itself supersensible" (CJ, §26). This experience, that the mind abandons imagination and still contains an idea as soaring as infinity, endows man with a renewed sense of worthiness and elevation. (In the context of his discussion of quantity, Hegel later attributed this shudder caused by – bad – infinity not to sublimity but merely to the boredom of the series that never finds an end; *Encyclopedia of Philosophical Sciences*, §104.)

Our encounters with the causes of the dynamical sublime, however, are different insofar as they contain a moment of anxiety. In these cases, we experience nature as a force strong enough to destroy us and, therefore, as "a source of fear." Our first response to a situation we later might come to call sublime is, therefore, intense displeasure since we feel vulnerable and inferior to the brute forces of nature. Kant famously mentions

> boldly overhanging and, as it were, threatening rocks, thunderclouds piled up in the sky, moving along with thunder and lightning, volcanoes in all their destructive power, hurricanes with the destruction in their track, the boundless ocean rising in anger, a high cataract of a mighty river and so on. (CJ, §28)

And yet this experience in itself has no sublime value at all because without a second step, we do not arrive at sublimity. The displeasure of inferiority must be turned into a sense of independence and even human superiority over nature. In order to achieve this, a process of reflection is needed. As long as we are in a position of safety – aesthetic sublimity has of course no place in the struggle for survival – the encounter with the forces of nature lets us discover in ourselves a "power of resistance" that stems from the discovery that human freedom is not subject to natural destruction, but transcends the sensory realm:

> The irresistability of it [nature] forces us on the one side to acknowledge our physical helplessness, but on the other side reveals a faculty of estimating ourselves independent of it. On this faculty rests a self-preservation of a very different kind as that which can be challenged and endangered by nature, so that humanity remains unhumiliated in our person, even though man would be defeated by that force. (CJ, §28)

Eventually, we do arrive at a sense of pleasure that results from our insight into the indestructibility of human nature. Therefore, what we ultimately call sublime is certainly not that phenomenon of nature that threatens to destroy us with its might, but exactly our feeling of independence from nature.

Whereas beauty has a calming effect on man, sublimity can be understood as an expression of moral energy. The sublime experience is the triumph of the supersensory part of the self over the material and finite part. While beauty rests on the basis of sensory experience, sublimity aims at abandoning the sensory and moving toward reason. Beauty and sublimity, therefore, have very little in common; in fact, they are opposed to each other. Schiller, as well as the idealists Schelling and Hegel, will attempt to overcome this opposition because they argue that without a unification of beauty and sublimity, the self will remain divided between sensibility and morality. In Kant's aesthetics, however, these two experiences stand problematically unconnected.

Fine Art, Genius

Kant had declared beauty not to be a quality of the object. And yet when he comes to talk about art, or fine art as he labels it, he does make attempts to define the beautiful features of the arts in question. For this purpose he distinguishes, much like Lessing in his *Laokoon,* between temporal and atemporal arts (he actually separates poetry and rhetoric from the temporal arts as a third category, but this need not concern us here). In the case of the atemporal arts of painting and sculpture, beauty rests with the draftsmanship, not with color. For Kant, only perceptible form should enter the aesthetic judgment, but not the play of colors that is merely agreeable. In music, beauty is seen to rest with the composition, although Kant remains rather vague about what we are to understand under this term. Kant leaves no doubt that for him the beauty of nature always surpasses that of art[15] because it lays claim to immediate interest, whereas artistic products always mediate between their subject matter and the recipient. This explains why Kant holds that the work of art should look like a product of nature:

> Hence the purposiveness in products of the fine arts must not seem purposeful, although they are purposeful; i.e. fine art must be able to be considered as nature, our consciousness of it as art notwithstanding. A product of art appears to be nature when it agrees exactly with the rules according to which alone the product can become what it is intended to be, yet without displaying the embarrassment of academic form, i.e. without indicating that the rule had guided the artist and restrained his mental powers. (CJ, §45)

Kant argues here that art must not negate its character as a human product, yet it shall look like nature nevertheless. How are we to resolve this new contradiction? It seems that Kant positions himself in a tradition of aesthetic thought that found its most coherent expression in the Renaissance ideal of *sprezzatura,* that is, the seemingly effortless production of works of art that was, for example, advocated by Baldassare Castiglione in *Il Cortegiano* of 1528. The final artistic product is supposed to look uncontrived, natural, and effortless, instead of showing traits of adherence to rules or imitating previous works of art.

For Kant, there is only one way to create artistic products that look like natural ones, namely, through genius: "Fine arts must necessarily be regarded as arts of *genius*" (CJ, §46). We should think of a genius as an outstandingly talented person brought forth by nature so that he or she can in turn produce works of art:

> Genius is the talent (natural endowment) which gives the rule to art. Because talent as an innate productive ability of the artist belongs itself to nature, one could also say: Genius is the innate, mental aptitude (ingenium) through which nature gives the rule to art. (CJ, §46)

Much has been made of this statement that nature gives the rule to art through the genius, and there are probably a number of readings possible. It seems clear, though, that art involves rules. But unlike the traditional rhetorical system, the poetics of the Baroque period, or the eighteenth-century Swiss critics Bodmer and Breitinger, Kant does not think that artistic products result from the adherence to previously established rules. And yet, if every work of art would establish rules that held true only for itself and no other product, the very notion of a rule would not make sense. There are no rules that apply to one case only. Therefore, the genius should probably be seen as one who knows about the established rules for the productions of works of art, but who also knows when to disregard them. The originality of the genius lies in the ability to adhere to rules and to expand them at the same time, and he or she does so in a seemingly effortless and unstrained way.

Taste, like artistic production, also does not proceed according to rules. And yet it, too, is in need of some kind of orientation that Kant finds in the outstanding works of art of our tradition:

> Among all faculties and talents taste, because its judgment is not determined by concepts and regulations, is the one most in need of those examples which have received applause for the longest time in the course of culture so that it does not fall back into the rudeness of its earliest efforts and become crude again. (CJ, §32)

Winckelmann had in his 1763 *Abhandlung von der Fähigkeit der Empfindung des Schönen in der Kunst und dem Unterrichte in derselben* (Treatise on the capability to perceive the beautiful in art and the instruction thereof) also declared – and both find themselves in agreement with the rhetorical tradition: "Thus true and complete knowledge of beauty in art can only be achieved through contemplation of the originals themselves, and ideally in Rome."[16] But despite this postulated necessity to provide schooling and corrective mechanisms for taste, it ultimately remains unclear how exactly the paradigms of tradition are supposed to fulfill this function, since they cannot achieve the status of regulations.

One more aspect should be pointed out in Kant's discussion of fine art. We already saw that the aesthetic judgment transcends the purely subjective sphere and invites everyone's agreement. Therefore, the encounter with beauty somehow seems to have a tendency to force us out of our isolation and to establish contact with the other members of our society:

Empirically, the beautiful only exists in society. And if we grant that the impulse to society is natural to man and that the fitness and liking for it, i.e. sociability, is a requirement for man as a social being and a predicate of humanity, then it follows that taste as a faculty of judgment through which we communicate our feeling to everyone else must be considered a means of promoting that which everyone's natural inclination calls for. (CJ, §41)

Kant states as the explicit purpose of the work of art: "Fine art, on the other hand, is a mode of representation that is purposeful in itself, and that, although without purpose, advances the culture of the mental powers in the interest of social communication" (CJ, §44). All forms of beauty, be they artistic or natural, incite in us a pleasureable feeling and the desire to communicate this pleasure so that others might share in it. Art, it could be argued, is one of the means to strengthen communal ties, if not a means to help establish a community in the first place.

Friedrich Schiller echoes this notion in his 1793 letters on aesthetics to his patron, the Prince Friedrich Christian of Schleswig-Holstein-Sonderburg-Augustenburg. These are now collected as the *Augustenburger Briefe* that constitute the raw material for the *Letters on the Aesthetic Education of Man.* There, Schiller claims that the communicative nature of judgments of taste unites individuals into a society (see Letter of December 1793). Johann Gottlieb Fichte (1762–1814) also takes up the same idea in his 1794 *On the Spirit and the Letter in Philosophy.* In the second of these fictional letters, Fichte states that artistic inspiration expands the individuality of the artist into a collective disposition [*Universalsinn*], so that in turn, the work of art unites individual men and women into a community – an idea that from this time on regularly reemerges in the context of the discussion of the social role of art.[17]

Beauty and Morality

Whereas the moral judgment relies upon concepts and achieves universal validity, the aesthetic judgment is nonconceptual and of merely subjective universality. Therefore, both belong to different categories and, accordingly, hardly any connection should exist between beauty and morality. And yet, throughout the *Critique of Judgment,*

Kant suggests several possibilities for how to tie up the one with the other.

Confronted with a work of art, it is not enough simply for us to take pleasure in it, Kant argues at one point. The pleasure we feel in beauty should ultimately be directed toward morality, because only moral ideas may be contemplated as ends in themselves:

> When fine arts are not, either proximately or remotely, united with moral ideas, which alone are contemplated with a self-sufficient pleasure, the above [a displeasure with the object] is the fate that ultimately awaits them. (CJ, §52)

Kant also argues that there is a hierarchy of beautiful forms at the top of which we can find the human figure as the ideal of beauty. The human figure achieves this superiority not because the beauty of its form surpasses that of roses or horses but because an extrasensual element manifests itself visibly in the human body. This nonsensory moment is man's morality that distinguishes him from all natural forms. The highest form of beauty must therefore "be sought in the human figure. Here the ideal consists in the expression of the moral, apart from which the object would not please at once universally and positively (not merely negatively in an academically correct presentation)" (CJ, §17).

Kant's most complicated attempt to bring together beauty and morality can be found in the famous Section 59, titled "Beauty as the Symbol of Morality." Here, too, several arguments seem to be lumped together, but the most discussed and complex one is set up roughly in the following way:

> Now, I say: The beautiful is the symbol of the morally good; and only in this respect (a relation that is natural to everyone and that everyone expects from others as their duty) does it please with the claim to everyone's agreement; simultaneously, the mind becomes aware of a certain ennoblement and an elevation above the mere receptivity to pleasure from sense perceptions, and it estimates the worth of others according to a similar maxim of their judgments. (CJ, §59)

The most important thing to figure out is what Kant means by the beautiful being a symbol of the morally good. A symbol here is defined as something that allows for a sensory experience of something else that is nonsensory. The morally good is such a nonsensory idea, or a rational idea, that always escapes experiential representation. Kant had called the aesthetic idea nonconceptualizable [*inexponibel*]; that is, it perpetually escapes its representation by means of a concept that understanding would supply. As a corollary, the rational idea (like the morally good) is inostensible [*indemonstrabel*], because it can never be exemplified by means of a sensory instance. Therefore, the impossibility of subsuming the aesthetic idea under a concept symbolizes, or demonstrates experientially, the complementary shortcoming of the concept of morality, namely, its indemonstrability. Thus, beauty hints symbolically at morality.

Taste has yet another function for morality, and this one is preparatory. The regular exercise of aesthetic judgments, which ultimately point beyond the sensory pleasure toward a moral interest, get the individual into the habit of finding delight more in moral ideas than in sensuality: "Taste allows, as it were, for a transition without too violent a leap from sensory stimulation to habitual moral interest" (§59). Not all of these arguments carry the same force of conviction, but they prove sufficiently that Kant had a strong interest in orienting the aesthetic judgment toward morality.[18] Although Kant demonstrated the independence of taste from morality and reason, he still wanted to make sure that no possibility existed for art to turn against morality. The person who enjoys his pleasurable encounters with the beautiful is the same who is subject to the universal moral law from which taste cannot and should not attempt to set him free.

It cannot be doubted that Kant's *Critique of Judgment* first established philosophical aesthetics as an independent discipline. This was the result of his argument that the object of aesthetics, namely beauty in its natural and artistic manifestation, is independent of conceptual knowledge, both theoretical and moral. Thus, beauty merits its own independent inquiry.

And yet the results of the Kantian aesthetics leave us strangely unsatisfied when viewed from a different perspective, namely, when questioned about the ontological status of the work of art, its epistemic value (the truth content) and its practical potential. First, Kant does not answer the ontological question at all. The aesthetic judgment does not relate to the object, but is merely the expression of the pleasurable subjective state of the free play of imagination and understanding.

Beauty for Kant does lie in the eye of the beholder, not in a relativistic sense but in an ontological one. There are no beautiful objects, only those that incite in us a response of aesthetic pleasure.[19] But since not every object we encounter is able to do just that, it is somewhat hard to comprehend why there shouldn't be a class of objects that are capable of arousing aesthetic pleasure, and these would be the objects we would call art or beautiful products of nature. Thus, subjective pleasure would lead to a classification of objects as either art or nonart.

It should also be pointed out that we must not understand pleasure to be simply an agreeable sensation. If that were the case, modern art with its emphasis on displeasing and disturbing elements and its license to outright ugliness would prove Kant outdated. (The same holds true for many Gothic representations of the crucified Christ, an image that invites contemplation in the form of compassion, not as "disinterested pleasure" in the beautiful.) His concept of pleasure, though, refers to the free play of faculties in which the imagination attempts to subsume the object in question under a concept that understanding is to provide. Nothing in this definition excludes ugly objects from participating in the same free play. The aesthetic idea that induces much thought without ever arriving at a conceptual conclusion is applicable to modern art as well, even if this art has given up on the project of pleasing viewers, readers, or listeners.

In regard to the truth-claim of art, Kant's theory takes a strong stance. He declares outright that the aesthetic judgment is not cognitive and that, therefore, matters of art and matters of knowledge must not be confused. This is one of the legacies of Kant's aesthetics that turned out to be one of the greatest objects of contention in the tradition of philosophical thought on art from then on.

The third issue, namely the practical relevance of art and beauty, is the only one for which Kant provides a positive answer. Although beautiful objects have no direct practical value, they still serve as symbols of the morally good, and to encounter them regularly establishes a habit, contradictory enough, of valuing them not for the pleasure they incite but for their supersensory appeal. In this theory, the most positive feature of art is to strengthen us in our efforts to lead a moral life.

Immanuel Kant establishes the first strong paradigm of aesthetics that is characterized by the independence of art from cognition and from morality, by its formal nature that is free from the influences of history and of concrete developments in the arts, and finally by its subjectivization of the aesthetic experience that is divorced from the object and firmly rooted in the subject. All of these elements of the Kantian paradigm serve as a starting point for the other paradigmatic aesthetics up to the system of Hegel, and each one of the following paradigms can be considered an attempt to correct one or more of Kant's assumptions.

3

Schiller

Friedrich Schiller (1759–1805) takes Kant's *Critique of Judgment* as the starting point for his philosophical investigations of beauty and art. As he writes in the first letter of *Über die ästhetische Erziehung des Menschen in einer Reihe von Briefen* (On the aesthetic education of man in a series of letters, 1795): "I will, to be sure, not conceal from you the fact that it is Kantian principles upon which the propositions that follow will for the most part be based."[1] And yet, from early on, the Kantian aesthetic paradigm does not satisfy Schiller. More and more Kant's division of nature and freedom comes to be seen as part of the problem of modernity in which man's faculties are pitched against each other and never come to a full development and a harmonious unification. As much as Kant served as the inspiration for Schiller's turn toward philosophical aesthetics, his subjective and ahistorical stance was soon considered by Schiller to be one of the main obstacles not only to a productive aesthetics but also to ethical thought as an investigation of the duties of man toward himself, as well as to his polity.[2]

Before Schiller's encounter with Kant's aesthetic theory – this fact is often forgotten in the reception of Schiller's thought on art and beauty – he went through a Baumgartenian phase characterized by the association of sensuality and beauty with inferior cognition. This period is most clearly manifested in his 1788 poem *Die Künstler* (The artists), in which art is assigned a preparatory role for rational cognition. Associated with a more infantile state of humanity's development, art in this early conception is understood to give way eventually to sensually untainted truth: "*Was wir als Schönheit hier empfunden, / Wird einst als Wahrheit uns entgegengehen*" (What we here perceived as beauty / will one day come to us as truth). Sensuality, however, is seen with Leibniz mainly as an obscuring of rationality, albeit one that can be redeemed to a certain extent when it manifests itself as beauty. Schiller soon overcomes this position, but the linkage of the metaphor of mankind's childhood with (naïve) art recurs in later writings, in which Schiller also attempts to balance the gains and losses of the inevitability of growing up.

In his first meditations on aesthetics after his encounter with the *Critique of Judgment,* Schiller regards it as his vocation to discover an objective principle of art that can overcome Kant's subjectivism. In his 1793 *Kallias oder Über die Schönheit* (Kallias or on beauty), Schiller criticizes previous philosophical theories of art because either they lack an objective principle or, if they adhere to one, they neglect sensuality to the point of its negation. Edmund Burke remains caught up in sensual subjectivism without any objective moment; Kant advances a subjective definition of beauty that equally fails to provide objective standards; Baumgarten and Mendelssohn adhere to a system of objective rationality that links art with perfection, but loses all sensuality in this alliance.[3] Incorrect as these assessments might be (Baumgarten and Mendelssohn can hardly be considered full-fledged supporters of the aesthetics of perfection), Schiller at this stage of his aesthetic investigations aims primarily at providing a sensual theory of art that encompasses objective criteria for its definition and evaluation.[4]

Although Schiller keeps coming back to this objective principle in later publications (*Aesthetic Letters,* letter 25), and although his own definition of beauty, as we shall see, proposes such an objective principle, his attention is more and more occupied by a different problem. Schiller's interest shifts from the investigation of the possibility of an objective aesthetic principle to a critique of Kant's ahistorical approach to aesthetics without abandoning the first quest. This criticism emerges from an attempt to elaborate on Kant's efforts to relate art and morality by introducing the dimension of history. Schiller clearly goes beyond the limits of Kant's transcendental idealism, not so much by supplanting his transcendental grounding of beauty but, rather, by introducing an additional anthropological and historical foundation. Because Schiller is not willing to give up the transcendental moment of art, his extension of the Kantian system ultimately leads to a permanent opposition of reality and the appearance of art, as will become apparent from the *Aesthetic Letters* (AL).

It is precisely this historical moment that lets us see Schiller as a bridge between Kant and Hegel, between transcendental and objective idealism. It is not so much Schiller's attempts to supply an objective principle of aesthetics that move him closer to the position of Hegel, as Georg Lukács explained it,[5] as it is the historical character of his thought. Hegel himself claimed Schiller as a precursor in his *Lectures on Aesthetics* for this very reason.[6]

In respect to morality, the collective aspect for Schiller is more prevalent than the individual one, and yet the encounter with the artwork remains in the realm of personal experience – an argument that will later cause him some difficulty.[7] In his efforts to unite art and morality, Schiller makes two presuppositions. The first is that despite the fact that every individual has a moral responsibility and also the capability to act according to moral principles, the achievement of a moral community transcends individual efforts and becomes a political task. Schiller's second presupposition is that it is impossible to achieve a moral community by direct political action, either by means of political education or by revolution. Therefore, the only way to build a republic of free and equal members is by detour through an aesthetic education that mediates between the natural state of man and the utopian vision of humanity. These opening pronouncements of the *Aesthetic Letters* are Schiller's strongest attempt to desubjectivize the Kantian aesthetics, and yet in the end, this project does not come to fruition.

Although Schiller's *Aesthetic Letters* are his most important contribution to the aesthetic tradition, he wrote a number of other texts dealing with philosophical issues of art. His period as a philosopher, however, was restricted mainly to roughly the half decade between 1790 and 1795. The beginning of this stage of Schiller's career was marked by his reception of the Kantian writings, whereas he "closed the philosophical shop" (letter to Goethe of December 17, 1795) shortly after his friendship with Goethe had begun in order to return to the writing of fiction. The first Kantian influence can be detected in the 1791 *Über den Grund des Vergnügens an tragischen Gegenständen* (On the reason for the pleasure in tragic subjects), in which he already states his great theme, namely, the conjunction of art and morality. In the letters to his friend Körner, published posthumously in 1847 under the title *Kallias oder Über die Schönheit* (Kallias or on beauty), Schiller formulates for the first time the thought that beauty is the sensual expression of freedom – a notion that will play a more important role in the *Aesthetic Letters.* Some smaller texts, *Über das Erhabene* (On the sublime, circa 1795), *Über die notwendigen Grenzen beim Gebrauch schöner Formen* (On the necessary limits of the usage of beautiful forms, 1795 – the only aesthetic text by Schiller that takes up the issue of cognition and art), and *Über das Pathetische* (On pathos, 1793), test the limits of Kantian aesthetics and push its boundaries without ever making a clear break with Kant. In *Über Anmut und Würde* (On grace and dignity, 1793), Schiller argues – taking up Cicero's distinction of *venustas* (grace) and *dignitas* (dignity) – that physical beauty, united with *grace,* the physical manifestation of the soul's achievement to act morally out of desire, and *dignity,* the adherence to the moral law even in suffering, accounts for the perfect image of humanity that we find represented in the sculpture of classical Greece. Finally, *Über naïve und sentimentalische Dichtung* (On naïve and sentimental poetry, 1796) can be considered an attempt to apply the categories he had developed in the *Aesthetic Letters* to poetry and its historical development, thus again uniting aesthetic with historic speculation. Not counting some philosophical poems, Schiller gave up philosophy in the middle of the 1790s to write plays, such as *Wallenstein, Maria Stuart,* and *Wilhelm Tell.*

The Aesthetic Education of Man – Social Critique of the Present

Schiller's *Aesthetic Letters* undertakes to establish a new aesthetic paradigm by uniting a formal and a historical aspect, that is, by combining a theory of human drives with the idea of education. The very thought of education, however, is not only historical insofar as it presupposes a development from a less to a more desirable individual or collective constitution; it also demands the analysis of the present. While the notion of education does not need a preestablished vision of where to move – better pedagogical theories set goals depending on the potential to be developed – all efforts at guidance and improvement must understand the shortcomings, distortions, and dormant possibilities of the present. Therefore, Schiller's presentation of an aesthetic education opens with a detailed analysis of the present stage of mankind seen in its disorder.

The *Aesthetic Letters* proposes to combine the motive of education as it had become dominant in the Enlightenment philosophy of the eighteenth century with the newly established discipline of aesthetics. Yet it was by no means the first time that a philosopher envisioned art to be used for pedagogical purposes. Plato repeatedly emphasized the role that art should play in the education of the youth, as, for example, when he writes in *The Republic:*

> We must seek out such artists as have the talent to pursue the beautiful and the graceful in their work, in order that our young men shall benefit from living, as it were, in a healthy place, whence something from these beautiful works will strike their eyes and ears like a breeze that brings health from salubrious places to, and harmony with, the beauty of reason." (401 c)[8]

The educational idea was much discussed again in the eighteenth century. Schiller writes to his friend Körner of his approval of the reading of Mirabeau's (1749–1791) essay *Sur l'education,* which he suggests for a translation into German (letter of October 15, 1792). Furthermore, both Immanuel Kant and Johann Gottlieb Fichte had elaborated on the relevance of education in the process that leads humanity to freedom. As we will see, Fichte's educational concept of freedom that transcends the social and political realm largely determined Schiller's definition of this term.

Kant's idea of education, on the other hand, is less relevant for the aesthetic pedagogical project. Although Kant also assumed that the moral state was a political goal that was to be reached only with the establishment of a universal republic, he thought that the educational preparation for this utopian vision was the responsibility of the state in its present constitution (*Idee zu einer Allgemeinen Geschichte in weltbürgerlicher Absicht,* 1784). Schiller dissents from this on two counts: He assumes that a direct achievement of a moral state is impossible, but requires the detour through the aesthetic state; and he strongly believes that the state cannot achieve these educational projects. Thus, the way to the moral betterment of all leads through individual, voluntary, and unorganized encounters with art – a somewhat anarchic vision for reform from the outset that can be seen to backfire later on. Yet Schiller clearly dismisses the state from all pedagogical responsibility:

Should we expect this effect [the education of man's entire faculties] from the state? That is not possible, because the state as it exists now has caused the evil, and the state as reason conceives it in the idea must itself be based on an improved mankind rather than bring it about. (AL, letter 7)

Schiller's analysis of his age draws a gloomy picture. Egotism has dissolved the communal spirit: "In the lap of the most refined society egoism has built its system, and we experience all the contagions and all the calamities of society without developing a communal sense" (AL, letter 5). All thought of the common good is absent in man, but the care for his own soul has also been displaced by the exclusive concern with material possessions: "like fugitives from a burning city everyone seeks only to rescue his personal possessions from the devastation" (AL, letter 5). The sciences cannot balance this development because they have become overspecialized and impotent; the division of labor, albeit necessary for societal development, has alienated man from both the product of his work and himself. Modernity allows man's potential to unfold only fragmentarily – "whole classes of human beings develop only a part of their capacities" (AL, letter 6) – and a vision of totality cannot even be found in the organized community, the state, because it remains alien to its citizens. The sixth letter presents one of the early analyses of alienation from a materialist perspective:

Eternally fettered to only one single fragment of the whole, man develops himself only fragmentarily; eternally listening to the monotonous noise of the wheel that he drives, he never develops the harmony of his nature, and instead of modeling himself after the idea of humanity he becomes the mere imprint of his occupation, his science. (AL, letter 6)

Culture, up to its highest expression in the philosophy of Kant, thus causes an internal schism in man, who finds his faculties opposed to each other, thereby leading to their mutual immobilization and degeneration:

Intuitive and speculative reason withdrew upon their respective fields and began to guard their boundaries with distrust and jealousy, yet by confining one's activity to a single sphere we have established a master who often ends up suppressing all other abilities. While in one case the luxurious imagination ravages the carefully tended plantations of reason, in another case the spirit of abstraction stifles the fire that was meant to warm the heart and kindle the fantasy. (AL, letter 6)

In addition to these ailments of modernity, both lower and upper classes suffer from specific disfigurations of the human ideal. With the lower strata of society it is "barbarity," the degeneration into savage patterns of behavior: "Among the lower and more numerous classes we find crude, lawless impulses which the loosening of the bonds of civil order has unleashed and which hurry with ungovernable anger toward their bestial satisfaction" (AL, letter 5). The upper classes, on the other hand, suffer from languor and stifling permissiveness. While the lower classes fall back upon precivilized states of vulgarity and savagery, the leisured class (to use this expression of Thorsten Veblen here) have lost all goals and sense of purpose in its overrefinement: "the civilized classes present to us the even more repugnant spectacle of languor and a depravity of character that is all the more outrageous because culture itself is its source" (letter 5).

Now this analysis of the ills of present society is neither new nor genuine to Schiller. He simply echoes much of the Enlightenment critique of society, and yet he differs significantly from it in the solution he offers. His own suggestion for overcoming the calamity of the age presents itself as the only viable one, since the other two possibilities that Schiller considers, enlightenment and revolution, both have failed in their efforts. Schiller concedes that "the age is enlightened" (AL, letter 8); that is, the problems and their causes have been detected and publicly discussed, and yet no improvement of the individual nor of the societal condition has come about as a result. He speculates that it is not enough to present the truth, but that man's moral character has to be prepared to receive it; otherwise, it will not fall on fertile ground. The present age, however, has not prepared man for enlightenment: "Since it does not reside in the objects, something must be present in the mind of man that hinders the reception of truth, no matter how bright it shines, and its acceptance, no matter how lively it persuades" (letter 8).

The other means of change, namely revolution, had just been demonstrated to fail by the Reign of Terror in France. More explicitly than in the *Aesthetic Letters,* Schiller dismisses the French Revolution in the *Augustenburger Briefe,* the first version of the letters that were written under the immediate impression of the orgy of slaughtering in 1793: "The attempt of the French people to institute itself into its holy human rights and to gain political freedom has only brought to light the impotence and unworthiness of it. This attempt has not only thrown back this unhappy people into barbarity and slavery, but together with it a considerable part of Europe".[9]

In Schiller's view, in order to overcome the malaise of the present, it is important to remember that mankind did not always live under these conditions. Much in the spirit of classicism, he turns to Greece for an image of unalienated and unfragmented life. In Greece, more precisely in the polis of Athens of roughly the fifth century B.C., sensuality and reason had not yet been divorced from each other, and their functioning in unison made for the happiest period of humanity. These childhood days of mankind continue to provide him with the image of man's fulfillment, although no return to it is possible. Instead, man must move forward from his present position in order to achieve yet again the ideal of his development. In his 1796 essay *On Naïve and Sentimental Poetry,* Schiller sketches out this philosophical notion of a historical development in more detail. Greece, that is, the naïve and natural state of mankind's development, brings forth out of itself art as the negation of nature through reason. And yet art does not simply negate nature, because as it develops nature to its full potential, art allows man the return to nature. This return, or *ideal,* is the perfection of man brought about by the perfection of art. The ideal bridges the gap between cold reason and unreflective sensibility, or as Schiller will put it, between beautiful form and moral energy. This notion of the ideal as a unifying moment of reason and feeling, beauty and morality, and form and energy recurs again in the philosophy of Hegel, who perceptively pointed out these moments in Schiller's writings.

The movement toward the ideal is the content of Schiller's aesthetic education. He, too, argues that man once lived in a natural state (which is not the hypothetical state of nature that the contractualists, such as Hobbes and Rousseau, paint in either terrifying or glorifying colors but, rather, the polity of Athens), and he needed to leave it in order to establish a self-determined ideal state – a process that Schiller compares to that of a child growing up to become an adult. Without this development, mankind would remain in the stage of pure potentiality, like a child who promises to become everything while abiding in the realm of numberless choices. The infinity of childhood is all capability and potentiality; adulthood is actuality and limitation. Yet despite the loss of the myriad possibilities that were eliminated by every choice, development also means the achievement of a higher level of reality. In order to fulfill its *telos,* mankind must become what it only promised to be in its naïve childhood stage. The ideal state remains the goal, yet the means to achieve it have failed so far. In fact, any attempt to move *directly* from the present state of self-interest and alienation to the moral state is bound to fail; therefore, a mediating stage has to be found and installed in order to guarantee a transition without violence. It is precisely this function that the aesthetic state is conceived to fulfill. Aesthetic education is at its outset the complement of enlightenment and the avoidance of revolutionary violence.

Therefore, Schiller's essay on aesthetics might only seem apolitical to his contemporaries, as Schiller argues with some concern, but it is in fact politically charged. The politics of the day is aesthetics, "since it is through beauty that we arrive at freedom" (AL, letter 2). In this context, the fragmentation of the totality of man's abilities and potential must not be considered a mere shortcoming of modernity. Instead, by means of specialization and the evolution of only select talents, the human species enables its own progress. Where the individual suffers, the collective profits. Yet the ideal is determined by the reconstitution of all faculties in all individuals. We all carry around in ourselves this ideal man who will emerge victorious in the ideal state – an idea that Schiller takes over from Fichte's *Über die Bestimmung des Gelehrten* (The vocation of the scholar, 1794).

Art is not only the means by which the present state will be transformed into the ideal state; it also reminds us of our childhood happiness that remains a vision and a responsibility. Whereas the political, social, and moral spheres have all been corrupted in the course of history, art is the reservoir for the ideal of the life of totality: "Humanity has lost its dignity, but art has rescued and preserved it in significant stone; truth lives on in the midst of deception, and from the copy the original will once again be restored" (AL, letter 9). Here, Schiller takes a strong stance against Plato who had charged the aesthetic appearance with a loss of truth. For Schiller, however, art has safeguarded the truth of man in times of decay, and from art will issue forth the regenerated man of the ideal. Political and moral change toward the better will be brought about by a change in taste – a thought that connects Schiller directly to Friedrich Nietzsche, who writes in 1886 that the renewal of philosophical thought depends on "the arrival of a new species of philosophers who have a new taste and tendency in opposition to the present ones" (*Beyond Good and Evil*, §2).

Art is assigned a very concrete historical function in this scheme, and yet Schiller's aesthetic philosophy is incomplete without its formal aspect that investigates the nature of mankind apart from its social deformation. This theory of drives provides the basis for the historical justification of art's central role in the political agenda. Schiller's paradigmatic aesthetics are founded on the endeavor to mediate the formal aspect of his aesthetic anthropology with the historical aspect of the progression from natural through aesthetic to moral state.

The Theory of Drives

Schiller's entire text of the *Aesthetic Letters* is structured around a series of oppositions that are mediated by a third term. His historical model pitched the natural state against the ideal state and posited the aesthetic state as the transition. Aesthetic man, in turn, is considered to mediate between natural and ideal man. This latter transition is further developed in Schiller's theory of drives, which is based on Fichte's model of impulses. In the context of his moral philosophy, Fichte had stated that the natural drive and the drive of freedom, the "pure drive," must be united in a third drive, namely that of morality. Schiller adopts this basic model, yet he makes decisive changes when working out his own conception of the three drives, most importantly in respect to the third.

Man, according to this theory, is governed by two drives that are both complementary and oppositional. The first is called the *Stofftrieb*, the *sense drive;* it is determined by sensuality, perception, and the primacy of the matter of the world over the ego. Since the ego is responsible for organizing the sense impressions, it is constantly threatened by the sense drive's anarchic onslaught up to the point of its complete dissolution. The sense drive remains committed to the individual instance of sense input without any attempt at abstraction and generalization. Its world is filled with examples that never exemplify a rule. Man under the rule of the sense drive is devoid of individuality, because he is nothing more than the receptive vessel of constantly changing impressions. As far as there is a personality to speak of, it is subject to constant modification, the toy of time and alteration. For this ego there is no freedom – an argument that Kant, Fichte, and Schiller all advance – since it remains subject to causality and, thus, to the determination by previous instances that in turn are determined by instances previous to them, and so on ad infinitum. The world of this sensual ego is pure materiality; its relation to this world is one of receptivity. The ego is passively given over to physical necessity, namely, the laws of nature. And yet this subjection of the sensual ego to matter and the forces of nature not only is a negative form of dependence but also is the principle of life, dynamism, and futurity.

The *Formtrieb,* the *form drive,* on the other hand, results from the unchangeable part of man. Since this part of the self cannot itself change, it can also not have its origin in any kind of outside causation and must, therefore, be the ground of itself, just as Fichte had argued for the pure ego. Whereas the sensual ego is determined by sensuality, the self operates under the principles of reason. Against constant change it pitches its own atemporality, and against matter, form. Whereas the sense drive receives sense data, the form drive impresses form on them. It is not the world as a material totality that determines the latter but, rather, the spirit. The spirit, however, is not passive but, rather, the principle of activity. The necessity of the form drive is not physical but moral, and it is not subject to the laws of nature but to those of reason. Whereas the sense drive not only aims at an abandoning of the self to the world but also hungers for ever more and new objects, the form drive has a chilling quality that freezes its objects in time and sets the eternal gestalt against life's principle of permanent mutation.

Since both of these drives inhabit distinct spheres, they cannot directly interact with each other. And yet both of them "require restriction" (AL, letter 14), because the uninhibited development of either drive would result in self-destruction. Therefore, Schiller posits the will as that force that keeps both drives in check, although it is not quite clear where exactly the will itself is supposed to originate: "It is therefore the will that acts toward both drives as an authority, but neither of the two can of its own accord act as an authority against the other" (AL, letter 19). Still, it is not enough merely to keep both drives in check by means of the will; in order to overcome man's fragmentation they need to be mediated.

Such mediation Schiller finds in the *Spieltrieb,* the *play drive* that is able to unify time and atemporality, becoming and being, change and identity. The very phrase "play drive" combines Kantian and Fichtean influences by its reference to Kant's free play of faculties in the aesthetic experience and Fichte's theory of drives: "Reason demands, on transcendental grounds, that a partnership between the sense drive and the form drive should exist, namely a play drive, because only the union of reality with form, of contingency with necessity, of suffering with freedom fulfills the conception of humanity" (AL, letter 15). This play drive, however, is exactly the aesthetic principle. The term play refers to the contemplation of the beautiful that frees man both from the atemporality of the law and from sensual desire by situating him in between both. Man takes seriously both the pleasure of the senses and the perfection of the moral law, but beauty is devoid of such earnestness – beauty is the object of play. In play, man expresses his complete nature, no longer divided into sensuality and morality. As Schiller famously writes: "Man plays only when he is in the full sense of the word a man, and *he is only wholly man when he is playing*" (AL, letter 15).

Beauty, both natural and artistic, restores the balance of human faculties, because "we find the actual and therefore limited man either in a condition of tension or in one of relaxation, depending on whether the one-sided activity of isolated faculties is disturbing the harmony of his being or if the unity of his nature is based on the overall degeneration of his sensual and rational faculties" (AL, letter 17). In man, who is too restricted by the demands of the moral law, beauty restores the harmony with the senses, and in languid man it infuses new energy. Since beauty is the mediator between the two drives, it also follows that it can be defined neither in purely empirical nor in purely transcendental terms because it needs to participate in both spheres.

It is clear, though, that the two sets of oppositions that Schiller sets up – the first being that between natural and ideal state, natural and ideal man; the second that between sensuality and reason, change and atemporality, pure and empirical I, matter and spirit, passivity and activity, physical and moral laws, and so on – and that are both supposed to be mediated by art, need mediation between them in turn. Whereas the first set of oppositions emerged from a critique of modernity and is, thus, rather firmly grounded in history, the second set refers to anthropological constants. Only insofar as they hint at the historically vague emancipation of man from nature and at the process of individuation by means of the Fichtean *Tathandlung,* which causes the differentiation not only between I and non-I but also between pure and empirical I, is a historical moment present here. Still, the opposition of reason and sensuality or of spirit and matter is hardly a modern phenomenon. In other words, the theory of drives has no intrinsic connection with Schiller's political critique and vision, and yet he needs to bring them together in order to ground his political project. Whereas man under the perspective of drives does not need to be situated in a historical context in order to be understood, man who suffers from the fragmented state of his being brought about by modernity is a radically historical creature. Schiller's task is, thus, to mediate between the formal and the historical aspect of his theory of aesthetic education by finding functions in the play drive that are both anthropological constants and historical agents.

Beauty, Formal and Historical

Schiller had argued that man can only achieve the transition from the sensual to the rational and moral state by means of the aesthetic intermediary in which both drives are present, the opposition of which does not lead to a deadlock but, rather, allows for freedom of both drives. This freedom of the play drive, however, is nothing else but beauty. Only beauty can manifest the union of the rational and the real, the person and his or her temporal states, causality and indeterminacy. Beauty, Schiller famously defines, "is the only possible expression of freedom in appearance" (AL, letter 23). This is Schiller's definition of beauty throughout all his aesthetic writings, and although it appears only in a footnote in the *Aesthetic Letters,* it is still central for the understanding of this text.

A more detailed description of the concept of freedom is put forth in the *Kallias Letters.* With Kant, Schiller there argues that true freedom can only be achieved by the supersensory, since all empirical objects remain determined by the chain of cause and effects. Freedom can thus never find a sensual expression. And yet some objects to us seem as if they had broken away from causality and had their raison d'être purely in themselves. Objects that strikes us as thus indetermined are beautiful: Beauty is freedom in appearance. This definition of beauty marks a distinct break with Kant's aesthetics. The principle of beauty as freedom in appearance is no longer a merely subjective response of disinterested pleasure but, rather, precisely that objective principle that Schiller had meant to introduce from the beginning of his aesthetic endeavor. The encounter with the beautiful transcends the subjective sphere and unites the subject and the object that is perceived as if free from all outside determination in the aesthetic experience.[10]

The unifying role attributed to art and natural beauty in this theory points forward to the systems of Schelling and Hegel and their grounding of both subject and object in a preceding principle.[11] The pleasure we take in beauty Schiller calls love, thereby introducing a term that will figure prominently in the speculative idealism of both Schelling and Hegel, the latter of whom credits Schiller with this notion. It would be more appropriate, however, to speak of the reintroduction of the concept of love in the philosophical search for a principle that can unify the sensual manifold. Thus, we are led back to Plotinus (ca. 204–270), who advanced love as the striving for unity and beauty as the expression of such unity:

> What do you feel in the presence of the grace you discern in actions, in manners, in sound morality, in all the works and fruits of virtue, in the beauty of Souls? When you see that you yourself are beautiful within, what do you feel? What is this Dionysiac exultation that thrills through your being, this straining upward of all your soul, this longing to break away from the body and live sunken within the veritable self? These are no other than the emotions of Souls under the spell of love.[12]

Even before Schiller, Karl Philipp Moritz (1756–1793) had pointed toward the moment of love in beauty that causes us to overcome our individual limitations and to participate in a higher existence: "The pleasure in beauty must therefore move ever closer to *love* if it wants to be real."[13]

For Schiller, love is that bond that conjoins reason to sensuality in beauty. This idea, however, constitutes an application to aesthetics of his early thinking on love as was expressed in the 1786 *Philosophische Briefe / Theosophie des Julius* (Philosophical letters / theosophy of Julius). In this early attempt at a monist philosophy that would overcome the denigration of sensuality by rationalism, Schiller had conceived of love as a cosmic principle more than a unifying power that overcame antinomies; he called it the "reflection of this one single ur-force."[14] In love, the loving subjects transcend the limits of individuality and realize the self in the other. Self and other are not eclipsed into each other; rather, a preceding commonality is experienced that exposes the strict opposition of subject and object as secondary and inadequate. In the context of beauty, love does not only refer to the inclination of the subject to be absorbed in the beautiful object; the beautiful object itself is seen as the loving unification of reason and sensuality. This concept of love, however, becomes problematic when – as can be rightfully expected – love is regarded as a voluntary union between equals. In this case, the Kantian framework – accepted in this respect by Schiller without much hesitation – that demands the dominance of reason over sensuality is too restrictive to be able to contain the concept of love in which we would have to attribute an egalitarian standing to both reason and sensuality.[15] Again, Schiller pushes the boundaries of transcendental idealism without arriving at the speculative system that will solve this aporia.

The transition between Schiller and the idealist concept of love is provided, as so often, by the poet Friedrich Hölderlin (1770–1843), who considers love to be the metaphorical expression both of the individual positions of the lovers and of the unity that dissolves those individualities. Hölderlin was the first of the three *Stiftler* – himself, Schelling, and Hegel all having been roommates at the seminary, the *Stift,* in Tübingen – to follow in the footsteps of Schiller and Jacobi and develop his own version of a *Vereinigungsphilosophie* (philosophy of unification) in which the concept of love figures prominently. In the three early fragments of *Hyperion oder Der Eremit in Griechenland* (Hyperion or the hermit in Greece, 1793), love is already seen as the principle that unites the opposite drives of man. In *Hyperions Jugend* (Hyperion's youth), it is written: "The opposition [*Widerstreit*] of the drives, of which none is dispensible, love unites, the daughter of riches and poverty."[16] The closing lines of the second part of the novel, written in 1799 toward the end of his phase of aesthetic speculation, phrase this ideal as follows: "Like the row of lovers are the dissonances of the world. Reconciliation is in the midst of quarrel and all that is separated becomes united again."[17]

Schiller can only achieve an approximation to objective idealism by turning away from Kant's understanding of freedom as the autonomy of reason and morality from sensuality. Instead, Schiller aims at a mediation of this concept with that of Fichte: "whenever I speak of freedom I do not mean the sort that is necessarily attached to man as a being of reason, and that can neither be given to him nor taken from him, but the sort that is based upon his composite nature" (AL, letter 19, footnote).[18]

Fichte's notion of freedom is, this is important to note, emphatically educational. He argues that sensuality is in need of guidance and development by means of reason, and that freedom consequently consists in the liberation from the power that an untamed sensuality has over man. And yet freedom is nothing transcendent. Man remains a sensual being even as a free agent, thereby defining freedom not in opposition to man's sensual nature, but as partaking in it. Schiller agrees with this notion, but instead of a general education of the senses he envisions a specifically aesthetic one.[19]

Beauty defined as freedom thus has no concrete content either. Individual manifestations of beauty serve no circumscribed moral purpose, nor do they reveal a hitherto unknown truth. Instead, the culture of beauty demonstrates the freedom of man to turn himself into whatever being he envisions while remaining under the law of morality. This freedom of self-creation is present in every encounter with the beautiful, because we leave the aesthetic mindset in a state of pure potentiality in which every actual activity is conceivable to us. At least ideally this is the case, because human existence never achieves purity, so that every aesthetic encounter must remain an approximation to the ideal aesthetic state (which, since it regenerates itself endlessly, would not lead back to reality at all, but leave us suspended in a state of aesthetic bliss from which only the imperfection of the phenomena saves us). Works of art can be classified for their merit according to the proximity to this pure aesthetic state that they allow us to achieve. As works of art, however, they do so exclusively on the basis of their form, leaving aside all considerations of content: "In a truly beautiful work of art the content should do nothing, the form everything, because form alone affects man in his entirety, while content affects only individual faculties" (AL, letter 22). The beauty of form alone is capable of uniting rationality and sensuality in man, whereas the content will appeal to one faculty more than the other at all times. In the contemplation of beauty, though, we enter the realm of ideas without leaving behind the realm of sensuality. Truth as an achievement of reason is only to be had for the price of sacrificing sensuality, but beauty's reign is benevolent and never asks to forfeit any of man's faculties. Instead, beauty introduces harmony into division.

Yet beauty's freedom remains restricted to the aesthetic realm. All beauty contains the promise of man's reconciliation with himself, but only so as strictly divorced from reality:

> Only insofar as it is truthful (expressly renouncing all claim to reality), and only insofar as it is self-reliant (dispensing with all assistance from reality), is appearance aesthetic. As soon as it is deceitful and simulates reality and as soon as it is impure and requires reality for its effect, it is nothing but a base tool for material ends and cannot aid the freedom of the spirit. (AL, letter 26)

In short, art and reality, aesthetic appearance and factuality, have to remain separate. Of this conclusion Schiller is convinced, and he repeats it in other contexts. In his foreword to *The Bride of Messina* (1803), he argues that "art is only true to the extent that it completely abandons reality and becomes purely ideal."[20] This notion of art as the principle of semblance, of appearance that is opposed to reality, will reappear roughly seventy-five years later in Nietzsche's conception of the Apollonian as he develops it in *The Birth of Tragedy*.

There are two ways to read this separation of the aesthetic and the real in Schiller. The first interpretation is suggested by the Marxist reception of the *Aesthetic Letters,* in which the work of art is considered as that which remains unreconciled with reality and, thus, harbors the potential to both negate this reality and keep alive the promise of a better one. Georg Lukács and Theodor W. Adorno both argue in this vein, and Ernst Bloch's concept of art as *Vorschein,* a *promesse de bonheur* of future times, owes much to Schiller's notion of aesthetic appearance. The other way to understand the separation of art from reality, however, is to consider it as yet another instance of Schiller's inability to successfully fuse the historical and the formal aspect of his aesthetic theory. If art remains divorced from political and social life without any chance of interfering with it, the project of aesthetic education must be considered a failure when judged according to its own premises. Aesthetic reconciliation must become factual for it to succeed, all the more so because it was set up as an alternative to all revolutionary action. For Marxist thinkers, art is not burdened with such responsibility, since they expect radical political action to bring about the transition from the alienating system of capitalism to harmonizing socialism as the cure to man's fragmentation. Art can, therefore, remain sheltered from action, whereas for Schiller, politics had been defined in terms of the aesthetic.

It was J. G. Fichte who pointed out this weakness in Schiller's theory as early as 1794 in his *Ueber Geist und Buchstab in der Philosophie* (On the spirit and the letter in philosophy), a submission to Schiller's journal *Die Horen* in which the *Aesthetic Letters* appeared in installments. Fichte's essay, however, was rejected by Schiller and did not appear in print before 1798:

> Therefore the times and regions of serfdom are also those of tastelessness; and if it is on the one hand not advisable to give freedom to man before his aesthetic sense is developed, it is on the other hand impossible to develop the latter before he is free; and the idea to lead man to the appreciation of freedom through aesthetic education and hence to freedom itself gets us into a vicious circle unless we find a means beforehand of awakening the courage in some individuals out of the great multitude to be nobody's master and nobody's slave.[21]

Schiller's turn from the politics of egalitarianism to a hierarchy of aesthetic awareness and thus of self-realization, that is, the separation of beauty as freedom in appearance from the unfreedom of society, remains an unsolved problem of the *Aesthetic Letters* that undercuts its own premises.

This is even more evident in the last of the twenty-seven letters on aesthetic education. Here, the discrepancy between the initial utopian vision of a moral state to which the aesthetic state constitutes the bridge and the abandonment of this political impetus becomes most discernible. Although Schiller repeats the claim that the aesthetic state already allows for the freedom of each and the equality of all, he no longer understands the term "state" to signify a polity. Instead, the term comes to designate small circles of aesthetically educated men who have risen above and outside society and have constituted elite groups of independent thinkers and artists:

> But does such a state of beautiful appearance exist and where can it be found? It exists as a need in every finely tuned soul; as a reality it can probably only be found, like the pure church and the pure republic, in some few select

circles where behavior is not governed by the mindless imitation of foreign manners but by one's own beautiful nature, where man moves through the most complicated situations with daring ease and quiet innocence and without the necessity to insult the freedom of others in order to assert his own, or to throw away his dignity to show grace. (AL, letter 27)

The aesthetic state, even in its reduced version as salon culture, is no longer advanced as the transition to the moral state but has become an aim in its own right. Schiller's project of reconciliation has failed; political egalitarianism has folded over into an apotheosis of elitism. As Hans-Georg Gadamer comments: "In the grounding of the aesthetic reconciliation of the Kantian dualism between Is and Ought yawns a deep, unsolved dualism."[22] Beauty, freedom, love, and the ideal have been so many attempts to bridge this gap, and yet the paradigm of a union of formal and historical aesthetics remains unattainable for Schiller.[23]

It has become apparent that Schiller's primary interest in aesthetics is practical. This strong emphasis on the moral function of beauty leads to a relatively weak stance regarding the epistemological and ontological aspect of art. In terms of ontology, Schiller advances an objective principle of beauty, namely, that of freedom in appearance, in order to overcome Kant's restriction of the beautiful to the subjective sphere. Rather, he suggests, we should consider beauty to be an attribute both of the object located in its form and of the subject, that is, the sense of love that is defined by our pleasure in the beautiful object in which we want to be absorbed: "Beauty is therefore certainly an *object* for us, since reflection is the condition under which we have a sensation of it; but it is at the same time a *state of the subject,* since feeling is the condition under which we have a representation of it" (AL, letter 25). An objective principle, however, that is attained by reflection and thus subject to cognition should consequently lead to a strong epistemological position. Instead, Schiller adheres to the Kantian view by repeating that our encounters with beauty are strictly separated from cognitive advances: "Beauty produces no individual result whatsoever, either for the reason or the will; it realizes no individual purpose, either intellectual or moral; it discovers no individual truth, helps us to perform no individual duty, and is, in a word, equally incapable of establishing the character and enlightening the mind" (AL, letter 21). This rift between art and truth is widened by Schiller's insistence on the radical foreignness of aesthetic appearance with respect to reality. Truth as a form of insight into reality cannot be distilled from a realm that does not touch upon reality. Ultimately, however, such separation calls for either revelation or a speculative idealism that explains this dualism as a secondary phenomenon. The latter is the path of Schelling and Hegel.

4

Schelling

If Kant's *Critique of Judgment* marks the low point of classical German philosophy in respect to the philosophical significance attributed to the work of art, the writings of Friedrich Wilhelm Joseph Schelling (1775–1854) mark the peak in the estimation of art's role for philosophy. In Schelling's early writings, art is not merely one of many possible objects of philosophy but, rather, an integral part of it. Moreover, art is considered indispensable insofar as it is seen as the only means of completing the philosophical system that Schelling proposes. It might go too far, though, to advance the thesis, as Dieter Jähnig does, that only in Schelling's work, even more precisely, only in the sixth chapter of the *System des transzendentalen Idealismus* (System of transcendental idealism) of 1800, did Western philosophy envision an intimate mutual dependency of art and philosophy.[1] The fact is that romantic philosophy in general esteemed art as the necessary completion of philosophical investigation. Schelling is probably the one who thought through this position with the most philosophical rigor and who contributed the most coherent investigation, but this is due to the fact that Schelling remained committed to the idea of the philosophical system, whereas most romantics took a much more ambivalent stance toward systematic philosophy and the demands it places on the form of argumentation. Friedrich Schlegel (1772–1829) declared: "It is equally deadly for the spirit to have and not to have a system. Thus, one will have to decide to combine both." (KA II, 173, no. 53)[2]

The romantic suspicion of totality as the object of conceptual knowledge manifests itself in the style employed for philosophizing. Romantic theorizing more often than not takes the form of the fragment that no longer is embedded in an overarching systematic discussion, and yet it differs from the aphorism by not being self-contained and by pointing toward a totality. This totality can no longer be the object of a comprehensive philosophical discourse, a point that Schelling argues forcefully without giving up on the idea of the system itself, but instead, the *gesture* toward totality takes the place of the system for most romantics. Needless to say, it is often harder to distill a coherent position from fragmentary philosophy, and partly for this reason, Schelling's more systematic attempts make him a philosophically more approachable (though by no means easier) representative of romanticism than Novalis or Friedrich Schlegel. Still, Schelling was not alone among the romantics in his defense of the system, since Karl Wilhelm Ferdinand Solger (1780–1819) also declared: "One can and may not philosophize without a system,"[3] although this system for Solger had to be presented in the form of a dialogue, which since Plato moves philosophy closer to art (leaving aside here the differences that Hegel, in his review of Solger, established between these two thinkers).

The romantic reverence for art as a medium of cognition is not unprecedented either. Some thirty-five years earlier, Johann Georg Hamann (1730–1788) had already opposed the rationalism of the Enlightenment, as well as the rationalist metaphysics of the Wolffians, by stressing the necessity of artistic creation for cognition. Artistic creation is primarily that of God, but to the process of divine creation man responds with poetic language. Poetic language is the translation of a cognition based on sensuality, as Hamann states in his *Aesthetica in nuce* (1762): "Senses and passions speak and understand nothing but images. Of images the entire treasure of human cognition and beatitude consists."[4] The artist re-creates the original creation and, thus, helps to reveal God's revelation in nature. Poetic language is most genuine to man because it allows for more insight into the being of God than speculative philosophy: "Poetry is the native language of mankind" (81). Not only did Hamann exert a strong influence on the generation of the *Sturm und Drang,* the Storm and Stress, but his religiously motivated opposition against the overvaluation of reason and his advocacy of art as a means of gaining insights otherwise unattainable to man also influenced romantic thinkers, such as Schleiermacher, Schelling, Novalis, and Friedrich Schlegel. But again it is Hölderlin who must be regarded as the immediate precursor of Schelling in the attempt to consider the aesthetic as the *via regia* to the absolute that remains unknowable by all conceptual means. His aesthetic fragments of the latter half of the 1790s contained both the idea of the rationally ever-elusive absolute and that of beauty as the means to enable its experiential realization.

Romanticism, like idealism, can be understood as a response to the Kantian dualism of noumena and phenomena, of nature and freedom, that was still unresolved. The romantics took up Fichte's suggestion that the pure ego constitutes the ground that precedes the division of subject and object, and in this they found themselves in agreement with idealist philosophy. Kant himself had already proposed that the faculty that allows one to attribute a manifold of sensory data to one and the same perceiving entity, namely, the "transcendental synthesis of apperception," must be considered as the "highest point" of philosophy (*Critique of Pure Reason,* B 136), although he did not take it to be the principle to bridge the noumenal and phenomenal realm. Only Fichte elevated the ego into the position of foundational being, but in romantic philosophy this ground is no longer accessible by means of reason. It can only be disclosed symbolically, and it is precisely this function of disclosure of the ground of being that Schelling and the other romantic thinkers attribute to the work of art.

Schelling is traditionally positioned between Fichte and Hegel as yet another step from subjective to objective idealism. While this holds true for his aesthetic writings, it is not necessarily the case for his overall position in the history of philosophy. While Schelling certainly helped to prepare the shift from the principle of the self as the ground of being to that of the absolute thinking itself as Hegel proposes it, he also survived Hegel by more than twenty years and advanced critical evaluations of Hegelian rationalism – even before the demise of his former friend and fellow student at the *Evangelisches Stift* at Tübingen – that argue from a vantage point comparable to Kierkegaard and Nietzsche. Therefore, Manfred Frank even suggests considering Hegel as the link between Fichte and Schelling.[5] Our concern here, however, is merely Schelling's contribution to philosophical aesthetics.

Yet Schelling's writings on the philosophy of art cannot be severed from his philosophy as a whole exactly because they derive their value from the position attributed to art in the system at large. Especially Schelling's most important pronouncement on aesthetics, that is, the final chapter of the *System of Transcendental Idealism,* cannot be understood without a comprehension of the system he attempts to set up. Systematic philosophy is characterized by the dependence of all argumentative elements on one central idea, as well as by their interdependence. Without the knowledge of the organizing idea, individual insights cannot be gained. Kant had defined the philosophical system in the *Critique of Pure Reason* as follows: "I understand a system to be the unity of the manifold insights [*Erkenntnisse*] under one idea. This is the concept of reason in the form of a totality, insofar as it determines *a priori* the scope of the manifold as well as the position of the parts in respect to each other" (B 860 ff.). Schelling, despite his failure to achieve this goal at all times, subscribes to this philosophical ideal as much as Fichte or Hegel, and thus the relevance of his aesthetics will only reveal itself in light of the entire *System of Transcendental Idealism.*

The *System,* however, is not the only text by Schelling that deals with aesthetics. In the years between 1800 and 1807, at least five of his publications deal exclusively, substantially, or at least partially with the subject of art. After the 1800 *System,* these are the dialogue *Bruno* (1802), his lecture series *Philosophie der Kunst* (Philosophy of art, 1802–3 and 1804–5, published posthumously 1859), the fourteenth lecture of the *Vorlesungen über die Methode des akademischen Studiums* (Lectures on the method of academic studies, 1803), and finally *Über das Verhältnis der bildenden Künste zu der Natur* (On the relation of the visual arts to nature, 1807), a speech given on the occasion of the christening day of the Bavarian king. After that, only occasional statements on individual works of art or brief meditations on the relation of art to the *Philosophy of Revelation* appear in Schelling's writings.

Before Schelling formulated his first approach to aesthetics, he had become a member of the circle of friends later known as the Jena romantics: Friedrich and August Wilhelm Schlegel, Caroline Schlegel, Ludwig Tieck, Friedrich Schleiermacher, Dorothea Veit, and Gotthilf Heinrich Schubert, to name only the most prominent ones. With Goethe's support – Schelling was an admirer of his theory of colors – the twenty-four-year-old had been awarded a professorship in Jena where he then taught as a colleague of Fichte. The romantic circle deeply influenced Schelling's thinking about art in the years 1798 to 1800, by which time the circle had by and large been destroyed, mainly due to the scandal surrounding the liaison between Schelling and Caroline Schlegel (August Wilhelm's wife), the consequent divorce of the couple, and Caroline's subsequent marriage to Schelling. Fichte also had had to leave Jena in 1799 due to accusations of atheism, which led Goethe to comment: "As one star falls, the other rises" (Fichte III, vol. 3, p. 346). The falling star is, of course, Fichte, the rising one, Schelling. The path was open for the latter to become the prime philosopher of the romantic generation – despite all his idealist leanings and the consequent criticism of both early romanticism and idealism.

Schelling's views on the relevance of art for philosophy changed during his lifetime. While he argued for art as the indispensable completion of the philosophical project in the 1800 *System*, he subjugated it to conceptual knowledge in his lectures on art of two years later. It might even be telling that Schelling never published the manuscript of these talks, although he repeated his Jena lectures of 1802–3 in Würzburg in 1804–5. Odo Marquard goes so far as to suggest that the *Philosophy of Art* was presented in lecture form "not *as* the execution of aesthetics but *instead of* it."[6] The fact is, though, that art loses its privileged status in Schelling's thought shortly after the completion of the *System*, although for some time it remains on a par with the philosophical concept or comes in behind it as a very close second – a position which resembles closely that of Hegel. In the last phase of his philosophical development, however, Schelling's evaluation of artistic creativity and its products becomes significantly more cautious and even moderately hostile. Under the perspective of Christian philosophy, art appears to be "worldly and pagan in its nature."[7] Schelling's most important and influential contribution to the philosophy of art undoubtedly is contained in the closing discussion of the *System* from which a direct line can be drawn to the philosophy of art as advanced by Heidegger and Adorno. For this reason, our discussion will focus on this text to a large extent, before we briefly consider the *Philosophy of Art.* In conclusion, we will examine the notion of irony as proposed primarily by F. Schlegel and Solger as an artistic strategy to bridge philosophy and art.

The System of Transcendental Idealism

Published in 1800 when Schelling was only twenty-five years old, *The System of Transcendental Idealism* is one of the most important texts of classical German philosophy. It brings to a close the first period of Schelling's philosophy that had begun in 1794 and is characterized by writings on natural and transcendental philosophy. The constant partner in the philosophical dialogue is Fichte, although Schelling's contributions achieve a considerable independence from this thinker, who strongly influenced the philosophical scene in Germany in the 1790s and who was widely admired by the romantics. Fichte himself had greeted Schelling's first publications with approval; he considered him to be his most talented follower, if not his equal, although Schelling moved away from Fichte by supplementing his writings on transcendental philosophy with those on the philosophy of nature. Without an attempt to reconcile these two aspects, however, a relapse into the Kantian dualism could not be avoided, and so nature and the transcendental must be shown to present two sides of one coin. It is one aim of the *System* to unite the philosophy of nature, which deduces the ideal from the real, with the transcendental philosophy, which understands nature as a reflex of spirit.

The *System,* much like Hegel's *Phenomenology of Spirit* (1806), presents the narrative of the stages of self-consciousness, so that Schelling states in his introduction that "philosophy ... is the ongoing history of self-consciousness" (*System,* VIII).[8] The aim of it is to demonstrate the identity of subject and object, self and nature, which becomes revealed in the history of mankind. Schelling attempts to unite his tendency toward an overarching totality, that is, the absolute that both idealists and romantics consider as that which precedes subject and object, as he inherited it from Spinoza with his allegiance to Fichte's *Wissenschaftslehre* (Science of knowledge).[9]

The absolute, however – and this is where idealism and romanticism part ways – cannot become an object of knowledge because this would precisely perpetuate the subject–object split that is meant to be overcome. Moreover, it would establish the primacy of the self over the absolute, since the self is able to embrace every object conceptually, and thus, a conceptually knowable absolute would result in a philosophical paradox. The absolute [*das Unbedingte*], Schelling puns, cannot be a thing [*ein Ding*], and whatever cannot be an object necessarily escapes conceptualization. The same opposition of absolute and objects, *Unbedingtes* and *Dinge*, is also advanced by Novalis in his collection of fragments called *Blüthenstaub* (Pollen, 1798). There he writes: *Wir suchen überall das Unbedingte, und finden immer nur Dinge.* (We search everywhere for the absolute, but we always only find things.)[10] If the absolute becomes an object of knowledge, this knowledge has to be phrased in terms of propositions, since no thinking is possible without language, that is, the propositional junction of subject and predicate.

Hölderlin had made this point in his 1795 fragment *Urtheil und Seyn* (Proposition or judgment and being) that was not published before 1961, but the content of which was certainly communicated to Hölderlin's friends. Written roughly one year after Fichte's *Science of Knowledge* – simultaneously with and yet independent of Schelling's *Das Ich als Prinzip der Philosophie* (The ego as principle of philosophy) – this text is intended as an argument against Fichte's principle of the ego as the foundation of philosophy. Hölderlin sets up an opposition between being and proposition (or judgment) in which *being* marks the indifference of subject and object, whereas *proposition* is the principle of separation: "Proposition [*Urtheil*] is in the highest and strictest sense the original separation of subject and object which were intimately united in the intellectual intuition, that separation which makes possible subject and object in the first place, the original separation [*Ur= Theilung*]."[11] Propositional thinking – a redundant expression – thus disables the appearance of being that precedes all relation of the subject to its object and, therefore, cannot become the object of cognition. Yet being is not identity either, because all identification demands an instance that can identify subject and object as the same and that, in turn, needs to precede the separation of subject and object. Thus, the self can under no circumstances be the final principle of philosophy. Being, in Dieter Henrich's words, becomes a "liminal concept of cognition."[12]

Despite the fact that conceptual knowledge cannot present access to the absolute, it can still be grasped in the intellectual intuition, a thought shared by Hölderlin and Schelling. Kant had called it "intuitive reason" and restricted it to God (*Critique of Judgment*, §77), whereas Fichte coined the term "intellectual intuition" [*intellektuelle*

Anschauung] in order to designate the philosopher's observation of that act in which the self posits itself, that is, the *Tathandlung*.[13] For Schelling, intellectual intuition is a form of certainty that is not mediated by concepts, but instead is an unmediated vision that reveals, much like for Fichte, the empirical self as freely posited. In it, the self acquires a certainty of itself without reaching knowledge of itself since the certainty remains unconceptualized. The absolute self as the ground of both subject and object cannot become an object for knowledge since it always precedes the reflexive self – in fact, the absolute is more than the ground that grounds subject and object, self and world. Objectivity and knowledge of the absolute can therefore not be achieved philosophically, that is, by means of concepts, but only symbolically, that is, through the work of art.[14] The state of intellectual intuition is precarious and unaccountable; it is like a "state of death"[15] from which we have no choice but to return to the state of reflection, knowledge of our empirical self and the division into subject and object. Schelling takes up the tradition of mythical knowledge as represented by Jakob Böhme and others by arguing that the absolute can be experienced in a deathlike state that transcends all concepts. And yet, this mythical certainty is not the ultimate point of Schelling's system, but rather, it is overcome by the knowledge of the absolute that the objective existence of the work of art grants us.

Schelling is not the first philosopher to consider art as possessing the power to unify subject and object by means of beauty where both practice and reflection fail in this effort. Again it is Hölderlin who constitutes the bridge between Schiller's advanced Kantianism and the idealism of Hegel and the romanticism of Schelling. In the latter half of the 1790s, Hölderlin sketches out his aesthetic ideas in a number of essays, none of which was published during his lifetime. He even planned to write a series of letters, tentatively titled *New Letters on the Aesthetic Education of Man,* in which the argument was to be advanced that the aesthetic sense will overcome the division of subject and object, reason and revelation (letter to Niethammer of February 24, 1796). These ideas were communicated to his student friends Schelling and Hegel both in letters and in personal conversations in Frankfurt, where both Hegel and Hölderlin lived briefly and where Schelling visited. Beauty, Hölderlin argues, makes the union that precedes subject and object accessible, a state of indifferentiation that he labels *Seyn* [being].[16] Sensual beauty, that is, beauty manifested as nature as well as art, will lead the way back to the *Seyn* – a slightly problematic concept, as Dieter Henrich has pointed out, for if beauty mirrors this original union only in the realm of the senses, then it is difficult to comprehend how it should overcome the split between thought and reality.[17]

The history of self-consciousness in Schelling's *System* that reaches its acme in the encounter with the work of art has to undergo a process of development in order to reach this final and highest stage, during which it passes from sensation to reflection to praxis. Sensation marks that stage in which the naïve consciousness regards objects as having an independent existence of the self and, thus, thinks of the object as a "thing in itself." The consciousness of mere sensation does not yet realize that it itself, that is, the productive intuition, posits the object. Consciousness forgets about its own productive activity and mistakes the object as independent (*System*, 138). In the state of reflexion, the self already distances itself from the object by means of thought, that is, linguistic operations, but only to realize the interdependence of its concepts and the object (*System*, 281 f.). In the state of praxis, finally, the realm of intersubjectivity is reached in which other individuals make demands on the self. But again the conscious erection of a moral order, the expression of the right of every individual to impose limits on the freedom of other individuals, leads to insight into the posited nature of the world of objects. The moral universe manifests itself as law, that is, the repudiating force that punishes "with iron necessity" (*System*, 406) the violation of another person's freedom. "History as a whole is an ongoing gradual revelation of the absolute" (*System*, 438) – although this process is itself endless. Therefore, the absolute can also not be known in history. It is, however, achieved in nature that represents the harmony of conscious and unconscious activities. This elevation of nature over history harks back to the importance that Schelling attributed to it in his natural philosophy. And still, nature's embodiment of the absolute is not the ultimate resting point for the *System*, either, because the identity that it presents is not knowable for the reflexive self as one that rests in the absolute self (*System*, 449 f.). Nature's harmony is without consciousness and demands yet another step – the knowledge of the absolute provided by art.

Neither the moral freedom of man demonstrated in the course of history nor the product of nature was able to fulfill the demand for the conscious realization of the absolute in which conscious and unconscious activity are known to be identical. Thus, yet another, higher level in the narrative of self-consciousness needs to be reached in order to achieve this aim, and what freedom and nature were incapable of providing reaches its *telos* in the work of art. While nature in its production begins unconsciously and ends in consciousness, namely, that of man, the artistic activity reverses this process by beginning consciously and continuing without consciousness. While the artist certainly decides to create a specific work and to make plans for it, the execution demands that an additional force beyond the control of the artist enter into the work. It is precisely the definition of genius – and all artistic creation for Schelling depends on genius – that the unconscious element joins the conscious effort. The true artist, after he has begun his work, is then visited by an outside power that adds the objective moment to the product, that is, that which transcends the merely personal and consciously drafted. These visitations, however, isolate the artist from his fellow beings and force him to represent things in his work that he himself fails to comprehend completely and that supply the infinite meaning that characterizes every work of art. Thus, every work of art conjoins two elements: one that Schelling calls "art" [*Kunst*] and that signifies art in the sense of τὲχνη, that is, skill, practice, and imitation of the established artistic paradigms, primarily the art of classical Greece; the other that Schelling labels "poetry" and that refers to the unconscious moment that enters the work of art not as a result of the effort of the artist but, instead, as the reflex of "grace" (*System*, 459). No work of art can come into existence without both moments present, although Schelling declares, more in allegiance with Goethe's classicism than with the credo of the romantic poets, that in the end the patient practice, especially as *imitatio,* as the study of and the inspiration by the ancient masters, wins precedence over inspiration. Inspiration alone will not lead to anything without technical skill and knowledge of the artistic tradition, whereas these qualities can still produce a respectable work, even though it will fall short of the requirements for great art.

Where conscious and unconscious activity unite in order to demonstrate their identity in the artistic product, a sense of wonder will be experienced, just like that which is said to set in motion all philosophical thought:

> Because this absolute consonance of the two opposed activities is fundamentally inexplicable, yet still a phenomenon that, though incomprehensible, is undeniable, art is the only and eternal revelation that exists as well as the miracle that, even if it had only existed once, would have to convince us of the absolute reality of the Highest. (*System*, 460)

Both the artistic creativity itself and the unsettled search of man for the absolute come to rest in the final product, the work of art. In it, the reflexive self understands itself to be merely a lower order [*Potenz der Selbstanschauung*] of the absolute self:

> Because it was the free tendency towards self-representation in that [original] identity that had incipiently caused this division, the feeling that accompanies this [aesthetic] intuition will be one of infinite satisfaction. All drive to produce stands still with the completion of the product, all contradictions are resolved [*aufgehoben*], all riddles solved. (*System*, 456)

The work of art represents the identity of conscious and unconscious activity, although it doesn't collapse these into each other. Instead, conscious and unconscious tendencies remain both intact and sublated at the same time, thereby guaranteeing an infinite opposition of these moments. Since no ultimate reconciliation can be achieved between them, the work of art never allows for just one interpretation, but for an infinite multitude: "Such is the case with every true work of art inasmuch as every one, as if an infinity of purposes were contained in it, is capable of infinite interpretation, and one can never say whether this infinity had its cause in the artist or lies merely in the work of art" (*System*, 463 f.).

With this idea of the infinite interpretability of art – a favorite concept of romantic thought in general – Schelling harks back to Kant's notion of the aesthetic idea that had been defined as one that causes an infinite amount of thought without ever subsuming the multitude of sensual riches under one concept. And yet the eternal strife of conscious and unconscious activity in the work of art does not cause it to give an impression of restlessness. Quite the opposite; the artwork, and here again Schelling's classicist leanings manifest themselves, is the "expression of quietude and of calm greatness" (*System*, 464). This formulation echoes almost verbatim Winckelmann's famous definition of Greek masterpieces as exhibiting "an noble simplicity and calm greatness."[18] Such impression prevails even if the subject matter portrays great emotional or physical perturbance like joy or pain.

The infinite strife of conscious and unconscious activity as united in a final product is nothing but a definition of beauty without which no work of art can exist as such. Beauty is manifest "where the infinite opposition is sublated [*aufgehoben*] in the object" (*System*, 465). Works of art are by definition and necessity beautiful, and they are also the prime examples of beauty. Schelling concedes that beauty certainly appears in natural objects as well, although in nature, it is random and can only be recognized due to our familiarity with the beauty as it shines in art:

> The organic product of nature will therefore not necessarily be *beautiful*, and if it is beautiful, its beauty, because the necessity for its existence cannot be thought as existing in nature, will appear as utterly arbitrary. ... This clarifies what ought to be thought of imitation of nature as the principle of art, since by no means does nature – which is only accidentally beautiful – prescribe the rule for art. Instead, that which art produces in its perfection is the principle and norm for the judgment of natural beauty. (*System*, 466 f.)

With such institution of the supremacy of beauty in art over that in nature, Schelling overturns Kant's hierarchy. Kant had argued that the genius is the person in whom nature prescribes the rule to art (CJ, §46), thereby placing nature above man-made objects. But it is Schelling's view that turned out to be more influential, so that Solger states in his *Lectures on Aesthetics*: "Nothing beautiful exists outside of art. If we consider nature under the aspect of beauty, we transfer the notion of art onto nature" (1).

Schelling argues vehemently against the notion that art might have any kind of use value, be it theoretical or practical. He reasons that art has no end outside itself, and only as an end in itself can it retain its "holiness and purity" (*System*, 467). To consider art a means for sensual pleasure is barbaric; to look for a use value in it reveals the spirit of an age in which economic principles reign supreme; even to connect it to morality is fruitless; and scientific knowledge cannot be expected from it, since all scientific inquiry is directed toward a specific goal and driven by specific questions and, therefore, has to remain subordinate to the absolute freedom of the work of art.

To be sure, it is not merely that art and science – and philosophy for Schelling is part of the scientific project – are not opposed in their respective quest; rather, it is that they have set identical tasks for themselves. Science, however, will never be able to fulfill its own task, whereas art is the very embodiment of this fulfillment. Art has already achieved what always remains an incomplete project for science. Philosophy is incapacitated by its own contradiction between its task – thinking the absolute – and the means at its disposal – knowledge achieved through concepts. Since the absolute cannot become the object of knowledge, philosophy finds itself in the role of Tantalus: The water is within reach, but every gesture toward it causes its withdrawal. The utmost that the philosopher can achieve is the state of intellectual intuition, although this state, despite the unmediated certainty that it grants, escapes philosophical justification. Only in the work of art does the intellectual intuition find its objective demonstration. Much like Schiller, Schelling argues that philosophy can lead only one fragment of man to the highest form of completion, whereas art overcomes fragmentation and achieves the unification of man in aesthetic intuition (*System*, 480). According to Schelling:

> This objectivity of the intellectual intuition that is generally accepted and by no means deniable is art itself. Because the aesthetic intuition is precisely the intellectual intuition gone objective. Only the artwork reflects for me what is not reflected in anything else, namely that absolute identity that had already divided itself in the self. What the philosopher regards as already divided in the first act of consciousness is being reflected through the miracle of art while it is inaccessible for every other intuition. (*System*, 472)

What has already been lost in every conscious act that rests on concepts is recovered in art. Only art is capable of representing the infinite, and nothing that does not contain such infinity is a work of art. And although every work of art naturally has a subject matter that represents only one aspect of the world, its true content nevertheless is the world as totality. This is why Schelling can claim that, in fact, only one true work of art exists, namely, one objective manifestation of the infinity of the world, although this work of art exists in many different exemplars. The Neoplatonism inherent in this concept of the one idea of art that emanates into the material multitude of factually existing artworks will become distinctly more prominent in Schelling's writings on art in the years after the *System.*

The *System* itself closes its discussion of art with a veritable hymn that sums up the preceding pages:

If the aesthetic intuition is merely the intellectual intuition gone objective, then it is self-understood that art is at once the only true and eternal organon and document of philosophy that always anew documents what philosophy cannot externally represent, namely the unconscious in act and production and its original identity with consciousness. Art is therefore the Highest to the philosopher, because as it were it opens the most holy where in eternal and primary union burns as if in one flame what is separated in nature and history and what must flee each other in life and act as well as in thought. (*System,* 475)

These much-quoted lines demonstrate how art is the capstone of the philosophical system as the harmonious objectification of consciousness and unconsciousness, subject and object, as identical in the absolute. Therefore, those branches of knowledge that can achieve this representation of identity only subjectively, that is, science and philosophy, have to be aligned with art. A utopian vision of a future in which all merely subjective knowledge gives way to a comprehensive poetic knowledge closes Schelling's *System.* Schelling calls for a New Mythology that will close the gap between the present and that future state in which all sciences have been dissolved in universal poetry:

... therefore it can be expected that philosophy, as it was born and raised by poetry, and with it all those sciences that it leads toward perfection will after their perfection flow back like individual rivers into the extensive ocean of poetry from where they originated. It is not hard to say what will be the mediator for the return of science to poetry, since such mediator existed as mythology before this division that now seems unbridgeable had occurred. Yet how a New Mythology could come into existence not as the invention of one single poet but of a new generation living as *one* poet is a problem to which the solution can be expected from the future fate of the world and the consequent course of history. (*System,* 477 f.)

Schelling's notion of a New Mythology was not unique; instead, it was very much in the air around the turn of the century.[19] Herder in his *Iduna* dialogue (1796) had called for a renewal of ancient Greek and Nordic mythology as a means for societal refurbishing. The most vigorous call for a New Mythology, however, came in the form of a "program for agitation" (Dieter Henrich), namely, the so-called *Das älteste Systemprogramm des deutschen Idealismus* (The oldest systematic program of German idealism, probably 1796). Although the brief text is written in Hegel's handwriting, the authorship – Schelling, Hölderlin, Hegel, or, less likely, an unknown fourth person – is still disputed. It declares that "the philosopher must possess as much aesthetic force as the poet," because it is the idea of beauty that unites all other ideas. In the context of an anarchist critique of the mechanized modern polity that does not allow for the symbolization of freedom as a concept of reason, since mechanical entities cannot represent ideas, poetry as the highest form of art is advanced as anticipation of a social existence that will have returned to a unity beyond mechanical functioning. Once this state has been reached, poetry will take over the functions of all other arts and sciences, including philosophy: "poetry alone will survive all other sciences and arts." To mediate between the present state and the poeticized one, a New Mythology is called for: "We must have a New Mythology, but this Mythology must be in the service of reason, it must become a Mythology of reason. Before we haven't rendered the ideas aesthetic, i.e., mythological, they hold no interest for the populace, and before the Mythology hasn't become reasonable the philosopher must be ashamed of it."[20] Thus, this type of mythology will reconcile the sphere of art with the – one is tempted to use a Hegelian term in Marx's sense: alienating – social reality.

In 1799, Novalis in his *Die Christenheit oder Europa* (Christianity or Europe) prophesied a rebirth of the Catholic Christian faith that would not only lead to a Europe that had overcome its nationalisms, but would also cause "a universal individuality, a new history, a new humanity, the sweetest embrace of a young surprised church and a loving God, and simultaneously the heartfelt [*innige*] reception of a new messiah in its thousand limbs."[21] Although the Christian faith cannot properly be called a mythology, the unifying function that Novalis attributes to its revival allows us to draw parallels to the present discussion. Finally, Friedrich Schlegel's centerpiece of the *Gespräch über die Poesie*

(Conversation about poetry, 1800), namely, the *Rede über die Mythologie* (Speech on mythology), was written with the knowledge of the *Systemprogramm.* Not distinguishing between poetry and mythology, Schlegel considers it its function to unite all of mankind through the aesthetic certainty of the absolute that it grants:

> Neither this [romantic] esprit nor a mythology can exist without something original and inimitable [*ein erstes Ursprüngliches und Unnachahmliches*] that is absolutely indivisible and that still lets its old nature and force shine through after all permutations. . . . Because it is the beginning of all poetry to suspend [*aufzuheben*] the way and the laws of reasonably thinking reason and to return us to the beautiful confusion of phantasy, to the original chaos of human nature of which I know thus far no symbol more beautiful than the colorful swarm of the ancient Gods.[22]

In general, the New Mythology has the function of unifying aesthetic intuition with the polity, that is, of reuniting art as an epistemological instrument with practical philosophy. This aspect is certainly of greater importance in the *Systemprogramm* than it is in Schlegel, who tends to emphasize the aesthetic moment over the social, yet it still remains the basis of the various conceptions of a New Mythology. Whereas aesthetic intuition is a merely private affair, its incorporation into a mythology is meant to guarantee the social aspect of art. And whereas a critical function is never attributed to the individual work, the New Mythology both takes a critical stance toward the present and anticipates a future reconciled in all its theoretical and practical aspects. And yet it should be mentioned, although a detailed discussion of this issue would lead far beyond our present scope, that it is somewhat difficult to comprehend how the transition from the apolitical individual work of art (this nature of the artwork will become even clearer in our discussion of irony) to the socially committed New Mythology is meant to be achieved.

Philosophy of Art

Continuities as well as discontinuities exist between Schelling's aesthetic theories of the *System of Transcendental Idealism* and the writings of the following seven years, especially the manuscript for his lecture on the *Philosophy of Art.* One thing, though, is clear beyond a doubt: Art loses its status as the capstone of the philosophical system in all of these texts. Despite its continuing relevance for philosophical thought, it no longer reaches what philosophy cannot achieve. Art is a vital contribution to thought because it still fulfills functions that cannot be executed by conceptual thought, yet ultimately it depends on the philosopher to interpret its exploits. Also, the emphasis on the genius as necessary producer of artworks gives way to a conception on a larger historical scale in which entire peoples serve as agents of artistic production[23] – yet another tendency that underscores Schelling's move from romanticism toward a Hegelian idealism during his middle period, the years of the so-called *Identitätsphilosophie* (philosophy of identity).

Our discussion of the *Philosophy of Art* will be limited to the general first part and leave out most of the second part in which Schelling develops a system of the individual arts. This half of the work, however, depends heavily on the manuscript of private lectures that August Wilhelm Schlegel (1767–1845), Friedrich's brother, had given in Berlin in the years 1801–3 and that Schelling had borrowed from him.[24]

It can even be argued that the absolute itself acquires a new quality in the *Philosophy of Art* (PA) that adds another dimension to that being that precedes the differentiation into subject and object, namely, those "romantic" features of chaos, night and darkness. The absolute itself is mere "bottomless nothingness" [*bodenlose Leere*] (PA, 393).[25] Only with the emergence of ideas [*Urbilder*] that introduce limitation, that is, the finite, into the absolute is the creation of the universe possible. What we know as the gods of ancient mythology are the first sensual manifestations of these ideas, the first emanations of the absolute. Whereas beauty is the reflection of the well-ordered universe, in the sublime we still encounter chaos (PA, 465), although the sublime must never be allowed to overpower order; that is, it must always retain a trace of beauty. Inversely, beauty must contain an aspect of sublimity, something faintly terrible (PA, 468 f.) – an idea that takes up the Aristotelian theory of catharsis and that is echoed in the verses of R. M. Rilke's first *Duino Elegies: Denn das Schöne ist nichts als des Schrecklichen Anfang / Den wir noch grade ertragen* (The beautiful is nothing but the beginning of the terrifying / that we can still endure).

Art, and now Schelling argues in the Neoplatonic tradition, does not represent objects; that is, it is not engaged in any naturalistic mimesis but, rather, represents the idea of the object. This metaphysical grounding of aesthetics can be considered an attempt to suspend the individualizing tendencies of Kant's aesthetic philosophy.[26] Even more explicit than in the *Philosophy of Art,* this Neoplatonic understanding of art informs the 1807 lecture *On the Relation of the Visual Arts to Nature.* Every object, Schelling affirms here, is determined by its idea: "every object is ruled by an eternal concept" (RN, 300).[27] A work of art can be considered successful when it represents the transcendental beauty of the idea – we remember that Schelling had defined the ideas as simultaneously true and beautiful – to the senses, a conception that anticipates Hegel's definition of beauty as the sensual splendor of the idea. In consequence, the artist in his work does not imitate the objects of nature that surround him; instead, he turns away from the visible world to directly imitate the ideas. This other aspect of the Platonic theory of mimesis, one that has been called "esoteric" and that is also taken up by Plotinus (e.g., *Ennead* V, 8, 1), will again play an important role in Schopenhauer's aesthetics:

> He [the artist] must distance himself from the product or the creation, but only in order to be elevated to the creative force and to grasp it mentally [*geistig*]. Through this he soars upward into the realm of pure concepts; he leaves the creation in order to regain it with thousandfold interest and thereby to return to it. That spirit of nature that labors inside the object through form and gestalt as if through images [*Sinnbilder*] the artist must imitate, and only insofar as he grasps it in his imitation does he achieve truth [*etwas Wahrhaftes*]. (RN, 301)

The work of art thus represents not the empirical object but its idea. Another way of putting this is by claiming that in art, every object is presented as the epitome of its existence, a state where it has reached its *telos.* Art captures the perfect moment and lifts the object out of the flow of time, allowing it to become eternal in its preservation through art.[28] The true being of the object is not its temporal existence by its timeless presence that it reclaims in the artwork. This idea of the perfect moment that reveals the true nature of the object, transcends time, and eternalizes the object in art will inform many poetic theories of modernist writers, as in James Joyce's theory of epiphany, Virginia Woolf's "moment of being," or Marcel Proust's *moment privilégié.*

As much as the material world as God's creation is the result of his emanation [*Entäusserung*], so the activity of the artist consists in pouring the idea into a form that is perceptible to the senses: "As much as all of creation is a work of the highest emanation, so the artist must negate himself and decend into the singular, not shying away from isolation, nor from agony and the pain of form" (RN, 304). Art is here likened to God's act of creation that is considered a painful event of individualization and materialization – a *kenosis,* in the term of the New Testament, and, hence, an idea more Christian in nature than Neoplatonic, since Plotinus speaks of the engendering of the cosmos as a "painless labor" (*Ennead* V, 8, 12).

Obviously, Schelling has not given up all moments of the theory of genius, since one of its standard topoi is the parallelization of the work of the artist with the divine creation. The painful aspect of this notion is also echoed in Karl Wilhelm Ferdinand Solger's tragic version of romantic irony. Without taking up the discussion of irony here, we can nevertheless point out that Solger regards the incorporation of the absolute (which he calls "idea") in an object of art as an event that destroys the eternal nature of the absolute and that thus causes sadness in the observer. In his dialogue *Erwin* he asserts:

> When the idea through artistic reason is incorporated in the individual object, it does not only express itself therein, nor does it appear as merely temporal and transient, but instead it becomes the present reality. Since nothing exists outside of it, only nothingness and transience, immense sadness must grip us when we see the most glorious dissolve into nothing through its necessary earthly existence.[29]

Whereas the intellectual intuition encounters the absolute in its transcendent state and sensual perception only considers the transient nature of objects, art hovers in between these two spheres. Art has a tragic aspect, but it is not tragic throughout, because from its vantage point both realms come into view. This view that observes the moment of the incarnation of the absolute in the artistic object is labeled "irony" by Solger. No matter what its achievements are, it will always retain its moment of sadness that is caused by the embodiment of the idea in a material object.

Returning to the *Philosophy of Art,* Schelling's Neoplatonic aesthetics define art and truth as two different perspectives on the absolute. An object is beautiful when it is so adequate to its idea that the infinite (the concept) enters the real. In fewer words, in beauty the real becomes ideal. Schelling repeats the ontological arguments from the *System of Transcendental Idealism* that had defined the artwork as the point of indifference between conscious and unconscious, freedom and necessity, subject and object. The work of art is not identical with the idea, but it is the reflection [*Gegenbild*] of the idea [*Urbild*]. Its beauty is not an achievement of the artist; rather, it is due to its reflecting quality of the infinite that is characterized by truth and beauty. Again, Schelling takes up a Neoplatonic motif in this definition of *pulchritudo* [beauty] as *splendor dei* [the splendor of God].[30]

If ideas are by necessity true and beautiful, it follows that the ugliness of some empirical objects cannot be traced back to ugly ideas; rather, it results from the merely temporal perspective on things. Ugliness is a mode of privation, the absence of almost all reflected splendor of the *Urbild,* the idea. Such interdependence of art and the transcendent naturally leads to a postulate of intimate ties between art and religion. At the end of his art historical essay on the allegorical representations of death and sleep in ancient art, *Wie die Alten den Tod gebildet* (How the ancients depicted death, 1768–9), Lessing had already come to the same Neoplatonic conclusion: "Only misunderstood religion can distance us from art: and it is a proof of the true, the correctly understood true religion when everywhere it leads us back to the beautiful."[31] And Solger affirms two decades after Schelling: "Religion cannot exist without art, as something merely rational; this is the other side of religion. Shall the religious principle reveal itself, it can only do this in manifestations that are capable of representing an idea [Solger's term for the absolute]. Similarly, the orientation toward religion is inherent in the sphere of art" (*Lectures on Aesthetics,* 94). In his *Lectures on the Method of Academic Studies,* Schelling states that no poetic world can exist outside religion and that no objective representation of religion is possible without art (LM, 352).[32] And although art causes the infinite to appear in the finite realm, the mere appearance is not sufficient but needs to be interpreted. Such interpretation can neither be undertaken by the artist himself nor by the untrained consumer of art.

The interpretation of the presence of the infinite in the finite object depends on the philosopher, and aesthetics therefore are defined as the investigation of the "representation of the absolute world in the form of art" (LM, 350).

Manfred Frank has pointed out rightly that a certain tension in Schelling's later conception of art cannot be overlooked. If philosophy can grasp the absolute through its interpretation of art, the infinite interpretability of art and, thus, the ever-elusive nature of the absolute is endangered. It seems that either thesis has to be given up to achieve coherence, unless a new philosophical conception of the absolute can be argued for that no longer depends on the embodiment of the absolute in privileged objects – a path that Hegel will soon take by advancing the notion that philosophy can dispense with the assistance of art when it comes to knowledge of the absolute.[33]

Irony

Irony is regarded by the romantics as the link between speculation and poetic practice, as that which philosophy can understand but only art can do. By becoming ironic, poetry enables itself to fulfill the promises of romantic philosophy. This claim, however, can only be comprehended if the definition of the term "irony" is clarified, since it has little to do with our quotidian understanding of that same word.

Two meanings can already be distinguished in the traditional sense of the concept of irony. The first is the one developed by the rhetorical system, especially Quintilian and Cicero, where irony is used as a figure of speech that means exactly the opposite of what it says. By employing some kind of hint through mimic or intonation, the so-called signal of irony, our interlocutor understands that we mean to debunk a book of which we ironically say: "This is a very good piece of writing!" Thus, rhetorical irony leaves us with a positive statement that is in no way unclear insofar as it is the reversal of the literal meaning.

The other traditional notion of irony is the Socratic one, which consisted in Socrates' pretense to always know less that his dialogue partner and thereby to dismantle the latter's presumed knowledge. It is not a figure of speech but an ethos of communication that only has the appearance of playfulness, but that turns out to be an instrument of the serious quest for knowledge.

Romantic irony distinguishes itself sharply from either position since it lacks the positive result of the rhetorical figure of speech, as well as the serious conviction of the attainability of a truth that can be grasped as a concept and communicated to others. Instead, romantic irony undermines all positions insofar as they are positive, final, and limited. In the words of Friedrich Schlegel:

> In it, all must be joke and all must be earnestness, all innocently open and all deeply concealed. It has its source in the unification of the artistic sense of life [*Lebenskunstsinn*] with the scientific spirit, in the engagement of completed natural philosophy and completed philosophy of art. It contains and produces a sense of the irreconcilable opposition of the infinite and the finite, the impossibility and necessity of a complete communication. It is the freest of all licenses, because through it one overcomes oneself [*setzt man sich über sich selbst hinweg*] and yet the most regulated, because it is absolutely necessary. (KA II, 159 f., no. 108)

This type of irony gestures toward the infinite by rendering all finitude unstable and incomplete. Through its use the empirical self transcends itself toward the absolute in a "constant change between self-creation and self-destruction" (KA II, 172, no. 51). The self never arrives at full self-knowledge or self-certainty, but remains elusive, the object of (romantic) longing.

Of course, irony cannot escape the necessity of all propositions to establish some positive meaning (even in propositions containing a negation) by means of its conjunction of subject and predicate. Thus, an ironic statement also posits something finite and positive, and yet – just like rhetorical irony – it overturns it through the way it is stated. But whereas the rhetorical figure of speech leaves it at that, romantic irony does not arrive at a stable position but overturns this again. Not coming to a rest in its constant back and forth between the proposition and its negation, it renders all finite positions equally meaningless. Schlegel writes: "Everything worth something must be simultaneously this and its opposite" (KA XVIII, 82, no. 633). And just before that: "Everything that does not annihilate itself is not free and worth nothing" (KA XVIII, 82, no. 628).

The result of this infinite process of mutual negation is not the sublation of both positions into a higher form of coexistence, a Hegelian synthesis but, rather, a sense of instability and of constant change between "chaos and system" (KA XVIII, 283, no. 1048). Solger elaborates on this point that not only does irony "annihilate" all that is finite – a form of "objective irony" that Hegel praises and likens to the dialectical force of negation – but the absolute itself at which this infinite process of negation hints also does not emerge as a positive moment. Irony can only provide an "intimation of totality" (KA II, 323) that is understood as that of which no perception can exist. Thus, philosophy can describe irony, but it is art that must practice it.

Georg Lukács has summarized this discussion in his 1920 *Die Theorie des Romans* (The theory of the novel):

> The irony of the poet is the negative mysticism of the godless ages: a *docta ignorantia* in respect to meaning; a demonstration of the merciful and ill-meaning labor of the demons; the decline to comprehend more than the fact of this labor and the deep certainty that can only be given form [*nur gestaltend ausdrückbar*]: in this refusal and impossibility to know one has seen and grasped the final, the true substance, the present, nonexisting God in its truth.[34]

In a somewhat dense manner, Lukács explains that the romantics held that by demonstrating the impossibility of all finite knowledge, they had grasped the absolute. And yet this absolute does not achieve presence either, because it cannot manifest itself as something positive. The absolute remains concealed in all its revelation; it is the "nonexisting God."

Ernst Behler, the editor of the critical edition of Schlegel's works, has argued that the romantic irony is nothing but an application of the Socratic irony to literature.[35] Taking his stance against Søren Kierkegaard, Behler seems to underestimate the negative force of romantic irony that Kierkegaard took issue with. For the latter, irony was the synonym of romanticism in general and – following in the footsteps of Hegel who had stated that this type of irony was symptomatic for a self-congratulatory ego that had cut all ties to reality[36] – thereby the symptom of a frivolous attitude that destroyed all seriousness by undermining every possibility to commit and to communicate.[37] Socratic irony, and Kierkegaard was right in this, rested precisely on these assumptions:

> Irony now functioned as that for which nothing was established, as that which was finished with everything, and also as that which had the absolute power to do everything. If it allowed something to remain established, it knew that it

had the power to destroy it, knew at the very same moment it let it continue. If it posited something, it knew it had the authority to annul it, knew at the very same moment it posited it. It knew that in general it possessed the absolute power to bind and to unbind. It was lord over the idea just as much as over the phenomenon, and it destroyed the one with the other. It destroyed the phenomenon by showing that it did not correspond to the idea; it destroyed the idea by showing that it did not correspond to the phenomenon. Both were correct, since the idea and the phenomenon are only in and with each other. And during all this, irony saved its carefree life, since the subject, man, was able to do all this, for who is as great as Allah, and who can endure before him?[38]

Kierkegaard, defending the ideal of the Socratic irony as a tool for the establishment of truth, fears that in romantic irony all seriousness, gratitude, and humility disappear from human existence. The romantic poet, in the absence the absolute, becomes the sole representative of the Highest. Far from being a humiliation of the narcissistic fantasies of grandeur, as Manfred Frank argues,[39] we would have to consider romantic irony as the function of a hypertrophic self. Similarly, art in the view of romantic philosophy would emerge as the supreme epistemic organ that has already undermined its own capacity of arriving at that conceptual knowledge that is necessary for the communication and the societal discourse of values. Romantic irony is obsessed with its own endless procedure and, thus, disables all agreement on valuation. The aestheticization of epistemology brings in its wake the loss of those foundations that are necessary for the establishment of communal ethical standards.

In the paradigm of aesthetics that Schelling and the other romantic philosophers develop, the epistemic function of art overrules all others; ontological functions are secondary, and any practical function is denied to the artwork. The result of this stance is that art takes precedence over science, of which philosophy is considered a part. Art is cast in a role in which it is celebrated as that product of the human spirit that reveals a kind of truth that is not only different from scientific truth; instead it is its foundation. The truth of art precedes scientific truth and enables it: Without the world-disclosing activity of art, no individual inquiry would be possible. From here, a direct line leads to Heidegger's theory of art as a disclosure of truth, as well as to the radical criticism of "instrumental reason," as Adorno and

Horkheimer termed the scientific project. Schelling's paradigm must be considered the grandfather of today's tendencies in philosophy to abort metaphysics, ontology, and epistemology all in favor of aesthetics. One cannot help but feel that philosophy somehow gets shortchanged with the establishment of romantic aesthetics – a sense that led Hegel to a reversal of the hierarchy of philosophy and art as expressed by the Schelling of the *System.*

5

Hegel

With Hegel the age of paradigms in aesthetics comes to an end. But there are two ways to understand the term "end." On the one hand, it can mean the goal of a structured development that brings something into its own, its telos, by fulfilling its inherent possibilities. On the other hand, end merely signifies the final point of a stretch of time, generally no better or worse than any previous one. Especially in the nineteenth century, Hegel's philosophy at large was understood in the former sense, namely, as the completion of German idealism as well as the epitome of its achievements. In regard to his philosophy of art, the analogous argument that portrays Hegel as the capstone of systematic aesthetic thought has been advanced.[1] Obviously, these are not value-neutral judgments, but they rest on the (Hegelian) assumption not that truth *is* a historical process but that it *becomes transparent* for itself in the course of history. Hence, the narrative that regards aesthetics as culminating in Hegel's version of it understands it as superior to the previous attempts, because its explanatory power is greater, its integration into the system of philosophy more convincing, and most of all, its claim to truth can be better substantiated. As is well known, such teleological narrative fell largely out of favor in the twentieth century, and it has mostly been replaced by the conviction that Hegel's *schlechte Unendlichkeit* (bad infinity, i.e., an open-ended historical process) provides the superior model over utopian and teleological versions of history. Nevertheless, we might indeed accede to the thesis that Hegel marks the end of a development, although this will not be *the* end, but *an* end.

The story of aesthetics after Hegel can, therefore, by no means be told as that of a decline, although the most influential contributions to aesthetics published during the remainder of the nineteenth century will often strike us as something of a loss in terms of argumentative rigor, boldness of speculation, and most importantly, the ability to relate art productively to other philosophical queries. Therefore, the nineteenth century after Hegel (although not always chronologically so, as Schopenhauer's case proves) can be understood as an interlude leading up to a new cycle of aesthetic investigation in the twentieth century that follows closely the pattern established by German idealism. Yet this pattern clearly ends with Hegel. Such "sense of an ending," to quote Frank Kermode's famous title here, should nevertheless not conjure up autumnal feelings of loss, finality, and retrospection. Instead, from Hegel's writings on art many vistas open into the future.

Not the least interesting of these is that which invited the honorific cognomen "father of art history" for Hegel, although historical accuracy demands that Winckelmann's 1764 *Geschichte der Kunst des Altertums* (History of the art of antiquity) at least be mentioned as a precursor to which Hegel also owes a certain debt.[2] Hegel's turn from a formal aesthetics to one of content – we shall see the precise meaning of this phrase later – has had the side effect that the newly established discipline of art history, which came into being together with the other humanities as we know them today in the beginning of the nineteenth century, received much inspiration from his theses. To be sure, Hegel was not the first philosopher of art to include a wide variety of artistic examples in his writings, since Schelling before him had devoted the second part of his *Philosophy of Art* to a system of artistic forms and genres. Yet Schelling's systematic approach to the empirical multitude of artistic objects had not been based on a concept of historical development but, rather, aimed for a synchronic systematicity. Thus, the historical investigation of art as practiced in the historical sciences of art – literary history, history of art and architecture, history of music, and so on – could hardly take any clues from Schelling, but found a model – albeit problematic – in Hegel.

The idea that there is a story to tell about the development of art slowly emerged during the period of German idealism. As we have seen, in Kant's third *Critique,* art was not viewed from a historical perspective, nor was any particular historical function attributed to it. This changed with Schiller's rewriting of the Kantian paradigm, at least so far as the second aspect is concerned. Art was still not considered to be historical in the sense that the emergence of concrete forms, genres, or works of art depends on specific historical constellations. Still, Schiller came to attribute a historical function to art nonetheless, namely, that of bridging the age of alienation and the moral state of the future. Only with Hegel does art come to be seen as both historical in its origin and its function.[3] We will have to consider both of these aspects in our discussion of Hegel's philosophy of art. Yet it is also evident that art transcends history insofar as the work of art allows the past to be present again. Far from being of mere historical interest, the art of the past speaks to the present age no less than the most contemporary product – or even more so. Thus, in the "essential simultaneity of all art" (Gadamer), art demonstrates its superiority over the constant flow of history. Even the Hegel student Karl Marx, who generally insists on the primacy of the economic base over the superstructure that contains all the forms of the absolute spirit, admits that art escapes its historical grounding and achieves an almost timeless existence: "The difficulty is not to understand that Greek art and epos are tied to certain social forms of development. The difficulty is that they still grant aesthetic pleasure and figure as norm and inimitable paradigms."[4]

Hegel presented his aesthetics repeatedly as a lecture course both in Heidelberg and Berlin. He did not, however, publish it in the form of a book. This only happened after his death in 1831 when the so-called *Freundeskreis* (Circle of friends) edited lecture notes not only on aesthetics but also on the philosophy of history, the philosophy of religion, and the history of philosophy. By now it is an established fact that these editions are not entirely reliable, and critical historical editions of the original unedited lecture notes of students present in the lecture courses have started to be published. In the case of the philosophy of art, Hegel's student Heinrich Gustav Hotho took some liberties in his transformation of lecture notes into a coherent book (one, we might add, that is a good bit more approachable than the texts that Hegel himself published), partly because the competing romantic school had presented itself very forcefully in the writings of Schelling and Solger. Thus, it might have seemed necessary to overstate some positions of Hegel's objective idealism in order to alert the contemporary public to the differences between the romantic and the idealist aesthetics. Somewhat simplified, it can be concluded that Hegel's lectures are marked by slightly different emphases than Hotho's polished version of 1835 (an improved second edition followed in 1842).

One charge that was repeatedly leveled against Hegel's aesthetics by future philosophers of art was that of a somwhat sterile classicism due to his strict separation of good and bad art, that is, beautiful and ugly artistic products. Art was seen as set in opposition to everyday life, beauty as removed from artifacts that were handicraft and not high art. And although Hegel's aesthetic certainly does not allow qualitative equality of high and low art, it also seems as if Hegel's sympathies for a "minor art" – to paraphrase a self-description of Kafka here – were censored in the published version of his lectures.[5] The main arguments, however, are hardly concerned with these editorial questions, since they are stated with the same clarity in the *Enzyklopädie der philosophischen Wissenschaften* (Encyclopedia of philosophical sciences – 1817/1827/1830) that Hegel had published as a textbook for his lectures. Hence, we will still rely mostly on the posthumously published version of Hegel's philosophy of art for our discussion.

In order to fully understand this last unfolding of idealist aesthetics, we need to briefly situate it within Hegel's larger philosophical system. With Hegel, not only does philosophical thought have a history, but it itself is also considered historical. Thus, Hegel's system narrates the story of the spirit (the concept that replaces that of love as it had been put forth by Schiller and Hölderlin as a resolution to the Kantian dilemma)[6] as a journey to itself – one that in fact has often been compared to the medieval *aventiure* epics, as well as to the *Bildungsroman* that emerged at the same time as Hegel's philosophy. Unlike adventure novels, however, the journey of the spirit does not lead through contingent episodes but, rather, follows a pattern of development that is strictly logical. Logic namely signifies for Hegel not the rules of reasoning but the investigation into the abstract existence of entities and their movement forward into different stages. The development of the spirit, as explicated in the *Encyclopedia of Philosophical Sciences*, is that from the in-itself of the spirit (mere spirit not knowing itself) to the for-itself (the material embodiment of the spirit) to the in-and-for-itself (the self-knowledge of the spirit as the outcome of its laborious movement through its materializations in the subject and in objective forms and institutions). Whereas the subjective spirit, that is, the spirit of individual man, develops from sensation to conscious perception and thought, objective spirit is embodied in law, morality, and mores [*Sittlichkeit*, i.e., the social praxis – understood in the Aristotelian sense – of a certain group at a certain time], the latter becoming manifest in the family, bourgeois society, and the state. Yet even the state as the highest form of communal life cannot incorporate full self-knowledge of the spirit, so that another step becomes necessary in which the spirit moves beyond institutions and finds its expression in the reflection of totality.

This last stage, that of the absolute spirit, again falls into three moments, namely art, the religion of revelation, and philosophy. In all three, the truth of absolute spirit can be found, in art in a fashion that we will discuss in detail, in religion as the representation [*Vorstellung*] of the absolute that combines image and idea, and finally, in philosophy as conceptual knowledge. Thus, art is just *one* way in which the truth of the absolute appears. Art, the Christian religion, and philosophy have the same content, namely, the truth of the absolute spirit, yet their form is obviously distinct. Hegel proceeds to argue that a dialectical relationship governs the movement of truth, from art as the thesis and religion as the antithesis to philosophy as the synthesis, which leads him to the violently disputed claim that art has been overcome by both of the other manifestations of the absolute spirit. We will refer back to this statement later; for the moment, it suffices to point out that a dialectical movement can hardly be proven with respect to the three forms of absolute spirit and that, instead, they might better be considered as linear.[7]

In Hegel's aesthetic, art does retain its truth-claim but, unlike for Schelling, is no longer the highest expression of truth. Instead, truth in the fullest sense of the word depends on the conceptual knowledge that only philosophy can achieve, and compared to which the truth of art seems to fall short. And although there is a way to argue that the truth of art cannot be subsumed under that of conceptual knowledge – a way that might have to rely on Kant's notion of the aesthetic idea – and is thus fundamentally *different* from that of philosophy, art's truth will turn out to be not that of the totality but that of the richness of the individual – and, therefore, still of a *lower* status. In order to salvage Hegel's aesthetic, it therefore must be brought closer to the romantic position, yet ultimately it can demonstrate its strength by being able to incorporate such modifications without giving up its fundamental claims.

Nature and Truth of the Work of Art

Hegel defines aesthetics as the philosophy of art, or to be more precise, of beautiful art. That could strike us initially as an unwelcome narrowing down of this field, since it would after all mean the double exclusion of both the beauty of nature and of nonbeautiful art, that is, the ugly and grotesque, comical and farcical, burlesque and satirical, and so on. Incidentally, Hegel's position on this question is not consistent, and in the course of his elaboration he undercuts or at least relativizes the above exclusions. But why does he introduce them in the first place?

Hegel's reasoning regarding the restriction of the category of art to beautiful (and man-made) objects is founded on the association of truth and beauty, as we shall see. Ugliness is therefore a mode of privation – a point on which Hegel's student Karl Rosenkranz will elaborate at length – and thus a secondary phenomenon. And since art is a way in which truth is present in the world, it must cohere with the objective laws of reality (and reality in turn is defined as that which is a truthful embodiment of ideas). Yet the ugly – much like the comical whose nature is to undermine those rules which govern our predictions and expectations and thus to produce laughter due to the unexpected[8] – does not know any rules and is characterized precisely by their violation.[9] Hence, it must be excluded from the discussion of art. Also, it later serves as one of the arguments Hegel advances to make plausible that art is superseded by religion. The depiction of Christ's suffering on the cross must necessarily be ugly; the relevance of this suffering can consequently not be grasped aesthetically, but only in religious contemplation. Thus, the art of Christianity is already one of decline, since it has broken with basic notions of beautiful art.

Still, Hegel's own position is not as rigorous as it seems at first. He does grant poetry the "right to advance internally to the utmost agony of despair and externally to ugliness itself"[10] (13. 268). This is because poetry as a temporal art must afterward return to beauty and, thus, incorporate ugliness as a moment that can successfully be overcome. This distinguishes it from painting or sculpture from which ugliness has to be absent entirely, since it cannot be reintegrated into a larger context in which beauty triumphs – an argument that is obviously close to Lessing's *Laokoon*. Yet there is some leeway for ugliness even in Hegel's aesthetics. The exclusion of nature also turns out to be less unyielding than it appears initially. While nature is certainly not the opposite of spirit, but a stage of its journey, it still lacks consciousness and therefore truth [*Wahrhaftigkeit*]. Beauty, however, must have a relation to the idea that depends on consciousness. Whereas the beauty of art is born out of spirit, natural beauty is merely a reflection of the former. We are able to perceive natural beauty only because we are familiar with the beauty of art to which, therefore, a higher status must be attributed (13. 14 f.). And yet, nature is not banned from the realm of beauty, as it might appear at first. The beauty of nature results, as Hegel argues later, from its "intimation of the concept" (13. 174) – a weak attribute in terms of aesthetics, to be sure, but one that prevents the dismissal of natural beauty altogether.[11]

Unlike for Schelling, the work of art for Hegel does not *contain* both nature and mind, but is *situated between* them insofar as it mediates between unmediated sensation and thought (13. 60). In fact, Hegel rejects the romantic aesthetics and its claim that art constitutes the capstone of the philosophical system. The free flotation of the romantic genius whose irony undercuts all fixed positions Hegel considers as a violation of the mores [*Sittlichkeit*] of society that demand assent if one wants to belong to it.[12] Irony, however, isolates its agent "for whom all ties have been broken and who lives only in the bliss of self-enjoyment" (13. 95). Although we will see that a certain amount of mediation between romantic philosophy and Hegel will be necessary in order to attribute significance to Hegel's thesis for today's aesthetics, Hegel himself had little tolerance for it. His admiration for Kant is much more obvious, despite all critical distance.

He agrees with Kant that the reception of art must be without desire and without attempting to treat it scientifically and to subsume it under a concept (13. 58 ff.): "Faced with such infinite richness of fantasy and its free products, thought seems to lose its courage to *completely* represent these, judge them and subsume them under a general formula" (13. 18). Far from falling back onto Kant's subjective foundation of aesthetics, however, Hegel criticizes it as untenable. To concentrate on sensibility and imagination in an aesthetic theory means to remain stuck in the subjective and to fail to make any claims about the work of art itself. Thus, the judgment of taste remains superficial (13. 55). All the more Hegel insists that art contains objective truth, no matter whether it is translatable into the language of concepts or not. This conception of the truth of art needs to be explored in some more detail.

"In its freedom," argues Hegel, "beautiful art is only true art and serves its highest purpose only when it has situated itself in a common circle together with religion and philosophy and is only one way to bring to consciousness and to express the deepest interests of man, the most comprehensive truths of the spirit" (13. 21). Unlike the truth of philosophy, however, the truth of art remains in the realm of the senses; hence, "appearance" does by no means signify a deception but, instead, the luminous emanation of the truth of essence [*Wesen*]:[13] "Yet the *appearance* itself is essential for the *essence*; truth would not be, if it did not shine [*schiene*] and appear [*erschiene*]" (13. 21). Therefore, not only does art not deceive, but it also strips the deceptive appearance off of objects and reveals their truth, that is, their essence: "The deception [*Schein*] of this bad, transitory world art strips away from all truthful content of appearances and bestows upon them a higher, spirit-born reality. Far from being mere deception, the appearances [*Erscheinungen*] of art must be considered the higher reality and the more truthful existence compared to ordinary reality" (13. 22). This is indeed the only function of art: to be one stage of the development of absolute spirit and to be the truth of this stage: "Because other ends like edification, purification, melioration, monetary income, striving for fame and honor do not concern the work of art as such and do not determine its concept" (13. 82).

Still, at least one welcome side effect of the artwork Hegel also concedes. Referring back to the Aristotelian theory of catharsis and giving it a rationalist spin, he argues that art's representation of sensations, passions, and human perturbations invites their reflection and thus loosens the grip that these emotions have on us. This thesis, however, seems hardly convincing, because the mere reflection on passions can be taken as much as an invitation to indulge them as a warning against them. Without an additional moral standard that art itself, according to Hegel, is incapable of supplying, the weakening of unwelcome emotions will hardly be an automatic consequence of encounters with artworks.

Works of art, to be sure, are objects for the senses, just like nonartistic objects, although they point beyond themselves toward a higher reality, namely, that of ideas. Still, this does not mean that they are devoid of truth as something that they can only hint at but not contain. On the contrary, works of art are already in themselves a way for the absolute spirit to manifest itself as truth. Despite his gesture toward Kant's *aesthetic idea,* Hegel argues later that art as a vessel of truth can be the object of conceptual thought [*begreifendes Denken*] and "is open on all sides" for conceptualization (13. 127). This contradiction cannot be solved; in fact, it might be the result of the editing process that tends to overemphasize the anti-romantic elements in Hegel's thought. The fact is, though, that Hegel famously defines beauty as "the sensual appearance of the idea [*das sinnliche Scheinen der Idee*]," that is, as a unification of a sensual object with its concept (13. 151 f.).[14] Therefore, the work of art not only pleases our senses but also satisfies our longing for truth insofar as it allows us to comprehend the concept as realized in a material object. Just as in Schelling, the Neoplatonic tradition – Plotinus, not Plato – finds a forceful expression in this formulation that presents art as a reconciliation of sensual and intelligible worlds. The scientific understanding of art is then, in turn, the sublation [*Aufhebung*] of the materialization of the idea and reverses thereby the process of aesthetic production. Aesthetics has to be kept strictly separate from poetics: Whereas the latter is prescriptive, the former is descriptive. Simultaneously, Hegel takes a strong stance against the romantic aestheticians by advancing the thesis that the reflection on the work of art is a philosophical task. Whereas the romantics, above all Friedrich Schlegel, had demanded that the reflection on art must itself become aesthetic, Hegel insists on the concept as the only means for aesthetic theory.

If the truth content of a work of art refers to the idea, the consequence is obviously that the category of mimesis, as Hegel understands it, will play no role in aesthetics. Mimesis has been a central concept for many theories of art since antiquity; in Greek thought, a fairly wide range of meanings was attributed to it. It is safe to assume, though, that Hegel reacted mainly against the theories of mimesis that were developed during the Baroque and the following century, and which oftentimes could be understood as advocating a naturalistic imitation of material objects in art. For Aristotle, however, mimesis also contained aspects of performance and potentiality. Hegel's critique of mimesis falls short of this conception, but we will later see that Adorno's revision of this category owes more to Aristotle than he admits. Also arguing against Hegel for the relevance of mimesis for aesthetics is Georg Lukács, who insists on the necessity of realist art, as will be discussed in a subsequent chapter.

Now what precisely is it that Hegel finds fault with in the concept of mimesis? First of all, we must not confuse the correctness [*Richtigkeit*] of a representation with the truth [*Wahrheit*] of a work of art (13. 205, 10. 368). A representation can be faithful and correct, yet still lack the truth that elevates it from a mere mirroring into a work of art. Three arguments speak against the sufficiency of mere correctness as a criterion for art. The first is that mimesis presents us with yet another version of what already exists in reality. If it does not add anything to its representation, its labor as a whole seems redundant. If art is nothing but a copy of the real, we would be hard put to explain why we might want to turn to it instead of to reality directly. Only laziness, fear of reality, or the desire to avoid it could be possible answers to these questions, but if art serves to eschew the real, it undercuts its truth-claim and turns into entertainment. The second argument is that mimesis remains a merely formal judgment that can pronounce a verdict on the correctness of the reproduction, but not on its beauty. Even the faithful reproduction of ugly objects would have to be called successful (and possibly, by extension, beautiful) if mimesis were to be the basis for aesthetics. Thirdly, mimesis can play a role only in certain arts, but not in others. Thus, in painting or sculpture it would be much easier to find mimetic elements than in dance, architecture, or music. And even the visual arts only go through very short periods of realistic portrayal – during most of their history, painting and sculpture neither aspired to nor achieved a correct representation of real objects (13. 64–70). Hence, Hegel concludes that art not merely doubles the existing reality in its respective media but that it presents a higher reality – an argument, however, to which both Aristotle and Lukács as proponents of a mimetic theory of art would probably also subscribe. As Charles Taylor put it in his erudite study of Hegel: "Art is a *mode of consciousness* of the Idea, but it is not a *representation* of it."[15]

As such, then, the work of art is not self-contained but reaches out to man: "But the work of art rests not merely freely in itself, but it is essentially a question, an address to the resonant chest, a call to the souls [*Gemüter*] and spirits [*Geister*]" (13. 102). It is interesting to note that Hegel here advances a principle that became the basis for the reflections on art as developed by philosophical hermeneutics, especially by Hans-Georg Gadamer.[16] Hegel emphasizes the dialogical principle of our encounters with art well in advance of philosophical hermeneutics and its offshoot, the aesthetics of reception, when he writes that "every work of art is a dialogue with whoever stands in front of it" (13. 341). But sentences like this: " . . . art turns every one of its products into an Argus with a thousand eyes so that the inner soul and spirit [*Geistigkeit*] shall be seen at all points" (13. 203) also reverberate in art. R. M. Rilke's sonnet *Archaischer Torso Apollos* remarks about the power of an ancient sculpture: "*denn da ist keine Stelle, / die dich nicht sieht*" [Because no part exists / that does not see you]. Yet for man as a social being to be addressed means to be under the obligation to answer; thus, art necessarily remains tied to both the social and the ethical sphere, albeit without prescriptive or normative content.

Art's History and Forms

The insight that art had different functions in different historical epochs cannot be attributed to Hegel as an entirely new thought, since G. Vico (1668–1744) in his philosophy of history had already claimed that a poetic spirit permeated the age of the gods that got lost during the reign of man. A similar argument was not unknown to the eighteenth century as, for example, in the work of Herder and Hamann. Yet no philosophical attempt had been made before to deduce the necessity of historical changes in art from an overarching principle that itself depends on its historical unfolding. It is precisely the narrative of art's permutations in history that comprises the largest part of Hegel's aesthetic lectures, which aim at a reconciliation of formal and historical reflections on art:

> Spirit, before it reaches the true knowledge of its absolute essence, has to run through a course of stages determined by its concept, and to the course of this content that spirit bestows upon itself corresponds an immediately connected course of forms of art in which the spirit as an artistic one produces the consciousness of itself. (13. 103)

The development of spirit on its way to absolute knowledge thus requires that art, too, must go through a process of development at the end of which stands its dismissal by higher forms of knowledge – a problematic thesis that shall be discussed in the next section. Hegel divides his discussion of the movement of spirit through art into two parts that he wants to be considered as running parallel. The first part of the discussion is devoted to the forms of art [*Kunstformen*], that is, a historical narrative about the interdependence of artistic expression and the changing worldviews [*Weltanschauungen*]. The second part, much like Schelling's *Philosophy of Art,* develops a system of the arts.

Despite the fact that the development of the historical artistic expressions is not entirely linear – outmoded forms of art can continue to exist for some time in the same way as future forms can be anticipated (13. 393) – Hegel by and large regards the story of art as the succession of three periods, namely, the symbolic, the classical, and the romantic. He associates the symbolic stage of art with the ancient oriental cultures of Persia, India, and Egypt and is, for the most part, unwilling to grant it the full status of art; instead, he labels it preart [*Vorkunst*– 13. 393]. It is a sublime expression of man's search for meaning, yet it does not move beyond a manifestation of the insufficient and vague idea in inadequate forms. Art then reaches its acme in the classical period, during which the ideal and the form achieve perfect harmony. This is the age of Greek sculpture that represents the spirit in its ideal sensual form, namely the human body. The artist of the classical period does not have to search for the meaning of the absolute, because it is already given to him in the form of the religion of the populace (that was, in turn, the creation of previous artistic, i.e., literary efforts, namely by Homer and Hesiod – 14. 28). Greek religion, hence, is a religion of art; no distinction between the manifestation of truth in religion and in art is possible. Romantic art, finally, subsumes all artistic creation of the Christian era under its concept. It marks a decline of art that is characterized by the withdrawal of the spirit into inwardness. The physical beauty of Greek sculpture gives way to the beauty of the spirit. Although this inward turn produced a deepening of the human spirit, it was hardly an adequate foundation to value the sensual aspect of art. Christ's suffering on the cross could not be depicted with the classical means of art, and its representation consequently undermined the ideal of beauty by introducing ugliness not only as permissible but as necessary. But even more than in the visual arts, the Christian soul expresses itself in music as that art which depends least on a material foundation. Yet when art devalues sensual reality and negates the exterior world, it must eventually lead to the overcoming of itself in a different form of knowledge. Therefore, the three historical forms of art consist of "the striving for, the achievement of and the abandoning of the ideal as the true idea of beauty" (13. 114).

It has been pointed out that the opposition of classical and romantic forms of art is a late echo of the *querelle des anciens et des modernes* that dominated much of the aesthetic discussion of the eighteenth century. Peter Szondi argued convincingly that this opposition can be found in much of the aesthetic thought during the age of Goethe.[17] Yet Hegel, as so often, turns an oppositional structure into a triadic one by adding the symbolic period that preceded the classical age. Such a triad, however, was also not a discovery of Hegel, since the philosophies of the New Mythology had prognosticated a third stage of art for the future. But Hegel's thesis of the end of art does not allow him to agree to this interpretation; instead, it forces him to situate the triadic third in the remote past.

Closely connected to this shift from the future to the past is Hegel's unwillingness to take much of the postmedieval art into consideration. Apart from some remarks on Dutch genre painting and still life, almost all of the outstanding achievements of the arts after the fifteenth century or so are absent from the discussion. Renaissance and Baroque sculpture and architecture are missing, as are the neoclassical contemporaries of Hegel, for example, Schinkel and von Klenze. This led to a criticism of Hegel's theory of the forms of art among his students, who attempted to rescue the dialectical force of the argument by introducing Renaissance art as the true triadic third. As they clearly saw, a narrative that peaks during its middle period cannot be a dialectical movement upward and must therefore be corrected.[18]

The third part of Hegel's aesthetics is a systematic grouping of the arts. This enterprise, however, is not meant to stand isolated from the elaboration on the historical forms of art, but Hegel proposes – yet another problematic feature – a parallel between these two. Certain arts are meant to be paradigmatic for certain historical worldviews, so that the system of the arts is itself the object of a process. Symbolic art is thus primarily architecture, which forms man's environment according to his needs. Classical art manifests itself as sculpture; here, spirit enters matter and permeates it completely. While contemplating a sculpture, the spirit recognizes itself precisely because the perfection of the body demonstrates that it has been formed entirely by its soul. Soul in Greek sculpture is body; no inner life – as would be announced by the soulful eye – is hidden from view (14. 389). That is why such sculpture is self-contained, a subject isolated from its surrounding. As works of art these statues sometimes "leave us cold" (15. 17), since their appeal reveals itself only after intense and repeated study. In this respect, the romantic arts differ. While the symbolic and the classical ages both are associated with only one art – architecture and sculpture, respectively – Hegel subsumes three arts under the romantic worldview.

As the first of these, painting unites the modeling of man's environment as practiced by architecture with the subjectivity of sculpture: "Painting represents the internal in the form of external objects, but the actual content that it expresses is the sensible subjectivity [of the artist]" (15. 25). Far from depicting the beauty of the body, at the center of painting as a romantic art stands the Christian interpretation of love, exemplified by the love of the Madonna for the child. Rather than on the self-contained physique, Christian painting focuses on the gaze that is exchanged between mother and child, at once causing and exploring the inwardness of the subject.

Music is the second of the romantic arts that is characterized by the elimination of spaciality. What remains is pure inwardness: "To musical expression only the entirely objectless interior lends itself, the abstract subjectivity as such. This is our completely empty self, the self without any content" (15. 135). Poetry, finally, is the last and highest of the romantic arts, and yet it also constitutes an exception to the system, insofar as it can rise to the acme of its possibilities during all historical ages: "poetry is adequate for all forms of beauty and extends itself across all of them" (13. 124). Having itself a triadic structure – lyric poetry, epic, and drama – poetry as an art encompasses all the other arts. Yet it also marks the point where the absolute spirit on its way to complete self-knowledge transcends its artistic manifestation and settles into philosophical thought: "Precisely on this highest level art transcends itself by leaving behind the element of reconciled sensuality of the spirit and moving from the poetry of imagination into the prose of thought" (13. 123).

These brief remarks nevertheless suffice to show that Hegel organizes the arts along two axes: one indicating the historical development from symbolic over classical to romantic art, the other denoting the materiality of the arts. Thus, architecture depends most on the material world, sculpture less so; painting represents it merely two-dimensionally, music abandons it almost entirely, and poetry marks the transition from sensuality to conceptual thought. Thus, an advance in time goes hand in hand with a decrease of the material foundation of art.

It is hard not to stumble over the inconsistencies and forced analogies of this part of Hegel's aesthetics. First of all, it is not plausible to remove poetry from the historical development and grant it exceptional status, since there is nothing that justifies this maneuver, as Hegel's students already pointed out. Secondly, to place poetry in this exceptional position means that two arts now compete for the highest honors, namely, classical sculpture and poetry. Thirdly, to subsume painting, music, and poetry as sister arts under one heading must strike us as somewhat bizarre, since the traditional grouping of architecture, sculpture, and painting into the category of visual arts seems rather more convincing. One interesting attempt to reorganize the arts along Hegelian lines has been put forward by V. Hösle, who follows the revisions of Hegel's students and further amends them. In this plausible version, the visual arts would mark a first historical stage, namely, that of the objectivity of spirit; music follows as the subjective state; and finally poetry, especially drama, marks the intersubjective state of the absolute spirit.[19] Still, this restructuring does not yet instantiate Hegel's problematic thesis that art moves beyond itself in its highest stage and is replaced by thought. We need to take a closer look at this speculation.

An End of Art?

Hegel's thesis that art has come to an end has always been one of the largest bones of contention of his aesthetic philosophy with which every engagement with his aesthetics must come to terms.[20] He argues that art is a manifestation of truth, but it fulfills this function only during one historical period, namely, that of the art-religion [*Kunstreligion*] of the Greek civilization. Beginning with Christianity, truth found its expression no longer in the sensual forms of art but in the images of the New Testament: "Thought and reflection have overtaken beautiful art. . . . In all of these respects art is and remains in terms of its highest function something bygone [*etwas Vergangenes*]" (13. 24–25). Although art still speaks to us, no matter from what period, we have nevertheless stopped to consider it the highest organon of truth and, therefore, also stopped revering it:

> Once the perfect content was manifested in perfect forms, the searching [*weiterblickende*] spirit turns away from this objectivity toward its own interior and shuns the former. Such a time is ours. We can still hope that art will continue to rise and to perfect itself, but its form has stopped to be the highest necessity for the spirit. We might find the Greek statues of the gods most excellent and God the father, Christ and Mary represented most dignified and perfect – it changes nothing, we still don't bow our knee anymore. (13. 142)

Hegel's thesis of the end of art much resembles his thesis of the end of history. The latter is now generally understood to mean not that history has factually ended but that after the discovery of the highest principle of historical development, namely, that of the freedom of all, historical development is merely the – probably always incomplete – realization of this principle in reality.[21] If we take both claims literally, to speak of an end of art would, therefore, be as counterintuitive and absurd as to speak of an end of history, because we all are familiar with works of art that have made a difference in our lives and that came into existence *after* the proclaimed end of art. Sociologically, it might even be the case that in a secularized age, art has regained a semireligious status as the only expression of something that transcends man's individual life.[22]

Hegel himself is also not entirely consistent in his story about the rise and fall of art, since repeatedly he places works of art from later epochs in their importance right beside those of the classical age – a procedure that can hardly be justified by recourse to his narrative.[23] Thus, we are well advised to consider other possible readings of the thesis about the end of art.

Many interpreters have taken up a suggestion that Hegel himself advances at one point when he explains:

> Being tied to one particular content and to one manner of representation suited to this content is for today's artist something bygone, and thus art has

become a free instrument that he can employ with respect to every content, no matter of which kind, depending on his subjective skill. (14. 235)

Gadamer has called this the "liberation of art as art," and Arthur Danto, something of a modern-day Hegelian in aesthetics, has also embraced the end of art as a liberating moment in history that marked the beginning of true artistic sovereignty.[24] In both Gadamer and Danto can be detected an echo of Arnold Gehlen, who had already declared in 1960, certainly not entirely without cynicism: "From now on there will be *no more art-immanent development!* Any meaningful, logical history of art is done with, even the consequence of the absurdities is done with, the development is derailed, and what comes next exists already: the syncretism of the confusion of all styles and possibilities, the post-histoire."[25] Despite the fact that such independence of the artist has produced outstanding works of art, it has also been perceived as burdensome and problematic, as Thomas Mann described masterfully in *Doctor Faustus.* Also, it is likely that some kind of normative principle needs to be found in order to judge the success of the individual work, because otherwise, the view that "anything goes" could hardly be avoided and a line between kitsch and art no longer drawn.

Although these readings can well explain the historical fact of the multitude of styles that have existed simultaneously since the nineteenth century, they do not really answer the question of the kind of relation in which art stands to truth. It is not convincing to argue that art remains one organon of truth among others (as Oelmüller and others do), since there would hardly be a reason to choose a less developed organon over a more highly developed means of truth, this is, philosophy. Thus, an explanation cannot come to an end after it has established the desirability of artistic independence and stylistic choice. Some theory of the truth of art is necessary as the complement hereof.

Before the necessary revisions to Hegel's aesthetics are discussed, a brief summary of his position should be attempted. The work of art is ontologically defined as the reconciliation of the finality of nature and the infinity of pure thought, of sensuality and spirit. Unlike for Schelling, however, art does not fulfill this mediating role independent of all historical developments. Rather, its specific embodiment of truth is limited to one historical period, namely, that of ancient Greece when religion and art fall into one. Here, the work of art allows man to cherish both the idea and sensuality in one and the same object, a balance that gets lost with Christianity's inward turn. In a practical respect, the work of art not only satisfies the need for the shaping of the external and internal world as one of the means of self-realization (13. 52), but also helps to control man's emotional life. Yet there is a danger in this as well, since the encounters with art are relaxing;[26] serious tasks, however, demand determination and not aesthetic contemplation (13. 16).

Hegel's integration of systematic and historical aspects in his aesthetic theory indeed produces what could still be considered the most comprehensive and convincing philosophy of art of German idealism, or what here has been called the age of paradigms. Still, some revisions are unavoidable if Hegel's aesthetics is meant to be of more than just historical interest. For one, his notion of art needs to be broadened so as to encompass artistic phenomena other then the beautiful. A philosophy of art must be able to account for ugliness, the grotesque, and so on other than by reducing them to moments that eventually feed back into an all-embracing form of beauty. This might not be entirely possible within a Hegelian framework, as Rosenkranz and Weisse assumed, but it will also not challenge the most fundamental aspects of Hegel's aesthetics.

It is even more important to address the issue of truth in the Hegelian conception. To adhere to Hegel's narrative inevitably leads to the classification of aesthetic truth as that of a bygone historical period and, thus, hardly as a reasonable choice when the most advanced organon of truth is called for. Therefore, art can only retain its claim to truth if it is not considered as containing the truth of totality, but that of the multiplicity of the real. The overarching truth can then be provided by the conceptual thought of philosophy, yet there exists a truth value of the real in its individual manifestations that cannot be subsumed under the concept. Above all, society's mores [*Sittlichkeit*] that differ from society to society and yet are an indispensable element of communal life might find more adequate expression in the truth of art than in abstract knowledge.

Yet it must also be admitted that art will not shed its moment of contingency that is due to its necessary sensual nature, as Hösle points out.[27] But a plurality of truth-claims of art and its contingent nature do not render it dispensable, either. Since Hegel agrees with Kant that no conceptual subsumption is possible regarding the artwork, it can consequently be seen as an invitation to discuss its truth content. Such an encouragement to consider possible competing truth contents of one and the same work of art is based on the hermeneutical structure of question and answer inherent in the work itself. More than in the case of philosophical propositions that generally do not demand the response of the reader, this hermeneutic ontology of art begs to be transferred to the community of recipients. Thus, the relevance of art can fully emerge in its existence as an incitement to intersubjective exchanges and, thus, as something that is an amendment to Hegel's aesthetics, more than the remnant of a bygone time.

Ugliness in Art

Ugliness, to be sure, has always existed in art. Even before the Crucifixion there were the Gorgon, the head of the Medusa (a curious mixture of beauty and ugliness), and the Erinyes. Likewise, philosophies of art and beauty have also acknowledged the existence of ugliness. Aristotle attributes a certain fascination to it by claiming – this being one of the reasons that Hegel rejects mimesis – that the successful artistic reproduction of ugly objects can indeed induce pleasure (*Poetics*, 1448b), whereas Plotinus declares that the soul becomes ugly when it is incorporated in the body (Ennead I; 6, 5). Aristotle's position was echoed by eighteenth-century poetics that considered the ugly as the reverse aspect of the beautiful, that is, as something interesting. In the context of German idealism, however, not much attention was paid to the ugly, although Friedrich Schlegel's 1795 *Über das Studium der griechischen Poesie* [About the study of Greek poety] must be considered one of the basic texts on the aesthetics of ugliness, or aischrology.[28] Hegel himself lacks a theory of ugliness, although we have seen that some remarks on this subject indicate that he was aware of the problem. It could very well be, though, that Hegel preferred to ignore those works or styles of art that he perceived as ugly, as one biographer suggested.[29] It is on record that Hegel had little liking for the music of C. M. von Weber, and if we concur with Adorno's characterization of romanticism in music as the victory of the variation over the theme, then Hegel's distance becomes understandable. Where there is no totality but merely the flow of variations, there can be no beauty. And that art could in fact *be* ugly, not only *contain* ugly moments, was something that Hegel was not ready to admit.

Hegels students, however, responded to the romantic turn toward the inclusion of ugliness into art by incorporating it in turn into their aesthetic theories. Whereas the ugly certainly continued to play a role in the aesthetic philosophy of the nineteenth and twentieth centuries, for example, in Nietzsche or Lukács, the heydays of ugliness in aesthetics were certainly those of the Hegelian school. Most of his students who worked in the field of philosophy of art felt the need to comment on the problem of ugliness: Chr. H. Weisse, A. Runge, K. Fischer, F. Th. Vischer, and Karl Rosenkranz.

In his *System der Ästhetik als Wissenschaft von der Idee des Schönen* [System of aesthetics as the science of the idea of the beautiful – 1830], Christian Hermann Weisse argues that beauty is the ground for both the sublime, that is, the transition of beauty to the good and the true, and the ugly, that is, the distortion of beauty through evil. Ugliness, in turn, marks the transition of the sublime to the comical – an idea that returns in K. Rosenkranz's theory.[30] Noteworthy is the connection of aesthetic and ethical categories, a feature that returns in many of the theories of ugliness by the Hegelians.

The most elaborate of these theories is laid down in Karl Rosenkranz's (1805–1879) *Ästhetik des Hässlichen* [Aesthetics of ugliness] of 1853. "Hell is not only a religio-ethical one, it is also aesthetical," he argues (3). And although he grants ugliness a greater sphere of existence within art, he agrees with his teacher Hegel that the ugly is a mode of privation, "a negative beauty" (III). Thus, it presupposes the beautiful that it then distorts, but it does not have any claim to an original existence (7, 39): "Were the beautiful not, the ugly were nevermore, because it exists only as the negation thereof. The beautiful is the divine, original idea and the ugly, its negation, has as such a merely secondary existence. It generates itself in contact with and out of the beautiful" (7).

Beauty, therefore, is absolute insofar as it is not defined by its opposition, whereas ugliness is relative and secondary – a theory that

Adorno later reverses for modern art by claiming that now beauty always emerges out of ugliness. For Rosenkranz, the secondary nature of ugliness, however, is most apparent in the fact that beauty is not enhanced by the existence of ugliness, yet the ugly itself depends on principles of beauty for its portrayal, namely, the shunning of contingency and a somewhat idealized representation; "art must also idealize the ugly, i.e., treat it according to the general laws of beauty which it negates through its existence" (42).

For Rosenkranz, ugliness has its own complex morphology that is a result of the many different ways in which the ugly negates beauty. Three basic forms of negation can be distinguished, each of which then falls again into three subcategories and so on for several more levels. The first form of ugliness is the lack of form. If beauty as a totality requires limits, that is, form, then ugliness suffers from the lack thereof. Secondly, Rosenkranz defines beauty with Hegel as the sensual truth of the idea. Yet unlike Hegel, he presupposes the validity of mimesis as an expression of this idea, since he defines ugliness as incorrect representation. The third form of the ugly, finally, is one that indicates how strongly ethical considerations are tied up with these philosophies of ugliness, since it is characterized by its lack of self-determination and freedom. Both illness of the organism and malice are expressions of such ugliness that figure both in the sensual and in the ethical realm.

This explains why it would be more or less impossible to grant ugliness its own right of existence, since that would come close to an endorsement of character flaws. Instead, Rosenkranz argues that the ugly has the potential to negate itself, not to return to beauty but to result in the comical. Of course, this cannot be taken to be a dialectical movement, yet it certainly explains the residue of ugliness in all forms of the comical. But also in the realm of beauty ugliness fulfills a function. Not only is it allowed to exist side by side with the ugly, but it can even be enjoyed as long as the ultimate outcome of the artwork is the conquest of the ugly by the beautiful and the successful integration of the former into a harmonious totality. That much we had already heard from Hegel or even Lessing. Yet Rosenkranz adds a new dimension to these considerations; the totality of the idea, he argues, must not merely tolerate the ugly; in order to be a totality, the idea depends on the ugly for its realization. Ugliness might only be a moment of totality, yet it nevertheless is indispensable for the whole.

It is this last thought that, more involuntarily than not, moves Rosenkranz out of the Hegelian sphere and toward an aesthetics that acknowledges the independent existence of the ugly. Thus, one of the great themes of the philosophy of art finds its first expression in this contribution of a student of Hegel. That his magnum opus remained out of print until very recently – not to mention untranslated – is an undeserved fate.

PART II

CHALLENGING THE PARADIGMS

6

Schopenhauer

Without much doubt, Arthur Schopenhauer (1788–1860) is the one philosopher of art with the largest influence on artists, on their understanding of themselves, and on their artistic production. The list of those who acknowledge debts to Schopenhauer is long: the writers Friedrich Hebbel, August Strindberg, Thomas Hardy, Emile Zola, Marcel Proust, Thomas Mann, Edgar Allan Poe, Charles Baudelaire, Stephane Mallarmé, Joseph Conrad, André Gide, Robert Musil, Samuel Beckett, W. B. Yeats, Jorge L. Borges, Thomas Bernhard, and Arno Schmidt; the painter Eugene Delacroix; the composers Richard Wagner, Arnold Schönberg, Sergey Prokofiev, and Nikolay Rimsky-Korsakoff, as well as numerous others. Yet as pronounced as Schopenhauer's influence on the artistic community itself is, his effect on significant philosophers in general and on philosophical aesthetics in particular is negligible. With the exception of Friedrich Nietzsche, who is less a disciple than an idiosyncratic commentator with his own agenda, Schopenhauer's thought on art remained isolated in the history of ideas. Hence, his writings do not mark the beginning of a new productive approach to the riddle of art as much as they signal the beginning of the dismantling of the idealist tradition. Historically, the importance of Schopenhauer does not result so much from his effect on future thinkers; it lies in the fact that with him, the skeptical reaction against the achievements of idealism sets in and is clearly visible.

Chronologically, to be sure, Schopenhauer's philosophical magnum opus *Die Welt als Wille und Vorstellung* [The world as will and representation, 1818] appeared before Hegel began his lectures on aesthetics, yet chronology does not matter much in this case. Clearly, Schopenhauer's philosophy is not part of German idealism – despite his self-stylization as the true heir of Kant. We will see that with respect to some of the most central positions of idealist philosophy of art, Schopenhauer not only strays from the lines of argumentation but also advocates a definite reversal of these positions. Despite the forcefulness of his writing and the self-assured declaration of his superiority over Hegel especially, Schopenhauer's thinking achieves neither the conceptual rigor nor the systematic breadth of his idealist precursors, as becomes apparent from the many contradictions and inconclusive arguments in his writings. Schopenhauer's aesthetic theory is part of his large treatise *The World as Will and Representation,* the book that he published as a young philosopher and kept amending and commenting on for the rest of his life. Of the four sections of this work, one is devoted to the philosophy of art. Some shorter essays that take up questions like the interesting and its relation to the beautiful, the question of style in art and the art of writing – art taken here in the sense of rhetorical skill – flesh out his ideas. Yet despite the obvious importance that art holds for Schopenhauer both personally and philosophically, his aesthetic theory is often unclear and inconsistent when we get down to the particulars. While this is not the place to explore all of the apparent aporias in detail,[1] we will still have to attend to some of them in order to realize that Schopenhauer's thought marks the beginning of a period of skepticism in aesthetic philosophy.

It will turn out that there are three problematic departures from idealist positions on aesthetics that are indicative of a reductive tendency in the philosophy of art. The first is an individualist turn that considers art as no longer tied to a community, be it a more or less universal community as for Kant or the nation-state as for Hegel. Art matters only under the perspective of the isolated individual and his need to escape from an unbearable existence that is partly made insufferable precisely by the necessary communal nature of human life. The communal moment is not absent from Schopenhauer's aesthetic considerations, but it now has to serve as a negative backdrop from which art offers liberation. Connected to this individualistic turn of aesthetics is a reversal of both the epistemological and the practical moment of aesthetics. Although Schopenhauer insists on art's capacity to grant insights otherwise unavailable, the mediation between this epistemologically optimistic stance and his general antirationalism is problematic. Equally questionable is the insistence on the practical dimension of the aesthetic encounter. The practical moment of aesthetics in Schopenhauer no longer leads to an engagement with the world but to a withdrawal from it. Thus, aesthetic experience is putatively a technique of liberation from the world in which the only practical element left is the one that aims to end all praxis – if not for good, then at least temporarily. As with all systematic philosophy – and Schopenhauer aims to provide an all-encompassing system – the individual elements, including the aesthetic one, can only be understood when situated within their proper context in the system. Therefore, we will briefly have to explore Schopenhauer's metaphysical system first.

The World as Will and Representation

Having said that Schopenhauer's aesthetics is part of his metaphysics, it becomes necessary to characterize the latter with greater precision, all the more so because Schopenhauer's understanding of metaphysics constitutes a departure from the metaphysical tradition in several respects. Traditional speculative metaphysics aims to comprehend the entirety of reality by reference to a principle that is not itself part of this reality but precedes it. And Schopenhauer goes along with this assumption. Yet whereas this tradition is based on the primacy of reason or spirit as the transcendent principle that had replaced the Judeo-Christian creator – God, Schopenhauer radically breaks with these teachings and proposes the will as a fundamental principle, thus giving precedence to an irrational principle over the rationalist metaphysical heritage. Schopenhauer defines the will so that it is no longer characterized as a supporting agent of rationality but as an irrational force.

Since Schopenhauer's teaching of the will is essential for his philosophy of art, we need to sketch out these fundamentals of his philosophy. As the title of his main work indicates, Schopenhauer argues that the world is given to us in a twofold manner. Claiming to follow Kant's epistemology of the *Critique of Pure Reason,* he advances the notion that the object can be known only because of faculties contributed by the subject, although he reduces Kant's categories and modalities to a single principle, namely, that of the principle of sufficient reason [*Satz vom Grund*].[2] Kant had advanced the notion that the thing-in-itself cannot be known because it is not a phenomenon that would present itself to our senses, yet it is nevertheless necessary in order to guarantee the identity of the objects as fixed points of reference in the flow of consciousness. Kant concluded that the objects of the world are merely products of our faculties of cognition but not the things-in-themselves. From that view, Schopenhauer takes a further step with his thesis that the world is merely representation, an appearance for the subject: "Everything that belongs to the world and can belong to it is inescapably marked by this being-determined [*Bedingtsein*] by the subject and only exists for the subject. The world is representation."[3]

Schopenhauer also calls the multitude of representations by the name of *Maya,* the term that in Hindu philosophy signifies the veil of appearance behind which the truth of existence, namely, the oneness of all beings, is hidden. With this, he becomes one of the nineteenth-century philosophers who is most influenced (at least in his terminology) by the discovery of the *Upanishads* by the romantic generation, although the late Schelling and others also point out the resemblance between their own thinking and that of India's great religious heritage. Behind the representation thus lies the thing-in-itself that is, strictly speaking, unknowable. Yet one exception allows us to grasp the nature of the thing-in-itself and then to generalize this experience so as to find in it the key that unlocks the metaphysical principle of the world. This exception is our body that we not only know as object among objects and thus as representation, but that also grants us immediate access to the will: "Every act of the will is immediately and necessarily also a movement of the body" (WWR, 164). Hence, Schopenhauer calls the body "the will that became visible" (WWR, 173), and he deduces from this individual access to the determining principle of empirical reality that all objects are driven by the same force, that is, that the thing-in-itself is not unknowable after all but must be the will. The will "is the essence of all singular existence and also of totality: it appears in every blind force of nature; it also appears in the contemplated acts of man" (WWR, 177).

By making the body the privileged site of cognition, Schopenhauer reverses the hierarchy of body and intellect that had characterized the Western philosophical tradition, most prominently in Descartes.[4]

Yet the generalization from the discovery of the individual will to the will as principle of the world is not entirely convincing, since Schopenhauer never clarifies in what relation the individual will stands to the world will. References to the Hindu theory of Atman and Brahman do not help to elucidate the issue, because it still needs to be explained whether the individual will is part of the one encompassing will and, if so, how it can be distinguished from it. Conceivably, it could also be argued that the former only participates in the latter in certain respects, yet in this case, it would have to contain elements that are not part of the world will, which in turn would need to be accounted for. Aristotle's discussion of the problematic relation of empirical object and Platonic idea, the question of *methexis,* can *mutatis mutandis* be applied to this puzzling connection of individual will and world will.

The will for Schopenhauer is an egoistic and blind drive that only asks for satisfaction yet never reaches it and, thus, produces ever-new needs and wants: "All willing is founded in need [*Bedürfniss*], hence in lack [*Mangel*], hence in suffering" (WWR, 288). The satisfaction of one desire gives birth immediately to new cravings, so that under the rule of will, no situation can ever exist in which man's needs have all been satisfied and he is at rest, not wanting anything more or different from what he has and is at present. So long as we are driven by the will, "there will never be permanent happiness nor peace" (WWR, 288). Moreover, since the world is such that the means to satisfy our wants are fewer than those wants, and there are many people with identical or similar desires, our existence is also one of constant strife and warfare with our fellow men. Again we are confronted with a devaluation of the communal that, unlike for Hobbes and other contractualists, cannot be salvaged by means of a rational agreement.

Schopenhauer thus reverses the traditional metaphysical hierarchy of the West in which reason took first place and will, understood as desire, was secondary. Schopenhauer declares outright: "Originally and essentially cognition is a function of the will" (WWR, 262). Whereas for Kant will was still closely associated with autonomy and practical reason, Schopenhauer understands it to be drive, unconscious strife, and desire.[5] With this definition of the will, Schopenhauer finds himself much closer to Schelling's conception of nature, demonstrating once more the influence of romantic philosophy and especially of that of Schelling. Yet whereas Schelling had conceived of nature as a teleological drive toward spirit, Schopenhauer reverses this optimistic concept. Instead of joyful productivity he regards deprivation and suffering as the hallmarks of will. There is no hope for development, but only a static and aimless circulation of desire, a nihilistic disappointment with all positive movement toward an ideal.[6]

As the ground of all being, the will objectifies itself and brings forth ideas. It is never made quite clear why the will should have such a desire for objectification in the first place, but Schopenhauer considers the world of representations the empirical manifestation of the ideas. The ideas, which Schopenhauer labels "Platonic ideas," also have a rather peculiar meaning for him. They are not identical with concepts, since the latter are abstractions from the empirical reality and, thus, secondary to phenomenal objects. Nor are they transcendent blueprints of individual objects, since ideas for Schopenhauer do not refer to single beings, but only to classes of beings that share the same ontological characteristics. Ideas are thus empirical levels of objectification of the will, according to which the strata of the empirical world are organized into inorganic nature, organic nature, animals, humans, and so on. Therefore, Schopenhauer would not agree with Plato that an empirical bed has a bed-idea as its model according to which it can be fabricated and used, because for him, only levels of empirical reality correspond to an idea. Ideas do not refer to objects in their entirety, but only to their ontological essence as determined by the will that manifests itself as mere persistence and heaviness in inorganic nature, dependence on the interchange with the environment in plants, movement in animals, and self-consciousness in human beings. Whereas the objects of phenomenal reality depend on the principle of sufficient reason and are thus always imbedded in a totality, ideas are free from causality. Scientific investigation can only make claims about appearances and never penetrates to the thing-in-itself. Yet nevertheless, there is one means of access to both the ideas and the will, and that is art. Following Schelling and the romantics, Schopenhauer, too, places aesthetic cognition above conceptual knowledge. While philosophy, understood as the highest of the sciences, can point the way toward such cognition, only aesthetic contemplation can achieve it.

Yet the aim of art is not merely to grant the viewer or listener an insight that would otherwise be unavailable; more important still is its ability to quiet the forces of the will, since the workings of the will are the sources of human misery. The upshot of Schopenhauer's philosophy is to overcome the subservience to the will and to find peace without desires, without aims, and without the pains of an individual existence that is merely a phenomenal illusion. The will is one, its individual manifestations – Schopenhauer calls the individualizing force of the will the *principium individuationis* – but an illusion. All suffering stems from the will's blind strife; hence, philosophy's task is to alleviate pain by overcoming the pressure of the will. While it cannot do so itself, it can prepare for the praxis of the circumvention of the will by alerting man to the means at his disposal to achieve this aim.

Schopenhauer lists three possibilities to achieve quietude of the will. The first is the aesthetic experience that we will discuss at length. The second is the attitude of compassion in which I make someone else's suffering my own. Such behavior, however, is directed against the egoism of the will and would under normal circumstances have to be considered harmful to the agent from the perspective of the will. The fact that I can act out of compassion therefore proves that man is able to overcome his egoism and forget himself in acts of charity. The last possibility of finding peace is the direct negation of the will that leads to the denial of one's own physical needs, that is, to ascetic withdrawal. While this last path to peace is difficult and only an option for some very few persons, both the experiences of art and of compassion are open to more individuals, although never to a majority. Their drawback, however, is their ephemeral nature. Both from art and from the act of good will – to use a paradoxical formulation – we have to return to our quotidian existence that is governed by strife and unrest. Because of the fleeting nature of the aesthetic experience, art can never grant redemption but is merely a palliative; it is not a way out of suffering, merely a "consolation" (WWR, 384). But now we must turn to those privileged moments of calm that art grants us as an escape from misery.

Art as Alleviation of Suffering

Since cognition serves the will as one of its instruments, it follows that its objects are restricted to the phenomenal world. Strictly speaking, we can only know those representations in time and space that are mere appearances and that, hence – according to the Platonic tradition – lack any intrinsic value. Yet Schopenhauer argues that there is an exception to this restriction of our cognitive faculties to the world of appearances:

> The possible, yet exceptional transition from the usual cognition of individual objects to the cognition of the idea happens suddenly when cognition tears itself free from the will. Through this act the subject ceases to be a mere individual and is now the pure, will-less subject of cognition which no longer follows relations [of objects], but rests in secure contemplation of the presented object removed from all context. Hereby the subject overcomes himself. (WWR, 264)

What Schopenhauer describes here as the overcoming of will and the possibility of a cognition free from self-interest is, of course, the aesthetic experience. Three characteristics define this aesthetic experience of which we find two in this quotation, namely, the suspension of will – a form of disinterestedness that had constituted one of Kant's four elements of the aesthetic judgment – as well as the cognition of an idea. The third is the requirement that the object of contemplation be beautiful, a proposition that we will have to investigate more closely shortly.

This formulation of the aesthetic experience is problematic in at least one respect because it appears that the contemplation that frees us from the will needs to begin with the will to contemplate, namely, to actively engage with the aesthetic object.[7] At the basis of this is a certain confusion on Schopenhauer's part regarding the active and passive moments of the aesthetic encounter. He never makes clear whether the aesthetic state is induced by the object without any contribution by the subject or whether it is initiated by the subject. Presumably the latter is the case, since Schopenhauer rejects an overpowering force on the side of the object as destructive of beauty and, therefore, *interesting* at best. The interesting he defines as that which forces us to respond to it, but this force is experienced as a pressure on our will and thus counterproductive in a situation that aims precisely at the suspension of the will.[8] Beauty, we can thus deduce, is not overpowering but inviting, yet every invitation must be pondered, decided upon, and result in an action before an encounter can follow. Since art requires beauty, it cannot overwhelm us and, consequently, needs our active response to its appeal. Also, Schopenhauer had defined genius as the exceptional power to actively bracket the will. Yet he argues – again confusing matters – that to this active power of the genius the receptivity of the one who contemplates the work of art corresponds, thus stressing again the positive factor. Either way, however, Schopenhauer's argumentation does not add up and lingers between an epistemological passivity and the demand for active participation in that act that lets all activity rest.

Since cognition must necessarily view every object in a context because it is restricted to the phenomenal realm and thus governed by the principle of sufficient reason, cognition cannot achieve insight into the ideas. These exist in isolation and free from causation. Every object that exists in a context can also never be sufficiently defined and thus known, because the attempt at a complete definition has to take into account the other objects to which the original object is contextually related. These in turn carry with them their own context to which they need to be related, and so on ad infinitum. The idea, however, could be fully known since it exists freely. Art, hence, "repeats the ideas, the essence and permanence of all phenomena of the world, that were comprehended in pure contemplation" (WWR, 273). It follows Schopenhauer's famous definition of art: "We can therefore define it [i.e., art] as the contemplation of objects independent of the principle of sufficient reason" (WWR, 273f.). With this definition, however, Schopenhauer maneuvered himself into another corner. He, to be sure, conceives of art as cognition. Closely following Schelling's lead, he argues that art is not only cognition but also a higher cognition than everyday experience or scientific insight, because only art can penetrate the veil of appearances, *Maya,* and progress to the ideas. Just as in romantic aesthetics, art's potential for cognition is thus elevated above the cognitive faculties of philosophy.

This thesis, however, is problematic since Schopenhauer is unable to explain exactly how the cognition of the aesthetic experience is supposed to function. He excludes reason and its means, that is, concepts, from the cognition of ideas that he had clearly distinguished from concepts. The specific cognition of art, Schopenhauer insists, is sensual and presupposes the breakdown of those mental faculties that remain tied to phenomena and their mental representations, namely, understanding and reason. But what other faculties are left for the cognition of ideas? Following Kant, we could point to imagination and sensuality, yet the former cannot distinguish ideas from phantasmagoric productions, and the latter cannot achieve any cognition without the aid of other faculties. Hence, Schopenhauer leaves a great lacuna where he should have explained his theory of the cognition of ideas by means of art. Instead, we find a confusing, vague, and shifting association of cognitive achievements with different mental faculties without any clear sense of the precise operations of any of them.[9]

The Objective Vision of Genius

Art, as we have already seen, must be produced by a genius, since only in the genius do the cognitive powers dominate the will. Genius, thus, "is nothing but absolute objectivity, i.e., the objective direction of the spirit in opposition to the subjective one that is directed toward the self and the will" (WWR, 274). And just as contemplation begins with an act of will, both for the genius himself and for the contemplator of a work of art, so the will is also involved in the artistic production. Schopenhauer conceives of only the contemplation of the idea itself as will-less, whereas his model of artistic production follows the model of *poiesis* as conscious creation. The execution of a work of art must be driven by the will, Schopenhauer argues, because only the will can initiate the search for the means that are most adequate for the communication of the idea.[10] Again we find that art is unimaginable without the will, both in its creation and its reception.

Schopenhauer's theory of genius, thus, is antirealist in the sense that the central feature of the genius is his participation in the ideal world.[11] As has been pointed out, this conception is influenced by the ideas of literary romanticism and its opposition between the genius and the philistine who remains stuck in the quotidian world of strife and care for personal welfare, as he has been depicted very amusingly, for example, in Ludwig Tieck's comedies.[12] But not only the romantics set the philistine in opposition to the cultivated person with a sense for art; Goethe, too, subscribes to the same antithesis in his poem "Gedichte sind gemalte Fensterscheiben!" (Poems are painted windows!). Against such philistinism Schopenhauer pitches the genius's potential for intellectual intuition – a concept that he criticizes severely in Fichte only to utilize himself in the aesthetic context. And while Schopenhauer celebrates the genius as much as the previous generation of Storm-and-Stress authors, he makes it clear that for him, genius is not the expression of subjective individuality but, rather, the overcoming of all individual aspects and the ascent to pure objectivity. There is certainly a strong mystical element in this conception, insofar as the genius achieves both quietude and a close connection to the source of being in his contemplation. Here, too, Schopenhauer allies himself with the romantics who had rediscovered the writings of Jakob Böhme, Meister Eckhart, and other mystics for themselves.

The aesthetic experience is, then, the repetition of the genius's vision mediated by the work of art. Again Schopenhauer argues for a certain involvement of the subject in this process that is not exclusively driven by the aesthetic object. Aesthetic experience presupposes a special talent as well, namely, the ability to become for a moment of time a pure subject of contemplation. Most people, however, although they posses this latent ability (WWR, 286), cannot actualize it. Some intellectual potential – the precise definition of which remains unclear – is necessary to comprehend the idea that is represented in the work of art, so that especially the most outstanding works of art "must remain incomprehensible and inaccessible to the dull majority of people" (WWR, 339). We do not find out what precisely the majority of people are missing, since Schopenhauer was unable to explain how the cognition of ideas is meant to function, yet it is clear that for him, art is certainly an elitist affair. While he conceded that the consolation of art is available to more human beings than the redemption from suffering by means of ascetic negation of the will, he leaves little doubt that the requirements for the aesthetic experience still exclude the large majority from finding a moment of peace.

We must now turn to Schopenhauer's conception of beauty. We have identified three requirements for the aesthetic experience, namely, the cognition of an idea, the liberation from the will, and finally, beauty as the third condition. Schopenhauer advances a definition of beauty at one point, although it leaves much to be desired when he writes: "the adequate objectification of the will by means of a spatial phenomenon is beauty in the objective sense" (WWR, 324 f.). The question here is what distinguishes an adequate from an inadequate representation (presumably, Schopenhauer does not mean to refer to an immediate representation of the will, but the representation of an idea, since the only objectification of the will that Schopenhauer can imagine is music, that is, precisely not a *spatial* phenomenon) and what mental faculty would be able to distinguish the two. Also, it remains vague why the adequate representation constitutes beauty in an objective sense, since Schopenhauer leaves it open what sort of subjective beauty there could be.

Yet more surprising still for an aesthetic theory is his claim that in every object its idea can be contemplated and that art, hence, is ontologically not fundamentally different from all other objects: "Since every object can be contemplated objectively and free from all context and since furthermore the will appears in every object as one level of its objectification and the object is therefore expression of an idea, every object is beautiful" (WWR, 307). It hardly needs to be emphasized that Schopenhauer contradicts himself again here, since before, he had argued that no path leads from the phenomenal world to the world of ideas by means of the cognitive faculties that are always subservient to the will, whereas according to this statement, nothing should prevent us from such ascent. Still, the thesis that every object can serve as the source of aesthetic experience and must at least be considered of potential beauty is most puzzling. Art seems to lose a good bit of its privileged status if we take Schopenhauer seriously on this point. To be sure, he backpedals quickly and relativizes his argument by stating that some objects are more beautiful than others because they "aid the objective contemplation, invite it, and even force it so that we then call it beautiful" (WWR, 307). Yet once more this definition leaves us discontented: What before had been excluded from art, namely the element of force as one that involves the will in a struggle and thus hinders contemplation, is here put forward as one defining element of beauty.

To be sure, beauty cannot be found only in art but also in nature: "The aesthetic pleasure is essentially the same, be it produced by a work of art or immediately by the contemplation of nature or life. The work of art is merely an aid to that cognition that constitutes said pleasure" (WWR, 287). The beauty of art is superior to that of nature only in the sense that the work of art represents the idea cleansed of all accidental elements. Natural beauty still requires that we prepare it and penetrate to its idea, whereas the artist has already done this work for us and serves the idea up straight. Even ugly art – although such art falls short of the aesthetic requirements and should *sensu strictu* not be labeled art at all – can serve an aesthetic function, Schopenhauer states. In it the idea still appears, yet the ugliness of the object does not further the cognition but hinders it (WWR, 308).

The other possible conduit of an aesthetic experience is the sublime. The sublime threatens the subject, that is, the self-perpetuating drive of the will. Once the subject manages to tear itself away from the sense of danger and thus to liberate itself from the will, it achieves the same state of quiet contemplation that the work of art provides. Thus, with the sublime a struggle against the will needs to be won before contemplation can ensue; beauty accomplishes the same end without any force: "What thus distinguishes the sense of sublimity from that of beauty is this: with the beautiful pure cognition has gotten the upper hand without any struggle . . . whereas this state of pure cognition must first be won in the case of the sublime by a conscious and violent tearing away from those conditions that the will had realized as adverse" (WWR, 296). Since the sublime depends on the willful negation of the threatening aspects and, thus, willful overcoming of the will even before cognition can be achieved, beauty is conceived as cognition without struggle.

Obviously, Schopenhauer's theory of beauty is also no less problematic. For him, beauty not only characterizes the successful work of art but also turns out to be an attribute of the ideas themselves that the genius contemplates in his ecstatic vision, as well as an attribute of every nonartistic object insofar as it can serve as an initiator of pure contemplation. While some commentators grant Schopenhauer the benefit of the doubt by claiming that this multifaceted definition of beauty can be read as a quasi-romantic opposition against the normative definition of classicism,[13] it seems to me that such vagueness of definition renders the term almost useless.

From Architecture to Music

Based on his metaphysics of will, Schopenhauer then develops a system of the forms of art. These forms he regards as aesthetic correspondences to the levels of objectification of the will, so that inorganic nature, organic nature of plants and animals, and the sphere of human life all find their respective artistic representation in one form of art. The lowest form of art that corresponds to the lowest manifestation of will is architecture. The function of architecture is "to clearly express some ideas that are part of the lowest levels of the objectification of the will: namely heaviness, cohesion, rigidity, hardness, these general qualities of stone, these first, simplest, vaguest appearances of the will, the bass line of nature" (WWR, 312). From here the hierarchy of the forms of art mirrors that of nature: The art of gardening presents the beauty of the vegetable kingdom; the art of landscaping does the same, but it contains a transposition from the actual material to the representational realm; the art of animal painting – a unique form of art for Schopenhauer – corresponds to the fauna; and with historical painting and sculpture we reach the sphere of human life and the embodiment of human beauty as the perfect objectification of will. Portraiture then moves from the general depiction of man to individual representation; poetry as a discursive art peaks in tragedy that constitutes the epitome of all representational arts. The tragic for Schopenhauer not only embodies "the struggle of the will against itself" (WWR, 364), but more importantly shows us that the demise of the tragic hero does not result from any individual flaw: "The true meaning of the tragedy is the deeper insight that the hero does not do penance for his particular sins, but rather for the original sin, the guilt of being" (WWR, 365).

At the highest rank in the hierarchy of art, yet no longer part of the representational forms of art, is located music. While all the other arts have a direct correspondence to an idea as the objectification of the will, music is the unmediated objectification of the will itself: "Hence we can regard the phenomenal world, or nature, and music as two different expressions of the same instance" (WWR, 376). Music grips us most of all the arts because through music we gain direct access to the will. Music is "embodied will," not embodied idea. Drawing on Scholastic vocabulary, Schopenhauer declares: "Concepts are the *universalia post rem,* while music gives *universalia ante rem* and reality the *universalia in re*" (WWR, 378). Following the romantic thinkers, Schopenhauer thus reverses Kant's hierarchy of arts in which music had taken the lowest rank, partly because in the interaction of imagination and understanding, music sticks closest to the pole of imagination and contains no aspect of thought, partly because musical performances can be obtrusive by necessarily affecting everyone in earshot (*Critique of Judgment,* §54).[14] And while it is certainly true that the aesthetics of the late eighteenth century in general (with the exception of Diderot) did not pay much heed to music, and that this form of art only came to prominence in aesthetic reflection with the romantic generation and with Schopenhauer himself, both were preceded by J. J. W. Heinse's (1746–1803) essay-novel *Hildegard von Hohenthal.* In this narrative, music is also considered as a means of access to the objects as they exist outside of any conceptual framework, although Heinse regards the necessary dispensation of the verbal as grounded in an outbreak of passion – a thought diametrically opposed to Schopenhauer, yet closely allied with the poetics of Storm-and-Stress.

In his theory of music, Schopenhauer comes closest to the very traditional definition of beauty as the harmonious integration of parts into a totality, thus presenting a requirement that was absent from previous attempts to define the beautiful. Still, this new approach to beauty might very well be at odds with his previous cognitivist definition of beauty. Yet it is the cognitive function of art that leads him to declare that if music could be translated into concepts, it would be the "true philosophy" (WWR, 380).

Obviously, Schopenhauer's theory of the forms of art is entirely ahistorical. For him, forms of art do not develop or change. This static picture of art results from his general rejection of history as a useful category for thought – an attitude that he shares with his idol Goethe:

> The history of humankind, the bustle of events, the change of ages, the multiple forms of human life in different periods and centuries – all this is merely the accidental form of the appearance of the idea, does not belong to the latter itself, but only to its representation which is the object of individual cognition and as foreign, inessential and unimportant to it as their shapes are to the clouds. (WWR, 270)

Having rejected history as an illusion, however, Schopenhauer is hard put to explain changes in the forms of art that he himself deplores. At one point in time, he argues, for example, that the rise of opera led to a corruption of music, because a medium foreign to music, namely, words as elements of the conceptual realm, dominate in it.[15] Yet an ahistorical conception of the arts must either have accounted for the form of opera beforehand, so that it could not be considered a corruption but merely an intermediate form between poetry and music, or it must regard such corruption as irrelevant, since historical developments can never pose a threat to transhistorical forms.

The problem with Schopenhauer's aesthetic theory is not so much that it is full of inconsistencies and that many questions remain open. That is also the case with Kant's *Critique of Judgment*, for example, although certainly to a much lesser extent. Much more problematic, however, are Schopenhauer's departures from central positions of idealism. For one, there is the individualistic turn in his aesthetics. Schopenhauer paves the way for an aestheticism free from all ties to moral, communal, practical, and even metaphysical considerations. With the German idealists, art always was considered in some kind of nexus to a larger whole. Yet Schopenhauer transforms aesthetics into an individualist endeavor. True to the soteriological impetus of his metaphysics at large, the importance of art results from its relevance as a means for relief that it provides for the consumer. This has two important consequences for the philosophy of art: The first is that a redemptive function is transposed from religion to art and that art thus turns into something of an ersatz religion.[16] Precisely this position made Schopenhauer a favorite with the bored, enlightened, politically powerless, and somewhat areligious bourgeoisie of the post-1848 period in which Schopenhauer came to fame. Secondly, the individualistic turn also emphasizes the role of *experience* in art over and above the *work of art* itself – possibly even more so than Kant's third *Critique.* Also, we find here one of the rare instances in which a theoretical position in aesthetics antedates a tendency in artistic practice. Although tendencies to subjectivize painting, to mention only one example, had been under way for a long time – in painting certainly since romanticism, if not in part since the Renaissance – they only became a credo within the impressionist art of the latter half of the nineteenth century.[17]

Furthermore, Schopenhauer's theory of art complicates both the epistemological and the practical moment of art to the point of reversing their traditional function. We have already seen that Schopenhauer couldn't sufficiently explain how his antirationalist metaphysics could go together with his cognitivist aesthetics. For a solution to that impasse he would have to show us what mental faculty exists beyond reason and understanding, both of which are said to be dependent functions of the will that can grant cognition free from the will. Since one of his aims is to dismantle rationality as a function of the will, that is, as secondary and subservient, it is hard to see how the cognitive aspect of aesthetics can win out over the rationalist skepticism.

A similar impasse results when we consider the practical function of art. Schopenhauer certainly attributes a didactic function to the aesthetic experience, namely, one that reveals to us the ephemeral nature of all appearances. As he states in a collection of aphorisms, literature can contribute to the necessary disillusionment of man: "In order to achieve the necessary, clear and profound understanding of the true and sad condition of man it is more than helpful to study their actions and manners in literature as a commentary on their actions and manners in real life and vice versa."[18] Literature, thus, should serve to undo our positive expectations of human intercourse. All art, in other words, has the practical function not to further our engagement with the world but to support our withdrawal from it.[19] Individualism, the emphasis on personal experience over and above reality, epistemological skepticism, and practical asceticism, however, are the signs of a philosophy in general and an aesthetic theory in particular that mark the farewell to a position that considers man's life valuable, worthy of improvement through individual and communal efforts, and joyous due to its participation in a totality that both precedes the individual and yet demands his engagement in order to become truly a home for him.

7

Kierkegaard, Nietzsche

Kierkegaard

Aesthetic thought is central to Søren Kierkegaard's (1813–1855) philosophy, yet hardly another thinker – with the possible exception of the early Emmanuel Levinas – regards aesthetics with such disdain. Whereas idealist philosophy had granted art and beauty a privileged position in its various systems, Kierkegaard's reaction against idealism at large also affects his valuation of the aesthetic sphere. Intentionally, he reaches past the idealists in his attempt to redefine aesthetics as a sphere of life and inquiry; but unintentionally, he falls beneath the level of discussion that aesthetics had achieved during the previous decades. Kierkegaard opposes the idealist systems, especially the one advanced by Hegel, since for him their intellectual efforts remain irrelevant to quotidian life. The categories of being and becoming, so prominent in Hegel's *Logic,* have to be replaced in Kierkegaard's view by that of existence. Ontology, logic, and metaphysics are all given an anthropological spin by Kierkegaard. Many areas of philosophical inquiry are left altogether untouched by him – there is no philosophy of nature, hardly an ontology, little in terms of a philosophy of history, barely any political philosophy, in short, nothing resembling a philosophical system. Instead, Kierkegaard's thinking centers around the notion of existence that for him denotes the act of living considered as a unity of thought and feeling (both emotionally and sensually), desire and action. Yet this unity not only is not given as a preexisting mode of being for man; it is perpetually in a most precarious balance.

Some attempts to achieve an existence in balance are more successful than others, and Kierkegaard reserves the term "faith" for a favorable type of self-development. In it, the self realizes its existence as a dialectical interaction of createdness and obligation to self-creation in the realm of freedom that is opened up by God's grace and acknowledged thankfully by man. The failed type of existence, on the other hand, Kierkegaard labels "despair," that is, that way of life that is characterized by its negation of God and the attempt to ground its own existence. As we will see, the latter existence has much in common with what Kierkegaard understands to be an aesthetic mode of life.

Neither the completeness of systematic philosophy nor any knowledge unrelated to ethical matters in the wider sense are of much concern for Kierkegaard, and the presentation of his philosophy consequently is equally personal. Kierkegaard's strategy of publishing his books under a variety of pseudonyms emphasizes the fact that such writings are not vehicles for the direct transfer of knowledge from author to reader. Rather, the fictive author of the work is included as a self-reflective persona in the text. Such "indirect communication," as Kierkegaard terms it, thus presents a fictive author, a literary figure or a personified attitude toward life that challenges the reader to respond to this attitude by reflecting upon it and by evaluating its merits and shortcomings. This engagement with the figure of the fictive author, however, demands a certain adaptation of literary techniques for use in the philosophical discourse into which consequently fictional elements enter. Accordingly, *Either Or* (1843) contains in it several literary genres, such as a fictional diary, a novella, aphorisms, and character sketches in the tradition of Theophrastus; similar fictional genres are to be found in several of his other works. Judged on their literary merit, however, these attempts remain unsatisfactory, largely because their intention to serve as examples for an attitude or an *ethos* interferes with the necessary independence, well-roundedness, and multifacetedness of a convincing literary figure. No matter how often critics label Kierkegaard a philosopher-poet, as a writer of fiction he remains somewhat uninteresting. Adorno has argued this point as well by claiming in his early study on Kierkegaard that in his literary production, being is always subordinated to thinking; the figures serve merely as illustrations of categories, and the result is nothing less than "artistic impotence."[1]

Kierkegaard distinguishes three different types of existence that he terms aesthetic, ethical, and religious. These three must be thought of as an ascending order in which the ethical mode of life overcomes the aesthetic and is, in turn, overcome by the religious, more precisely the Christian existence. Despite all of his opposition against Hegel, Kierkegaard here takes up his opponent's notion that the aesthetic is transcended by the religious.[2] Yet there is a decisive difference between the two conceptions. Whereas Hegel had argued that art contains truth, no matter if superior expressions of truth have developed in the course of history, Kierkegaard associates the aesthetic more or less with deception and corruption. The aesthetic existence is one of sensuality; it is characterized by an immediacy in which man exists as a being governed by drives and sensuality, determined exclusively by his nature and driven by the search for pleasure as his highest principle. While for Kierkegaard most human beings exist in the aesthetic state, it is nevertheless a mode of life characterized by despair because it is painfully self-absorbed and unengaged. It should by all means be a temporary state, akin to the childhood of man, and the inability to leave it must be considered a form of arrested development. This serious critique of the aesthetic will concern us in more detail later when we investigate Kierkegaard's attempt to redefine the aesthetic in terms of sensuality.

In the hierarchy of modes of existence, Kierkegaard calls for a displacement of the aesthetic by the ethical that can only be achieved through a leap out of the sensual immediacy into the situation of choice governed by categories of good and evil. Only through this leap into the situation of choice does man leave the terror of sensual satisfaction behind, and choose himself as a human being. He therefore finds freedom precisely through his submission to the ethical obligation. In the ethical existence, however, the aesthetic moments of life are not negated but *aufgehoben,* that is, integrated into a higher form of existence, preserved and yet made subservient to a freely chosen cause. Still, the ethical existence is not yet the highest one achievable for man but is, in turn, overcome by the religious way of life. Unlike the achievement of the ethical existence, however, the religious existence results not from a choice alone; it depends on something outside of man. To move from the ethical to the religious life can only be accomplished as a response to that grace that calls out to man and demands his response, the *kerygma* of the New Testament. Unsummoned, man cannot realize that the ethical existence does not rest on freedom, precisely because man has lost his freedom by severing his ties to the eternal, and finds himself thus in a state that theologians call sin. Faith, on the other hand, reestablishes man's bond with the eternal and allows for the only truly successful existence.

Such is the context of Kierkegaard's philosophy in which his discussion of the aesthetic is situated. The term "aesthetic" has at least two different meanings for Kierkegaard. The first refers to the sphere of art and beauty – both of which are for Kierkegaard as synonymous as they were for Hegel – as well as to the attitude created in the recipient by individual works of art or by the (inappropriately) high valuation of art. Despite an admirably developed aesthetic sensibility – especially for the music of Mozart – Kierkegaard's discussions of art nevertheless do not move beyond the individual analysis into the realm of a general theoretical discussion of art. His statements on art of a more fundamental nature are few and mostly restricted to the adherence to the classical form–content coherence:

> Only when the idea reposes with transparent clearness in a definite form, can it be called a classic work; but then it will also be able to withstand the attacks of time. This unity, this mutual intensity within itself, is a property of every classical work, and hence it is readily evident that every attempt at a classification of the different classic works, which has for its basis a separation of form and content, or idea and form, is *eo ipso* doomed to failure. (I, 52)[3]

Later in life, Kierkegaard voices a more fundamental skepticism toward art as when he writes: "Christianly understood, every poet-existence (esthetics notwithstanding) is sin, the sin of poetizing instead of being, of relating to the good and the true through the imagination instead of being that – that is, existentially striving to that."[4]

Much more relevant, though, is Kierkegaard's understanding of the aesthetic as an attitude toward life, namely, that mode of existence characterized by immediacy, sensuality, desire, and natural inclinations. Yet man does not give himself over completely to his instincts – that would be a merely beastly form of life – but labors to give his sensuality shape, to develop and fine-tune his faculties of perception, and to create himself as an individual capable of more and more varied responses to outside stimuli. As often as to art the aesthetic life responds to the erotic fascination with human beauty, so that sensuality acquires a strong seductive undertone.[5] "This is the glory and divinity of aesthetics, that it enters into relation only with the beautiful: it has to do essentially only with fiction and the fair sex" (I, 423). This conception of aesthetics manifests the attempt to return to a pre-Baumgartenian understanding of aesthetics as a theory of sensuality as in the original meaning of the term *aisthesis,* namely, sensual perception. Yet Kierkegaard is not interested in the epistemological aspect of sensuality, as were Baumgarten's precursors Leibniz and Wolff. Rather, he wants to understand it as a new combination of sensual perception with artistic creativity, predominantly self-creation. The latter moment is by no means genuine to Kierkegaard but harks back to the Romantics' appeal "to live poetically." Hence, Kierkegaard constitutes the bridge between the Romantic aestheticization of life and Nietzsche's and Foucault's aestheticization of the self. In the end, however, this attempt to wed the rationalist metaphysical *aisthesis*-conception to the existential focus of his philosophy leads to a weak aesthetic philosophy. Yet in order to understand Kierkegaard's attempt at redefining the aesthetic, it is necessary first to lay out his critique of the aesthetic life.

Against the aesthetic existence, Kierkegaard claims that it is a life of indifference. Although we might not be entirely convinced by this argument – self-creation and erotic refinement, after all, both seem to call for discrimination of taste and, hence, for choice – he nevertheless wants to restrict the application of the category of decision to the ethical realm:

> ...for the aesthetical is not the evil but neutrality, and that is the reason why I affirmed that it is the ethical which constitutes the choice. It is, therefore, not so much a question of choosing between willing the good *or* the evil, as of choosing to will, but by this in turn the good and the evil are posited. (II, 173)

Equally problematic, and from a point of view of self-creation possibly even self-defeating, is Kierkegaard's thesis that the aesthetic life depends on the moment. To exist aesthetically means to want to maximize and intensify sensual experience, and these experiences manifest themselves in the psyche as moods – a concept that will later influence Heidegger's analysis of the *Gestimmtheit* of *Dasein* in *Being and Time* (1927):

The aesthetic view takes account of the personality in its relation to the environment, and the expression for this relation in its repercussion upon the individual is pleasure. But the aesthetic expression for pleasure in its relation to the individual is mood. In mood the personality is present but only dimly present. For he who lives aesthetically seeks as far as possible to be absorbed in mood, he seeks to hide himself entirely in it, so that there remains nothing in him which cannot be inflected into it; for such a remainder has always a disturbing effect, it is a continuity which would hold him back. (II, 234)

Being given over to the flow of moods and moments precludes any continuity of self, because this self would have to be precisely that which does not depend on the flood of impressions, as Kant had argued when he advanced the notion of the transcendental unity of apperception in his *Critique of Pure Reason.* Obviously, the aesthetic life is at odds with the ethical one, not so much because its decisions are inevitably immoral – one could possibly conceive of a long series of aesthetic choices that would not conflict with ethical principles – but, rather, because it disables all virtue, since virtue depends on the habitual practice of ethical choices, as we have learned from Aristotle. Without *ethos* – the continuity of character that is established through the continuous practice of behavior considered correct – no character formation is conceivable. What remains is a fragmented character in the romantic tradition, one that is appropriately presented by Kierkegaard in the form of fragments in one of the literary texts that make up the first part of *Either Or,* namely the *Diapsalmata.*[6] The fragment, however, carries with it the sadness of the impossible, since it still relates to a totality that it can no longer hope to achieve, yet that it cannot let go of either.

Ultimately, the aesthetic personality negates the claims of the world and reduces it to a mere reservoir for poetic construction.[7] The aesthetic life presupposes, therefore, not so much the engagement with but the distance from the world as it is expressed in that ironic attitude that Kierkegaard criticized so vehemently in his dissertation. Aesthetic freedom is always purchased at the cost of loneliness. And worse, the aesthetic existence is by necessity disrespectful, because no other being can be granted its own right that would set limits to the freedom of self-creation of the aesthete: "Aesthetic freedom precludes respect, for respect obliges."[8]

In respect to their temporal implications, Kierkegaard's two conceptions of the aesthetic – one referring to art and the other to life – are contradictory. Whereas he subscribes to a classical conception of art in which the work of art overcomes temporality and exists in a transhistorical realm, he simultaneously holds that life considered as a work of art can never escape the flow of time and that the eternal cannot be achieved by artistic enterprises. Not even the ethical life can grasp the eternal, only the religious one, yet in order to reach the third state, life must first pass from the aesthetic to the ethical mode. The latter then replaces aesthetic indifference through choice without negating the aesthetic altogether. The ethical life contains the aesthetic in it as its *Aufhebung*, its preservation, reformulation, and elevation to a higher level. This is why Kierkegaard speaks of ethical beauty: "Therefore, only when I regard life ethically do I see it with a view to its beauty, and only when I regard my own life ethically do I see it with a view to its beauty" (II, 279). Such reflex of beauty in the ethical personality is a reformulation of Schiller's notion of *Anmut* (grace), yet conceptually it is neither as precise nor as lucid as the latter's.

A good exemplification of the postulated interdependence of the aesthetic and the ethical is Kierkegaard's theory of tragedy. The aesthetic view of life that conceives of the self as an artistic product ultimately destroys the possibility of tragedy, which rests precisely on the inner conflict of the individual who is torn between two powers that are superior to him, and that both constitute central and valued aspects of his personality and have the power to destroy him. A self that owes everything to itself can never be tragic:

> Our age has lost all the substantial categories of family, state, and race. It must leave the individual entirely to himself, so that in a stricter sense he becomes his own creator, his guilt is consequently sin, his pain remorse; but this nullifies the tragic. (I, 147)

In other words, the aesthetic as a mode of life destroys the aesthetic as a form of art. If the art of the tragedy is to be revived – a topic that will also concern the young Nietzsche a few decades later – it can only be done by sacrificing the aesthetic life and reintegrating the personality into the ethical spheres of family, community, and state:

> If a man, however, were to contemplate regeneration in terms of ancient tragedy, then must every individual contemplate his own regeneration, not merely in a spiritual sense, but in the definite sense of rebirth from the matrix

of family and race. The dialectic which sets the individual in connection with family and race is no subjective dialectic, for such a dialectic lifts the connection and the individual out of the continuity; it is an objective dialectic. It is essentially piety. To preserve this cannot be regarded as something injurious to the individual. (I, 157)

As convincing as this analysis of the communal as a necessary condition not only for the tragic but also, by extension, for all great art might be – it is echoed by several twentieth-century thinkers of both socialist-revolutionary and conservative leanings – it is problematic for Kierkegaard's conception of the aesthetic as a whole. To redefine aesthetics in terms of sensuality is certainly a permissible and possibly even productive attempt – current discussions in aesthetics aim to achieve a similar end in order to be able to construct an ecological aesthetics, to mention just one example. Yet Kierkegaard's association of the sensual with the erotic leads to a loss of the cognitive element in aesthetics that had always been present in pre-idealist versions of aesthetics as a theory of sense perception. Even the *gnoseologia inferior* of the Leibniz-Wolff school conceived of aesthetics as fulfilling an epistemologically relevant function, but this cognitive moment disappears entirely in Kierkegaard's attempt to go back beyond the idealist tradition.

Problematic is also the practical function that he ascribes to art. Not much needs to be said about his occasional dismissal of art as an incitement to an immature and immoral aesthetic life – it is merely another version of religiously motivated iconoclasm of the unsophisticated sort. Of greater interest is Kierkegaard's idea of reintegrating aesthetics and ethics, but unfortunately, it remains vague to a great degree. If he can offer any solutions, they are restricted to the conception of aesthetics as a *mode of existence*, but here he does not move beyond Schiller; in fact, he doesn't even reach Schiller's sophistication of argumentation. No solution whatsoever is presented to the question of how to reconcile *art* and ethics. Kierkegaard does not even seem to be convinced that there are forms of art appropriate to the ethical and religious modes of life. Hence, one cannot help but conclude that Kierkegaard's redefinition of aesthetics in the light of a philosophy of existence impoverishes it and falls back behind idealist positions instead of developing them further.

Nietzsche

In Friedrich Nietzsche's (1844–1900) writings, the anti-idealist reaction reaches its self-assured, bombastic, and rhetorically most splendid peak, yet there is a seductive lightness about these texts that can easily tempt the reader to take rhetorical demonstration for argument and forcefulness for careful analysis. Equally undeniable is the fact that Nietzsche produces texts that are oftentimes pleasurable to read due to their stylistic brilliance and wit and the rhythmic flow of the syntax that often seems modeled on musical tempi. Still, the style at times can also overstep the *genus grande* and become hysterical; the wit can become vulgar insult and the musicality of the prose rhetorical Asianism: entertaining, but ultimately empty, ornamental speech. Just like Kierkegaard, Nietzsche does not succeed as a poet; his *Zarathustra* is written in loud prose that lacks all self-irony, and its fictional characters remain even more schematic and unpleasantly didactic than those of the Danish philosopher (whom Nietzsche never read). For reasons of fairness, however, it must be stated that Nietzsche certainly possessed more than just a modicum of artistic talent. His early musical compositions, mainly for piano, are at least a talented emulation of Franz Schubert, and some of his poems from later years hold up to scrutiny rather well.

Nietzsche's thought on aesthetics, however, is well in line with that of Schopenhauer and Kierkegaard insofar as he, too, attempts to rejuvenate aesthetics by going back beyond the idealist positions. In fact, there are strong similarities to Kierkegaard's undertaking of the redefinition of aesthetics in terms of sensuality, although Nietzsche uses the term physiology instead. Even though Nietzsche's invectives against Kant and his aesthetic theory are, as will become apparent, actually directed against the idol of his youth, Arthur Schopenhauer, he still faults idealism with the continuation of the Platonic metaphysics that devalues the empirical world.

When dealing with Nietzsche's aesthetic theory, a caveat is in order: One must expect neither too much precision nor too much consistency in Nietzsche's terminology. Generally, he offers few definitions for concepts, but what is worse is that many terms take on several meanings, sometimes simultaneously and in the same text, sometimes so that they change their meaning from one publication to the next. To mention just one example, the term "Dionysian" in Nietzsche's early writings refers to self-abandon, while the late Nietzsche uses the very same term to designate the ethos of self-discipline that is asked of those who want to initiate a morality of strength that is meant to overcome Christian meekness ("Dionysus against the Crucified," as Nietzsche writes). In the course of fifteen or so years, the term undergoes a volte-face. Much the same can be said about terms like "art," "aesthetics," "artist," and so forth; their meaning is in flux in Nietzsche's oeuvre as well.

Nevertheless, we can distinguish three phases in Nietzsche's aesthetic philosophizing. The first phase understands "aesthetics" to mean "philosophy of art." It finds its expression in Nietzsche's first publication as a Basel professor of classical philology – one that nevertheless failed to establish the coveted reputation as a serious scholar in the field – namely, *Die Geburt der Tragödie aus dem Geiste der Musik* (The birth of tragedy from the spirit of music, 1872). In this first phase, Nietzsche's aesthetic thought is concerned with the problem of artistic genius and the critique of science (including philosophy) from the perspective of art.

Nietzsche subsequently revised his stand on aesthetics during his positivistic years and becomes rather critical of art. The aim was for a new culture to overcome art altogether, for which purpose art must first be criticized from the perspective of science, which is now expected to lead the way into a rejuvenated culture. Although Nietzsche backtracks on his brief alliance with the positivists soon enough, this phase nevertheless marks the end of aesthetics understood as a philosophy of art. Art, and the term is still used a good bit in the late writings, no longer signifies primarily drama or music (the arts to which Nietzsche relates most – very few substantial remarks can be found about architecture or painting), but any product created by humans, including the production of social groups, attitudes, and even the self. Nietzsche here returns to the Greek understanding of art as *techne* that does not distinguish between the products of the craftsman and the artist. The term "art" *can* still signify poetry or music in Nietzsche's texts of this period, yet it generally carries a much wider meaning. Especially in the late fragments, there is often no context from which to deduce the intended connotation, but mostly it is safe to assume that Nietzsche has departed from the close association of art with the fine arts.

The third phase marks a radical aesthetization of philosophy at large in which artistic creation becomes paradigmatic for each and every philosophical discipline. Just as for Schelling, aesthetics replaces metaphysics as the *prima philosophia*, yet not as an organon of truth but as one of creative, unavoidable, and welcome deception, as we will see.

These phases are not neatly separated from one another, but some overlap occurs between them. Even in the first phase, Nietzsche introduces a meaning of art that does not refer to drama or music but to a much broader conception of creation. Although it is still a thoroughly metaphysical concept at this time, it still anticipates the usage of the term art in Nietzsche's third phase. Roughly speaking, we can read Nietzsche as slowly widening the meaning of the terms art and aesthetics throughout his career as a writer – and possibly overstretching them in the process.

The Birth of Tragedy

Two idols of the youthful Nietzsche influence the conception of the *Birth of Tragedy:* Arthur Schopenhauer and his philosophy of the will and Richard Wagner, both as a writer of cultural-aesthetic essays and as a composer. While Nietzsche takes up the ideas of the former mainly to reverse them – a strategy that he will practice throughout his writing life – he champions the latter as the composer who will bring about the rebirth of tragedy after it had lain dead for two millennia. This latter alliance, however, will not last for long, since a few years after the publication of *The Birth of Tragedy,* Nietzsche turned away from his former paternal friend to accuse him of being part of cultural decadence and of being a follower of Catholic Rome.

The Birth of Tragedy can be roughly divided into two parts, the first of which contains the first fifteen sections and has a cultural-historical focus. Here, Nietzsche examines the nature of Greek tragedy according to the duality of the Apollonian and Dionysian principles. Sections 16 to 25, then, are more concerned with the possibilities for a rebirth of tragedy and the general renewal of the European spirit, as well as Germany's role in this process. Nietzsche's style, even though still much more cautious and conventional than in later works, is already far from academic: The organization of the material is not linear but includes repetitions and revisitations; here and there Nietzsche becomes insistent and apodictic without bothering to argue, and frequently he attempts to bond with the reader by using the plural "we" and addressing him as "interested friend."

"Aesthetics" in the context of this early work means primarily, though not exclusively, philosophy of art. Art is discussed as the result of the ever-shifting and precarious arrangement that results from the struggle of two opposing principles that Nietzsche labels Apollonian and Dionysian. Later we will see that he understands these to be not only principles of art but much more fundamental forces of nature. Apollo is the Greek god of sunlight and daytime, of individuality, rationality, and order. In life, his *ethos* is *sophrosyne,* as Aristotle calls the knowledge of right measure. In art, his contribution to painting, for example, would be the *desegno,* the composition and the drawing of the outlines. But even more than painting, sculpture is most akin to Apollo. Among the poetic forms it is the epic. Both man's ethical conduct and his aesthetic attitude are determined by contemplation and cogitation when ruled by Apollo. Living the Apollonian life lets the individual stand out against the crowd, ruled as he is by the *principium individuationis.* But such life does not come easily to the Greek; rather, it is the result of a struggle against the most fundamental Greek attitude toward life in which existence is experienced as terrible, incomprehensible, and altogether too dreadful to be lived. Apollonian existence means the rescue from such sense of terror. With this assertion, Nietzsche turns the classicism of the previous generations upside down: Against Winckelmann he argues that the calmness and grandeur of the ancient civilization is nothing genuine but, rather, a secondary reflex born of the necessity of self-preservation. Both Apollonian art and the Olympian gods are products of an imagination searching for means for survival in the face of despair: "The Greek knew and sensed the terrors and dreadfulness of existence: in order to live at all he had to place the shining dream-products of the Olympians in front of those terrors"[9] (§3). Nietzsche thus claims that both art and the gods have the same anthropological origin, namely, as a defense mechanism against life's atrocities, an argument he had already advanced in his unpublished 1870 essay "Die dionysische Weltanschauung" (The Dionysian worldview).[10] This also explains why Nietzsche can agree with Schiller as little as with Winckelmann when it comes to the naïve as a form of art, for him, naïve art is not the sign of a culture's innocent youth but already the result of the highest conscious effort directed against the horror of being.

Dionysus, on the other hand, is a new addition to the Olympian gods, a newcomer from the East. He is the god who – at least in one version of his myth – was torn to pieces by the Titans; this fate of dismemberment he shared with his Egyptian precursor Osiris. Yet he is not only the god who died but also the god who returns from the dead, thus transgressing the boundary of life and death, as transgression generally is his prime characteristic. Most transgressions associated with the Dionysian festival occur in a state of intoxication and frenzy, an orgiastic abandon during which dichotomies such as male and female, subject and object, are collapsed. The *principium individuationis* breaks apart, the individual disappears like foam on the crest of a wave (or like Foucault's man drawn in the sand by the side of the ocean[11]), and "something unheard of forces its expression, the destruction of the veil of Maja, oneness as the genius of the species, of nature" (§2). And while Dionysian forms of art exist – music, especially its melodic and harmonious elements, qualifies as such – the true Dionysian work of art is not an artwork but man as a work of art: "Man is no longer artist, he became work of art: all of nature's forceful art, to the highest pleasure of the ur-oneness, reveals itself here in the shivers of intoxication" (§1). The Dionysian is nothing but an onslaught on the Apollonian, a threat to the carefully erected shield of form against the powers of chaos that now threaten to return. Since the Dionysian could not be denied or ignored – it was all too familiar to the Greek soul – the only way to handle it was by incorporating it into the culture. This taming of Dionysus happened in the tragedy. Tragedy is the invention that grants an outlet to the Dionysian forces and simultaneously ritualizes their triumph and forces them into a form.

Greek tragedy begins and ends with the chorus, the Dionysian mass that knows no individuality. This chorus is first of all a musical phenomenon, and out of it the Apollonian hero is born: "According to this insight we have to understand Greek tragedy as the chorus that always discharges itself anew in an Apollonian world of images" (§8). The events of the tragedy are a vision, an Apollonian dream, of the chorus. Yet the individual in the end must return to the unity of existence represented by the chorus. Underneath all single beings lies the oneness of existence. Hence, the death of the protagonist is no event to be mourned but reason for consolation. The teachings of the tragedy are "the basic insight into the unity of all beings, the consideration of individuality as the basis of all evil, art as the joyful hope that the spell of individuation can be broken, as the intimation of a renewed unity" (§10). Neither religion nor philosophy can provide man with the knowledge about the conditions of his existence, but in art he can experience them. That is the reason that Nietzsche speaks in the Preface of *The Birth of Tragedy* of "art as the highest task and the truly metaphysical practice of this life."

Nietzsche does not merely explain Greek tragedy as the successful accommodation of Apollonian and Dionysian principles. Rather, all art for him rests on precisely this interaction, and the individual arts can be arranged on a scale according to the predominance of either principle. Sculpture is the most purely Apollonian art; it celebrates the lie of the triumph of individuality and an existence without suffering. Lyric poetry begins in music, a Dionysian mood, but advances from here to Apollonian form. Music marks the other end of the scale where the Dionysian has achieved predominance and expresses the pain of existence unabashedly. Although painting and architecture are missing from Nietzsche's list, it would be possible to group architecture together with sculpture on the Apollonian end, drawings and etchings somewhat more toward the middle and painting, where color joins line, even closer to the Dionysian.

Nietzsche tells the story not only of the birth of the tragedy but also of its decline and death. He regards the tragedies of Euripides as the end of the genre, because in them tragedy is cleansed of its Dionysian element and the hero is replaced by the average man.[12] With Euripides and his philosophical counterpart Socrates, for Nietzsche, the scientific age begins, and it has not ceased since.[13] In it, beauty is falsely considered as in need of cognition. The delusion that existence can be understood rationally permeates everything and destroys precisely that tragic knowledge that had wisely understood all insight as limited by the incomprehensible and had, thus, required art as "protection and cure" (§16). In his lecture "Das griechische Musikdrama" (The Greek musical drama) from the same period, Nietzsche argues that it is precisely knowledge that has stifled the development of the arts in the modern age, because "all growth and becoming in the realm of art must occur in deep night."[14]

Yet Nietzsche finds hope for a renewal of the tragic culture of antiquity for two reasons. The first is negative, namely, the necessary failure of the scientific optimism that must precede a rebirth of culture. Nietzsche considers Kant's *Critique of Pure Reason* and its subsequent appropriation by Schopenhauer as two instances of a much-needed restriction of the scientific culture, for both had argued for the rational inaccessibility of the noumenal. Nietzsche finds a positive reason in the tradition of German music from Bach to Beethoven and beyond ("music reaches the heart unmediatedly," Nietzsche claims with Schopenhauer),[15] reaching its peak in the *Gesamtkunstwerk* of Richard Wagner, who is hailed as the instigator of a cultural renascence. His musical dramas are viewed as the foundation of a new mythology – the romantic discussion of around 1800 is echoed here – since no culture can exist without myths: "only a horizon surrounded by myths can give unity to a cultural movement" (§23).

Considered as a moment of Nietzsche's call for a new mythology, his reversal of Schopenhauer's metaphysics of will from an ascetic pessimism into an affirmative celebration of the oneness of being looks much less inventive and a good bit more like the renewal of a romantic theme under changed circumstances. Generally, it can be said that Nietzsche's philosophy of art as we find it in *The Birth of Tragedy* owes much more to idealist and romantic motifs of aesthetic philosophy than it wants to acknowledge. Nietzsche's claim that existence must remain rationally incomprehensible, yet that in art there can be found a means for its elucidation, is another of the assertions that harks back to Schelling and other romantic authors. Much the same can be said about Nietzsche's argument that the self is not opposed to the absolute, but that it discovers itself to be ultimately – tragically and joyfully – identical with it.

Also, Nietzsche's assertion that ugliness is part of art does not move beyond Rosenkranz's reformulation of Hegelian aesthetics, since for Nietzsche, too, the ugly is only a moment that ultimately feeds back into a larger harmonious totality. He acknowledges the "pleasurable sensation of dissonance in music" (§24), yet does not regard it as a moment that would burst asunder the work of art as a unified whole. Nietzsche's positive metaphysics of the will celebrates art as "triumph over the subject, redemption from the 'self.'" His formulation describing the aesthetic state of mind – "distinterested contemplation" (§5) – even seems to be taken directly from Kant, whose notion of disinterested pleasure Nietzsche will repeatedly attack in his later writings.

Finally, Nietzsche's notion of aesthetic play as he develops it with reference to Heraclitus also owes a fair amount to the discussion of this concept in Kant and Schiller. Nietzsche, too, conceives of the aesthetic play as an ultimately purposeless activity that finds its end and pleasure in itself, childlike, innocent even in its destruction and driven by a primordial pleasure that is the active ground of all art, as well as of the world at large (§24). Nietzsche echoes this motif of the innocent aesthetic playfulness in the *Zarathustra* section titled "About the Three Transformations," in which the carefree creativity of the child is celebrated as the highest stage of development. Here, however, the originally aesthetic motif has already been transformed largely into an ethical one and thus removed from the context of aesthetic discussion in the last decade of the eighteenth century and even turned against it.

To sum up, Nietzsche's discussion of art in *The Birth of Tragedy* owes much more to the idealist and romantic discussion than it is willing to acknowledge. Were it for this text only, Nietzsche's aesthetics, despite the introduction of the dichotomies of Apollo and Dionysus, as well as of Dionysus and Socrates, would be read merely as a belated echo of the heydays of German paradigmatic aesthetic philosophy. Yet there is another moment contained in the text that does not come to the forefront yet, although it will be the prominent focus of Nietzsche's later discussions of aesthetics. This is a second definition of the term art that departs from the context of cultural history, drama, music, and the rebirth of the German nation out of the spirit of Wagner's compositions.

There are a few passages in *The Birth of Tragedy* where Nietzsche argues that the Apollonian and Dionysian are not merely the two necessary forces of all artistic production, but that they are principles of nature. Hence, nature ceases to be an oppositional term to art; art, instead, includes nature. Nietzsche speaks of the Apollonian and Dionysian as "artistic powers which, without any mediation by the human artist, erupt from nature"; compared to these primary artistic forces of nature, "every artist is imitator" (§2). At another point he claims that the oneness of being is itself in need of redemption by means of a beautiful vision for which purpose it creates the world as a spectacle (§4). Although reminiscences to Plotinus run strong here, Nietzsche's assertion lacks a proper explanation as to why the originary One requires its redemption and how this could be accomplished through the world as theatrical creation. Yet there is a certain consistency with which he suggests repeatedly that the artist emulates that creative process that brought the world into being. While this takes up the well-established topos of God as the *creator mundi,* it signifies that Nietzsche operates with a concept of art that already at this early stage is broader than what meets the eye. As his involvement with aesthetics continues, the relation between the notion of art as fine art and the notion of art as a way of being and thinking is reversed. While the second concept of art is still thoroughly metaphysical in *The Birth of Tragedy* by being based on the notion of an ur-oneness, it will later be cleansed of metaphysical underpinnings.

Interestingly enough, it is not the Nietzsche who writes on the philosophy of art who is of primary interest for the history of aesthetics, but the Nietzsche who views all other traditional philosophical undertakings from the perspective of aesthetics. In order to reach that stage, however, Nietzsche first needed to overcome the association of aesthetics with the fine arts for himself. This is what happened during his positivist stage.

Positivist Interlude

Nietzsche concluded *The Birth of Tragedy* by expressing his hope for the failure of scientific culture, from the ruins of which a new artistic culture was to spring. A note to himself from the year 1876, however, demonstrates that he had already revoked this position of aesthetic optimism: "I will explicitly explain to readers of my earlier writings that I have given up the metaphysical-artistic views that basically govern these: they are pleasant, but untenable."[16] Now, in his positivist phase, the hope is for a scientific overcoming of art and a truly enlightened and rational culture. This reversal of his early view occurs less than a decade after the publication of the tragedy treatise and finds its most vivid expression in the fourth chapter of *Menschliches, Allzumenschliches I* (Human, all-too-human, 1878), titled "From the Soul of Artists and Writers."

One basic position, however, does not change – despite its changed valuation – and never will in Nietzsche's writings on aesthetics, namely, his view that art is a stimulant to life. This does still not raise its value for the positivist Nietzsche, since art's means to achieve this goal are more or less reprehensible themselves, as he now argues: "Art makes the vision of life bearable by covering it with the veil of impure thought" (§151). What he labels impure is that metaphysical residue that makes art the heir of religion in the sense that the two share many traits of underdevelopment. The artist, as much as the religious believer, cannot shed his faith in "the fantastic, mythical, insecure, extreme, the predilection for the symbolic, the overvaluation of the person, the belief in something miraculous in the genius" (§146). With these attitudes, the artist remains stuck at an infantile stage of development – "he [the artist] has remained child or youth all his life" (§147) – and even intends to bring back humanity as a whole to this juvenile state. (The parallel to Kierkegaard's notion of the aesthetic stage as a form of arrested development is obvious.) The artists "even hold back humanity from a true improvement of its situation by dissolving [*aufheben*] the passions of the unsatisfied ones that urge to action and by discharging them palliatively" (§148).

In other words, the production of artworks is a trait of a less-developed age; the artists are "the glorifiers of the religious and philosophical errors of mankind" (§220). Nietzsche reverses his own metaphysical positions as formulated in *The Birth of Tragedy*. In the case of music, this means that it must not be considered the revelation of the will itself, an unmediated access to the ground of being, but rather, is now regarded as deriving its force from the association with language. By no means, however, does music speak of the will or the thing in itself (§215).

Art, Nietzsche now argues, must give way to science: "Scientific man is the higher development of artistic man" (§222). An enlightened scientific culture will no longer have a need for art – a faint Hegelian echo of philosophical truth as the heir of artistic truth can be detected – but art will turn into a memory for mankind, still charming but powerless (§223). Thus, Nietzsche's positivist phase ends with a farewell to the fine arts. Yet this dismissal of the fine arts does not signify the end of aesthetic philosophy in Nietzsche. Aesthetics, though, from now on is merely unconcerned with the philosophical investigation of the fine arts. Instead, it busies itself aestheticizing all other philosophical fields.

Aestheticizing Philosophy

Nietzsche's thinking about aesthetics in the last productive decade of his life, namely the 1880s, must be considered his unique legacy to aesthetic philosophy, more so than the early book on tragedy and the positivist vision of overcoming art. Heidegger, in fact, went so far as to claim that Nietzsche's thought on art can only be understood from the perspective of *The Will to Power,* the collection of fragments that was edited posthumously and is now restored to the fragmentary state in which Nietzsche left it behind. The most relevant development of this last period of Nietzsche's dealings with aesthetics is the broadening of the notion of aesthetics itself so as to encompass ontology, cosmology, ethics, anthropology, and epistemology. In fact, nothing remains in his philosophy that is not viewed from an aesthetic perspective. The question remains, however, what meaning the term aesthetics now acquires and if there is any one meaning that could cover all of its different applications.

By now the opposition of Apollonian form and Dionysian frenzy has given way to the dominance of the Dionysian principle, so that both aesthetic principles are "considered as forms of intoxication."[17] This intoxication still serves the same purpose as in *The Birth of Tragedy,* namely, to stimulate life and to overcome all sense of "heaviness." This is why Nietzsche now repeatedly and vehemently argues against Kant's notion of disinterestedness, although, as has convincingly been shown, his actual target is not so much Kant as Schopenhauer's notion of art as panacea and escape from the will.[18] One of the fragments from the year 1883 reads: "Since Kant, all talk about art, beauty, cognition, wisdom is muddled and dirtied by the notion 'without interest.'"[19] Nietzsche takes the idea of *l'art pour l'art* to be just another symptom of decadence, since for him there is no doubt that art always serves a purpose, namely, that of stimulating a person's vital energies. Much like the good, the beautiful for Nietzsche consists of an increase of power; ugliness is what brings man down, depresses him, depletes his energies, in short, everything that Nietzsche considers decadent and unhealthy. Nietzsche does not shy away from regarding artistic production as a spin-off of sexual creation: "To make music is also a way to make children."[20] (*Note:* This is not an anticipation of Freud's theory of sublimation, but the perfectly conscious shifting of outlets for a somewhat mysterious vital energy.)

Yet what is most remarkable about Nietzsche's aesthetics is that he applies it to all possible philosophical inquiries. What we deal with is nothing less than an aesthetization of philosophy at large – at the cost of independent ethical and epistemological standards. As Habermas writes: "Nietzsche's aesthetic philosophy demands the reformulation of all ontic and moral phenomena in terms of aesthetics."[21] Nietzsche considers not only the cosmos a work of art (the Greek word itself that means both universe and ornament reveals that it is an ancient notion) but also the self: "As aesthetic phenomenon existence is always bearable, and art gives us the eye and hand and especially the good conscience to turn ourselves into such a phenomenon."[22] And elsewhere he writes: "We, however, want to be the poets of our lives."[23] Alexander Nehamas's interpretation of Nietzsche is largely based on this moment of aesthetization of the self; he presents Nietzsche as practicing this aesthetization of his own life by living it as a series of author-figures of his books.[24] As much as that may be the case, Nietzsche's aesthetization of philosophy extends beyond the aesthetization of the self in any case.

Closely connected to this motif, however, is Nietzsche's attempt to reformulate aesthetics in terms of sensual perception – the same attempt that had motivated Kierkegaard to go back beyond the idealists in an effort to revive elements of the rationalist metaphysics of the eighteenth century and its *cognitio sensitiva.* When Nietzsche revisits his early idolization of Wagner in order to reverse it, he argues for an understanding of aesthetics that investigates neither qualities of the object nor intentions or procedures of the artists, but merely the subjective response to the aesthetic object. This position is closer to Kant than Nietzsche wants to admit, since Kant had detected a "quickening of the faculties" in the aesthetic encounter, and Nietzsche reformulates this notion to signify a strengthening of the vital energies. Instead of mental faculties, however, he speaks of bodily functions, of physiology: "My arguments against Wagner's music are physiological arguments: why hide them under aesthetic formula? Aesthetics is nothing but applied physiology."[25] In a fragment meant to be included in *The Will to Power* and titled "About the Physiology of Art," he notes that physiological judgments have replaced aesthetic ones: "I know no more aesthetics!"[26] As much as the self is viewed as a work of art, it remains a physiological self, a self that needs to feel strong, act strong, and react to all outside stimuli physiologically.

Nietzsche's aesthetization of philosophy also includes epistemological questions. Already in his early essay "On Truth and Lie in an Extra-Moral Sense," he had defined truth in aesthetic terms, namely, as "a mobile army of metaphors, metonymies, anthropomorphisms."[27] And while in his *Zarathustra* he admits to the ancient charge that the poets are liars ("the poets lie too much"),[28] he generalizes this position so as to say that everyone is a liar and hence a poet. "One is much more of an artist than one knows," Nietzsche reminds those who are in danger of taking their own fabrications for truth.[29] One cannot help but think of Oscar Wilde's essay on the decay of lying as an art. Hence, there is precious little difference between the aesthetic attitude and the epistemological perspectivism for which Nietzsche is famed, that is, his theory that there is not one truth, as both correspondence and coherence theories of truth argue, but a multitude of truths that derive their particular truth-value from the beliefs and desires of the individual who holds them, in short, his or her private perspective.[30] Heidegger might have been the first to connect Nietzsche's epistemological perspectivism to his physiological aesthetics by arguing that the constantly shifting aesthetic perspective is the only adequate response to a life that develops itself creatively when all search for eternal truths would stifle progress.[31]

Philosophy as a whole, therefore, becomes redefined in aesthetic terms, namely, as an enterprise of taste. Here again, Nietzsche's attempt to go back behind idealist aesthetics manifests itself, since in the eighteenth century, taste as a category still applied to both moral and aesthetic phenomena, although this conjunction was becoming more and more questionable.[32] Kant's aesthetics, in which taste figured as a central category, already marks the end point of a development, and consequent idealist thinkers relegated taste to a minor position in their aesthetic writings. In Hegel this development comes to a conclusion, since for him the category of taste hardly matters at all.[33] Yet Nietzsche is adamant in reintroducing the notion of taste as a fundamental one for philosophy. Philosophy, he claims, does not succeed by argumentation but by changing the taste of its readers: "The change of the common taste is more important than opinions; opinions with all their demonstrations, refutations and all the intellectual masquerade are only symptoms of a changed taste and precisely not what one often takes them to be, namely its cause."[34] Philosophy moves along due to changes in taste, not due to better arguments (*Beyond Good and Evil*, §2). Hence, Nietzsche follows a double strategy: firstly by introducing taste back into aesthetics, secondly by making aesthetics fundamental for all philosophy.

However, it is questionable whether philosophy can remain standing on such a basis. Rather, it seems that Habermas is right when he argues that Nietzsche cannot legitimize his aesthetic principles, since he conceives of them as an alternative to and escape from a rationality that has become all-pervasive and burdensome. Yet like all radical critiques of rationalism, such a stance must lead to self-contradiction, since it cannot advance criteria by which to judge the alleged failure of rationality.[35] Furthermore, the coherence of aesthetic and moral values that was expressed as taste up until the eighteenth century depended on a largely unquestioned, commonly shared ideal of man and of social life that came to an end with the individualism of bourgeois society. Hence, Nietzsche's attempt to reestablish taste as a fundamental aesthetic category does not only remain vaguely defined and without argumentative backing; it also looks like an altogether futile project in the context of his individualistic philosophy that aims to erode all socially shared beliefs and desires.

Finally, the corollary to Nietzsche's aesthetization of anthropology is his anthropomorphic conception of beauty. "Nothing is beautiful, but only man is beautiful," he writes in *Twilight of the Idols*.[36] Yet unlike for Kant, man's beauty does not result from his exceptional status as the only moral being; for Nietzsche, any object that increases our sense of power or pleases any of our interests is beautiful: "Ultimately I only perceive as beautiful what corresponds to an ideal ("the happy person") of my own drives; for example wealth, splendor, piety, outflow of power, meekness can feel "beautiful" for different nations."[37] Such an anthropomorphic and interest-based definition of beauty, however, excludes all forms of beauty, notably among them the beauty of nature, that could offer man an encounter with something other than himself. Hence, Nietzsche's position is much more the expression of nineteenth-century scientism that revels in the domination over nature than the opposition against the positivistic and scientific spirit of the age that Nietzsche claims to advance in his writings.

There can be little doubt that Nietzsche's late aesthetic philosophy is the most ambitious expansion of aesthetics ever undertaken. Aesthetics becomes the *via regia* of philosophy, and nothing escapes the aesthetic revaluation. Yet while the central categories of Nietzsche's aesthetic thought – taste, beauty, aesthetics as physiology – claim to have shed the meanings they had acquired in previous aesthetic thought, their definition in Nietzsche's texts remains frustratingly vague. We can, therefore, detect a double movement in Nietzsche: On the one hand, he narrows down all philosophical inquiries to aesthetic questions; on the other hand, he broadens the field of aesthetics so as to be able to cover ontic, moral, epistemological, anthropological, and historical ground. Hence, what originally might look like the final liberation of aesthetics turns out to be the despotism of aesthetics that refuses to acknowledge any perspective other than its own. Nietzsche ultimately champions an aesthetics of terror that eliminates all nonaesthetic criteria in the discussion of moral and social philosophy and the inquiries into truth, being, and the good life.

Such radicalism naturally has to produce a backlash in the aesthetic discussion. It appears that it attacks Nietzsche's thought from two different angles. The first challenge is posed by those who argue that aesthetics must be brought back into narrow confines as one field of philosophical inquiry among many, and likely a minor one at that. They claim that aesthetics stands in need of precise definition and should be anchored within a scientific program of philosophy at large. This is the direction that the neo-Kantian school takes.

The other reaction against Nietzsche takes issue with his aesthetization of the self that it regards as paradigmatic for the failure of such aesthetic theory in general. An aesthetic philosophy that focuses on the self as a work of art eliminates the social dimension of art that was central to the idealist philosophy. If the self is regarded only as something to be created by the individual and not as something that at least partly precedes him or her, art can no longer grant man that joyous experience of understanding how through language and other symbolic expressions he is part of a larger whole. The other reaction against Nietzsche, therefore, emphasizes the social and historical role of art. While the neo-Kantian aesthetics goes back to Kant's scientific project of philosophy, this second reaction against Nietzsche's dissolution of the idealist paradigms resembles that of Schiller's sociohistorical aesthetics. We find it again in the writings of Georg Lukács.

PART III

RENEWING THE PARADIGMS

8

Cassirer, Lukács

Ernst Cassirer's neo-Kantianism

By and large, the neo-Kantian schools in Germany were not very interested in questions of aesthetics. Art and beauty mostly took second place to epistemology and ethics. Two notable exceptions are the Kant scholar Ernst Cassirer (1874–1945) and the young Georg Lukács (1885–1971), who also began his philosophical career under the influence of neo-Kantianism. Cassirer was, in fact, one of the founders of the *Kulturwissenschaftliche Bibliothek,* better known as the Warburg Institute, where he collaborated closely with the art historians and theoreticians Erwin Panofsky and Fritz Saxl during the years 1926–33. Still, despite a multivolume study on the philosophy of symbolic forms, Cassirer never presented a unified and fully developed theory of art. It is nevertheless possible to reconstruct his position based on a number of essays, lectures, and book chapters all dealing with the problems of aesthetics and its history. In this context, however, the main focus will be Cassirer's attempt to "rejuvenate" Kant's aesthetic theory, because after the challenge to the paradigmatic aesthetics of the idealists by Schopenhauer, Kierkegaard, and Nietzsche, we now return to precisely these paradigmatic positions.

Against the positivist notions of aesthetics that had been developed toward the end of the nineteenth century in the works of Helmholtz, Fechner, and others, who had attempted to reduce the sense for beauty and art to a physiological response, Cassirer stresses the uniqueness of the aesthetic experience as something that cannot be elucidated by scientific research. Cassirer returns to Kant in order to find a justification for the autonomy of art from science and morality. Yet this means consequently that science and morality cannot be reduced to aesthetic enterprises either, as Nietzsche had wanted it. Neither science nor art can subsume the other under itself, and the same holds true for morality. In his *Essay on Man,* the 1944 summary of his *Philosophie der symbolischen Formen* (Philosophy of symbolic forms) for an English audience, Cassirer writes in the chapter that deals with art: "The aesthetic experience – the experience of contemplation – is a different state of mind from the coolness of our theoretical and the sobriety of our moral judgement.... Science gives us order in thoughts; morality gives us order in actions; art gives us order in the apprehension of visible, tangible, and audible appearances."[1] The insistence on the autonomy of art, science, and morality, respectively, is the most important aspect of his philosophy that Cassirer owes to Kant. Yet unfortunately, this also means that he inherits Kant's problems that result from the separation of the notions of freedom and nature, beauty and morality: Both thinkers are at pains to reconnect the autonomous spheres to each other. Kant's failure to make this connection convincingly had given rise to one of the most exciting periods in the history of philosophy, namely, German idealism. And while the renewed interest in the aesthetic positions of the idealists in the twentieth century hardly depends on Cassirer's neo-Kantianism, the resulting philosophies of art very much resemble the paradigmatic reactions to Kant's *Critique of Judgment.*

The basis for Cassirer's philosophy is anthropological, namely, the idea that man is not so much the Aristotelian *animal rationale* but an *animal symbolicum.*[2]

> The ego, the individual mind, cannot create reality. Man is surrounded by a reality that he did not make, that he has to accept as an ultimate fact. But it is for him to interpret reality, to make it coherent, understandable, intelligible – and this task is performed in different ways in the various human activities, in religion and art, in science and philosophy. In all of them man proves to be not only the passive recipient of an external world; he is active and creative. But what he creates is not a new substantial thing; it is a representation, an objective description of the empirical world.[3]

Cassirer argues that art together with myth, religion, language, and science is a basic phenomenon of human life and culture; and with all these spheres art shares the nature of a symbolic expression of man. It would lead us too far astray in the present context to examine Cassirer's notion of the symbol; hence, it must suffice to state that for him symbols constitute human reality as the result of a process of inquiry into and discovery of new aspects of a preexisting reality. One of Cassirer's most important concerns in his aesthetic theory is, therefore, to establish an autonomous sphere of art by delineating it against myth, language, science, and morality and vice versa.

Cassirer argues that both language and science remove man from the immediacy of his lived experience and introduce a mediating symbolic sphere between man and reality. As much as this process of abstraction from the real is a necessary condition for scientific discovery and progress, as well as the basis for all linguistic communication, it inevitably leads to reduced vividness of life as well: "Language and science are abbreviations of reality; art is an intensification of reality. Language and science depend upon one and the same process of abstraction; art may be described as a continuous process of concentration."[4] Yet not only does art salvage the richness of life against linguistic and scientific impoverishment, it is also the necessary counterbalance to the scientific hubris claiming that reality is completely knowable and by extension controllable:

> It would seem as though reality were not only accessible to our scientific abstractions but exhaustible by them. But as soon as we approach the field of art this proves to be an illusion. For the aspects of things are innumerable, and they vary from one moment to another.... The revelation of this inexhaustability of the aspects of things is one of the great privileges and one of the deepest charms of art.[5]

Cassirer mobilizes Kant's notion of the *aesthetic idea* in order to limit not only the enterprise of scientific reason but also the possibilities of language. By pitching art against language, Cassirer demonstrates a conception of language that is closer to twentieth-century structuralism than to the tradition of Hamann, Herder, and Humboldt.[6] Their notion, on the other hand, was taken up by Nietzsche and revived in Heidegger, Gadamer, and others, who emphasize the creative and unscientific nature of language. (We will return to these positions of the latter thinkers in the next chapter.) But Cassirer, too, realizes that a radical opposition of language and art is unthinkable because it would disqualify plays, novels, and poetry from being art altogether, so in the end he allows for aesthetic speech to mediate between scientific objectivity and the intensity of personal experience. Yet Cassirer only hints at the uniqueness of such aesthetic language without stating explicitly how and why language can escape its abstract nature and incorporate the vividness of myth and art.

The autonomy of art also extends to morality. Cassirer argues against Plato and Tolstoy, both of whom had charged art with inciting passions that rational man is obliged to keep under control, by siding with Aristotle and his notion of catharsis. Instead of arousing unwanted emotions, Cassirer states, art helps to bring about the harmonious balance of the soul that the Greeks called *euthymia*. He argues that both Plato and Tolstoy forget that art is not a direct expression of pain, anger, jealousy, greed, lust, or rage but, rather, their representation in a new medium. This new medium, the work of art, is characterized by the predominance of form over content so that in it "all our feelings undergo a sort of transubstantiation with respect to their essence and their character. The passions themselves are relieved of their material burden. We feel their form and their life but not their encumbrance."[7] Cassirer goes on to state that art is less about single emotions like grief or anger than about "the dynamic process of life itself." The passions from which we might suffer in everyday life and which indeed might need to be controlled are liberated in art from their urgency and captivating power. The form of the artwork reigns over its content. Hence, art does not incite passions but supports the moral life by allowing us to live them vicariously. Just as Kant took pains to prove that some connection must exist between art and morality, Cassirer asserts that art's portrayed emotions lead to "an inner freedom which cannot be attained in any other way." Whereas Kant's notion of art as a symbol of the morally good restricts art to the beautiful, Cassirer's theory of art as a cleansing representation of imprudent, immodest, or immoral emotions also allows for the representation of the ugly as it manifests itself in violent, disgusting, or pornographic acts. Despite Cassirer's upholding of high culture, his aesthetics in this respect comes closer to the reality of art in the twentieth century than does that of Kant.

Still, for Cassirer, content ultimately has to take second place to form, and ugliness is only permissible as an element of content, not of form. Yet form is the more important aspect of art, and it is precisely the harmony of form that we call beauty. The beautiful form, however, is not a quality of the object but a "formative act" of the mind. Cassirer here renews Kant's attempt to shift aesthetics from the objective to the subjective pole. Although he acknowledges that beauty and pleasure depend on something objective, that is, the material existence of the artwork, its form first needs to be recognized as beautiful by the recipient. Hence, "beauty is not an immediate property of things" but the constitution of the form of the things in the mind of the reader, viewer, or listener. Such focus on the subjective side of the aesthetic experience, however, tends to bring in its wake a rather ahistorical conception of art that leaves out social factors and historical changes in the functions and forms of art. For Cassirer, these moments play almost as little a role as for Kant, and therefore, their absence opens his theory to the same charges that had been leveled against his precursor.

From this Kantian perspective, Cassirer also reads Plato's theory of artistic mimesis, thus bringing up one of the most discussed topics in twentieth-century aesthetics. In his essay "Eidos und Eidolon," Cassirer aims to revise the traditional reading of Plato's purported devaluation of the empirical world. Not only does the late Plato admit in his dialogue *Timaeus* that the world as the creation of a demiurg is an empirical manifestation of truth; beauty, characterized by proportion and right measure, also plays an essential role in this world because it mediates between art and truth. Hence, Plato's aesthetic thought is much more ambivalent than hitherto admitted and cannot be reduced to a paradigmatic criticism of mimesis understood in a naturalistic sense. Cassirer argues that Plato had not understood art to be a mere mirroring of nature, or at least he had not exclusively understood it this way. Therefore, Cassirer can find his own position anticipated in Plato: "Art is not a mere repetition of nature and life; it is a sort of transformation and transubstantiation. This transubstantiation is brought about by the power of aesthetic form."[8]

Interestingly enough, Cassirer again shies away from a concrete analysis of the transformative moment of art and resorts to religious language by using the metaphor of the Eucharist. While there is little reason to deny a connection of the religious and the aesthetic discourses, the metaphorical use of religious language cannot cover up Cassirer's main difficulty, namely, to reconnect the autonomous sphere of art back to man's other symbolic expressions. In fact, repeatedly, Cassirer finds himself arguing against the suspicion that the autonomy of art is identical to the position of *l'art pour l'art* that he rejects. In order to escape this association, he must demonstrate that some connection exists between the forms of art and the reality of everyday life. He does so by postulating art as a double reality of both autonomous forms *and* representation of reality: "Art is not a display and an enjoyment of empty forms. What we intuit in the medium of art and artistic forms is a double reality, the reality of nature and of human life. And every great work of art gives us a new approach to and a new interpretation of nature and life."[9] In the end, however, Cassirer merely gestures in the direction of a connection between reality and art, life and form. Yet his aesthetics ultimately fails to assign a place to the historical and social in connection with art. These, however, are the questions that Georg Lukács becomes most interested in when he leaves his early Kantianism behind, driven by the question of art's possibilities to help meliorate social reality.

The other question that emerges from the interconnection of art and reality is that of the truth of art. Cassirer claims that "art gives us a new kind of truth – a truth not of empirical things but of pure forms."[10] With this statement he echoes a fundamental position of the neo-Kantian theoretician of art and private collector Konrad Fiedler (1841–1895), whose theory of aesthetic vision as an enrichment of quotidian viewing patterns also influenced the young Lukács, Vasily Kandinsky, Paul Klee, and other aestheticians and artists. But unless Cassirer wants to resort to a Platonic understanding of pure forms and thus undercut his own position, he needs to supply an explanation of how the truth of pure forms relates to the truth of things. Yet on this issue Cassirer falls silent. Still, the question of the truth value of art is another constant element of the aesthetic discourse of the twentieth century. Even more than Lukács, however, it concerns Heidegger and Adorno.

Neo-Kantian aesthetics are thus challenged by Lukács from a sociohistorical position that takes up many of the charges that Schiller had leveled against Kant. The other challenge comes from Heidegger who, much like Schelling, insists on art as an organon of truth.

Neo-Marxism as neo-Schillerianism?

The history of aesthetics knows no neo-Schillerianism proper. Yet there are sufficient similarities in neo-Marxist aesthetic positions to suggest a historical parallel. Obviously, important differences exist as well, and to overlook them or gloss over them would mean to distort philosophical history. Schiller, despite his turn toward the realities of social and political history, stands firmly on idealist philosophical ground. Neo-Marxism, on the other hand, notwithstanding its more complex discussions of the base–superstructure relationship, regards dialectical and historical materialism as the historical successor of idealism. From this perspective, Schiller is frequently considered a mere intermediate step, albeit an important one, from the subjective idealism of Kant to the objective idealism of Hegel – and from there to Marx, Engels, and oftentimes Lenin (and in some cases, certainly in those of Ernst Bloch and Georg Lukács, also Stalin). While Schiller made it explicit that his notion of aesthetic education is meant to take place in lieu of revolution, the neo-Marxist aestheticians want both: art *and* revolution. Therefore, Lukács credits Schiller for being the first to attempt to discover the dialectics of history and aesthetics, yet still faults him for ending up in the apologetic camp of bourgeois culture due to his decrying of revolutionary activity.[11]

Likewise, Schiller's conclusion that art always remains separated from reality and that man's reconciliation with himself only happens in the aesthetic sphere has been interpreted differently. While in this case the moderate and bourgeois interpreters were the ones to charge Schiller with quietism and aestheticism, Marxist thinkers took him to state that art always remains unreconciled with reality and, hence, harbors the potential both to negate the existing reality and to advocate a better one. Still, there are more similarities to be found. Despite different suggested solutions, both Schiller and Lukács are concerned with a similar problem, namely, how to reconcile the autonomy of art with its practical role in the the process of social melioration. In other words, both wonder how art can facilitate the establishment of a utopian republic of free men without being reduced to a mere tool for political purposes.

Schiller's new paradigm in aesthetics, the combination of formal and historical moments (i.e., of a theory of human drives and one of aesthetic education), also provides the basis of Lukács's neo-Marxist aesthetics. With Schiller, Lukács shares the humanist ideal of man as free, unalienated, and completely developed.[12] Art, then, is seen by both as the reservoir of the vision of uncorrupted and unalienated humanity, and it is hailed for its potential to tap into the anthropological substance and to serve as a reminder that man has not yet reached his telos.[13] These similarities will become more evident after the discussion of Lukács's aesthetic theory; for the moment, it shall suffice to point out the historical pattern according to which a Schillerian paradigm is taken up in response to neo-Kantian aesthetics. Before we turn to the Marxist writings of Lukács, however, we shall briefly examine his development as a philosopher from neo-Kantianism to a historical and materialist dialectics.

Georg Lukács (1885–1971) wrote a large number of articles and books dealing with aesthetics in general. Starting with his earliest works, art, especially literature, stood at the center of his interest. In 1908 he published a history of modern drama, thought by some to be his best book ever, followed in 1911 by the collection of essays *Die Seele und die Formen* (Soul and forms) that appeared first in Hungarian and was soon after translated into German, the principle language of his writings, by Lukács himself. During the years 1912 to 1914, Lukács wrote down his first attempt at a systematic aesthetics, the *Philosophie der Kunst* (Philosophy of art), which was never finished and also not published until very late in the author's life. This was followed in 1916–18 by the so-called *Heidelberger Ästhetik,* equally unfinished and long unpublished. Then came the still much-read *Theorie des Romans* (Theory of the novel, 1916–20); *Es geht um den Realismus* (Realism is at stake, 1936); *Beiträge zur Geschichte der Ästhetik* (Contributions to the history of aesthetics, 1954); *Kunst und objektive Wahrheit* (Art and objective truth, 1954); *Über die Besonderheit als Kategorie des Ästhetischen* (On typicality as a category of aesthetics, 1957); *Wider den missverstandenen Realismus* (Against misunderstood realism, 1958); and the voluminous *Die Eigenart des Ästhetischen* (The quality of the aesthetic, 1963), the first of three conceived parts of what was meant to be Lukács's final and systematic word on aesthetics. This list is only a selection and excludes a fair number of books primarily on the subject of literature.[14]

The work of the early Lukács, that is, the books and articles before his conversion to communism in 1918 that led to his becoming a member in the Communist Party of Hungry in the same year, share the attitude of what Lukács himself later critically called "romantic anticapitalism." The essays of *Soul and Forms* and the chapters of the *Heidelberg Aesthetics* display influences from several thinkers, either teachers of the young Lukács or historical ideals. To the latter group belongs Kierkegaard, whom Lukács rediscovers for the twentieth century even before Heidegger, and with whom he shares the repulsion for the commercialized bourgeois life and the consequent search for an authentic existence. Max Weber, on the other hand, was a personal friend with whose diagnosis of the modern world as disenchanted Lukács agrees. Then there was Georg Simmel, also a teacher of Lukács, whose opposition of *life* as something heterogenous, unorderly, and almost anarchic and *form* as homogeneity and law was to inform the basic opposition of *Soul and Forms.*[15]

Just like Schiller, Lukács begins his aesthetic considerations with a diagnosis of contemporary culture at large. Better than in the essays of *Soul and Form* itself, this position is worked out in his article "Ästhetische Kultur" (Aesthetic culture) of 1912. In keeping with the vitalist convictions of his time, Lukács defines culture as "unity of life; force of the unity that enhances life, enriches life."[16] Yet in the present age, this culture has only managed to produce the type of the expert who administers life without even thinking about its contents and the aesthete who withdraws into himself – a distinction that goes back to Max Weber and that in one form or the other becomes a staple in the critique of the process of the modernization of society, from Adorno and Horkheimer to MacIntyre's *After Virtue.* Lukács echoes Kierkegaard when he claims that aesthetic culture is based on mood, that is, the arbitrary and nonrational relation between subject and object, and that hence, nothing can transcend the moment: The individual remains locked in his solitary moods. To reduce all objects to mere incitements for moods, however, prevents all true life of the soul. Both the soul and art must presuppose the independence of the object that resists the effort to turn it into a mood maker and forces a struggle upon the subject. Both the form of the soul and the form of great art then result from this struggle with the object, and only this self-formation, coupled with true artistic form, will allow for the overcoming of isolation. Contemporary culture, however, has not only produced alienated man but also reduced art, one of the few means of rescue, to trivial entertainment. Still, Lukács is not willing to give up on his ideal of unalienated, fraternal life, even if he considers present culture as unable to provide a home for the meaningful art of the past. Yet there is a glimmer of hope that precisely this past art will prove to be the storage for those forces that enable man to overcome his present alienation.[17]

While Lukács's first attempt at a systematic aesthetics aims to fuse vitalism with a Kantian aesthetic subjectivism, his *Heidelberg Aesthetics* of four years later has shed the vitalist elements and even takes a turn from Kant to Hegel. After leaving his Hegelian stage of *Theory of the Novel* behind, Lukács develops a Marxist aesthetics in the thirties and forties, primarily through his readings of nineteenth-century literary realism. Yet Hegel, more than any other idealist philosopher, nevertheless remains his constant point of reference in future ventures into aesthetics.

The Quality of the Aesthetic

Lukács's numerous volumes on art are written mostly from a Marxist-Leninist perspective. Some of these are of greater clarity and perceptiveness of the artistic object than the 1963 *Aesthetics*; others are still more dogmatic, including apologetic misjudgments of Stalin's contributions to linguistics and, by extension, to aesthetics that border on the ridiculous.[18] The late aesthetics itself is lengthy and repetitious[19] and, moreover, fails to offer the systematic coherence at which it is aimed.[20] Instead of a unified whole, we are confronted with loosely connected detailed discussions of central categories of Lukács's aesthetic theory, many of which had been developed more than thirty years before. Other central concepts had already made their appearance in the *Heidelberg Aesthetics,* yet of course had to be reinterpreted in a Marxist light. Still, the reason to turn to the 1963 *Aesthetics* is that the volume presents something of a *summa,* a last and final word on the matter of aesthetics that had been central to Lukács's thought throughout his life and political activity.

The 1963 *Aesthetics,* despite its length of roughly two thousand pages, remains unfinished. It presents only the first of three intended parts. The conceived but never-written sections were meant to deal with the structure of the work of art (Part 2) and the social history of art (Part 3).[21] Part 1, then, titled *Die Eigenart des Ästhetischen* (The quality of the aesthetic), examines art as a genuine form of the representation of reality.

Before we begin to discuss Lukács's work, a brief recapitulation of the basic theses of orthodox Marxist aesthetics, to which Lukács more or less subscribes, will help to provide a context for the discussion. A brief yet precise summary of this position can be found in Marcuse's *The Aesthetic Dimension:*

1. There is a definite connection between art and the material base, between art and the totality of the relations of production. With the change in production relations, art itself is transformed as part of the superstructure, although, like other ideologies, it can lag behind or anticipate social changes.
2. There is a definite connection between art and social class. The only authentic, true, progressive art is the art of an ascending class. It expresses the consciousness of this class.
3. Consequently, the political and the aesthetic, the revolutionary content and the artistic quality tend to coincide.
4. The writer has an obligation to articulate and express the interests and needs of the ascending class. (In capitalism, this would be the proletariat.)
5. A declining class or its representatives are unable to produce anything but "decadent" art.
6. Realism (in various senses) is considered as the art form which corresponds most adequately to the social relationships, and thus is the "correct" art form.[22]

Lukács's central concern is to develop a theory of art as mimesis.[23] His first task in this endeavor is to delineate artistic mimesis against scientific mimesis, because both art and science deal with the same objective reality and both reflect this reality cognitively. Yet whereas science must cleanse all subjective moments from its study of the object, this does not hold true for art. Lukács calls scientific mimesis "desanthropomorphizing" and explains that in science "appearance and essence must be neatly separated," while in art an "obvious sensual inseparability of appearance and essence" prevails (II, 174).[24] Furthermore, this means that in science the universal must rule over the individual, yet in art, Lukács argues with Aristotle, "aesthetic mimesis presents humanity always in the form of individuals and of individual fates" (I, 155). Yet not every particular can stand in for the universal, as Lukács emphasizes in his discussion of the category of *Besonderheit* (typicality). While the particular remains an isolated individual, the typical represents a unity of individual and universal (III, 175). Art can, therefore, portray objective historical tendencies in the typical.

Neither can it achieve the generality of science nor must it remain tied to the mere likings, fancies, and preferences with which we respond to particulars. Only the typical fulfills art's social calling: "The mimesis of society's metabolism [*Stoffwechsel*] with nature is the final, truly ultimate object of aesthetic mimesis" (I, 144).

Mimesis must not be understood as a photocopy of reality, but for Lukács it is based on a selection of features of reality, as well as on a positive or negative evaluation of the objects it portrays. This attitude constitutes one of the principles of socialist realism in art and is generally called *Parteilichkeit* (partisanship) (I, 155).[25] Moreover, selection also refers to the fact that mimesis does not merely reproduce reality; it aims to improve upon it by presenting it as adequate to man through the elimination of reality's alien and careless aspects. Art, therefore, is an autonomous reality that was selected, appraised, and formed. The difference between a mechanical copying and a realistic mimesis is all-important in art: The former is naturalistic and apologetic, the latter realistic and critical. Whereas naturalist art "fetishizes" the brute facts, realistic art is based on an analysis of their historical function. Naturalist art never penetrates the surface of reality and, hence, lacks a central requirement of all art, namely, the union of essence and appearance. Only realism in art overcomes the particular and presents the typical. As we will see shortly, precisely this privileged access to reality that Lukács reserves for realist art poses a problem that undermines the very foundation of his aesthetic theory. Before we discuss this point, we must examine the achievements that Lukács attributes to his conception of mimesis.

In the work of art, man beholds himself as the creator of an autonomous world, thus merging the experiences of self and world. Yet while man's everyday experience thus far has always been one of alienation, that is, a situation in which the products of man's labor are experienced by himself as something foreign, in the experience of art alienation is overcome. Art, in essence, is therefore a higher, more conscious form of labor. The product of labor in capitalist societies remains alienated from the laborer because he doesn't control and comprehend the process of production, nor does he profit from the surplus that his labor has added to the raw material. Art, on the other hand, allows the subject to undergo the necessary alienation without which no progress in self-awareness can be achieved, as Hegel demonstrated in the *Phenomenology of Spirit,* as well as the sublation [*Aufhebung*] of the alienation.

The experience of art nevertheless does not remain isolated from everyday life. Instead, Lukács conceives of a dialectical relation of aesthetic and quotidian experiences. The mimetic work of art incites both a cognitive and emotional change in the beholder, so that a hitherto unknown aspect of reality becomes cognizable. As we will see in Lukács's discussion of the notion of catharsis, the aspect of art that changes patterns of everyday life also has an emotional side to it. Taking up a distinction that he had already developed in his *Heidelberg Aesthetics,* Lukács describes the transformation that the recipient undergoes vis-à-vis a work of art as one from complete man [*der ganze Mensch*] to whole man [*der Mensch ganz*]. The artwork

> breaks into the life of the soul of the recipient, subjugates his ordinary way of looking at the world, forces a new "world" upon him, fills him with new or newly perceived contents, and precisely all this causes him to absorb this "world" with renewed, with rejuvenated sense organs and modes of cognition. The transformation of complete man into whole man gives rise to a factual and formal, actual and potential broadening and enriching of his psyche. (III, 10)

Yet in order for art to achieve these transformations in the beholder, it must be both a container of the past and a guide to the future. Man overcomes his alienation from humanity's past in the work of art, just as he overcomes self-alienation. Art is the reservoir of mankind's history, as Lukács echoes Schiller, but the artwork does not only contain the sociohistorical determinants of the time of its origin. Great art is also characterized by the "inseparability of its historical nature and its fulfillment of the aesthetic norm that holds for all mankind" (II, 34). Lukács, however, makes no attempt to deduce this transhistorical aesthetic norm, and we can assume that he would be hard put to square this notion with a thoroughly materialist aesthetics. The corollary of the transhistorical moment in the artwork is his concept of an anthropological essence that responds to art and that we will encounter as an argument in Lukács's attack on modernism. For the moment, suffice it to say that Lukács insists on the fact that art's vision of man as a fully developed human being is nothing transcendent but, rather, the necessary reflection of historical teleology, "the reflection of the true existence, of the true development of mankind" (III, 17).

The way to achieve progress by means of art is precisely through art's effects on everyday life that consist in a changed emotional and cognitive attitude. To analyze the process of such change, Lukács refers back to Aristotle's theory of catharsis that he reads through the eyes of Lessing. Catharsis is not merely an emotional upheaval with which the spectator responds to the plight of the hero in tragedy but, rather, a unified response of the whole man to great works of art in general. For Lukács, a restriction of catharsis to the emotional level, as cleansing as it might be, carries the danger of isolating it from our ethos, the habitual behavior that governs most of our actions. In short, he fears that emotional cleansing could occur without any moral consequences. Against this conception of catharsis he pitches the one he finds prefigured in Lessing's *Hamburgische Dramaturgie,* and repeatedly he quotes Lessing's definition of catharsis as a "transformation of the passions into virtuous skills [*tugendhafte Fertigkeiten*]." To base the cathartic effect solely on emotional responses means to degrade great art to the status of entertainment. But true catharsis presupposes an ethical renewal based on insight. Such a cathartic event is one "that forces the complete man of everyday life to a true conversion [*Umkehr*] by means of a rational upheaval" (III, 28). Thus, a cycle of cathartic aesthetic experiences and quotidian life exists, because the catharsis results in a change of interests in man that, in turn, leads to the seeking out of different – presumably worthier and more challenging – works of art: "So much is for sure, that man's approaches to art are never of a disinterested nature. The entire field of aesthetic reception is shot through completely with human interests" (III, 150). Without making it explicit, Lukács here takes up Schiller's notion of aesthetic education. Man's tastes and insights into reality change due to encounters with artworks.

Such aesthetic transformative power, however, Lukács grants only to works of art. While he admits that beauty exists in nature as well – yet without working out a theory of beauty – he argues against any relevant aesthetic experience that would originate in nature. In fact, for Lukács, the beauty of nature is not an aesthetic phenomenon at all, because it fails to rise to the level of typicality where it could present a unity of the particular and the universal. The beauty of nature never transcends the particular (III, 79). Much like the erotic experience of beauty, although without the desire that for Lukács generally accompanies the former, the encounter with natural beauty is merely pleasurable, but it lacks all cognitive moments that in art are supplied by a notion of totality.

A similar argument is advanced when Lukács takes modernist art to task, as he does in the so-called expressionism debate and on numerous other occasions. This, however, is not the place to recapitulate this debate in detail in which Lukács, together with such writers as Johannes R. Becher (later to become secretary of culture in the German Democratic Republic), argued against Bertolt Brecht, Walter Benjamin, and Ernst Bloch. Suffice it to say that Lukács charged the expressionist movement in art for having apologetic and decadent underpinnings. We must take note in this context that Lukács tends to collapse the terms modernism, decadence, and avant-garde into each other and uses these terms more or less synonymously to refer to movements like naturalism, symbolism, and expressionism. From a historical point of view, this is hardly correct, since the one encompassing notion is modernism, under which rubric decadence, symbolism, naturalism, expressionism, and so forth are grouped. However, those writers that Lukács hails as the true avant-garde, such as Thomas Mann and Maxim Gorki, are also part of the modernist movement in literature.

Yet more important than this quarrel about classifications in literary history is the fact that Lukács attempts to redefine the meaning of both realism and avant-garde. For him, realism is neither a literary style nor a period (like the second half of the nineteenth century) but an artistic practice that shows the "objective social totality," whereas modernist literature "takes reality to be as it appears immediately to the writer."[26] If realism presents an objective view of reality as a totality, modernist forms of art necessarily remain tied to the particular perspectives of the artists. Yet to turn away from art's responsibility for presenting an image of totality means nothing less than to fall into decadence. The particular never reaches the typical and is far from all universality that is meant to appear in it. Hence, all that modernist writers like Proust, Kafka, Beckett, or Joyce, to name but a few, can achieve is to present an aesthetically interesting form without granting any insight into the objective forces of history. Art, Lukács insists, must not only present the negative, fallen, and degenerate but also contain images of the worthy and noble, because against all social distortions these positive images tap into the anthropological substance of man where they are meant to keep awake the longing for an unalienated life.[27] Consequently, only this type of literature deserves to be called avant-garde.

This dismissal of almost all modernist art as merely decadent and devoid of true insight can certainly not hold up to scrutiny. One of the most convincing criticisms of Lukács's notion of realism was put forward by Adorno in his essay "Erpresste Versöhnung" (Reconciliation under duress). Therein, Adorno demonstrates convincingly that Lukács's understanding of modernist literature is limited, misguided, and often self-contradictory. And while it is true that Lukács values content over form, he does not, as his ontology of art shows, remain blind toward the formal aspect of aesthetic creation. Hence, Adorno is wrong to make the general claim that Lukács "refuses to acknowledge the central relevance of literary technique."[28] But he is all the more right to argue that Lukács's advocacy of socialist realism in literature amounts to a defense of oftentimes mediocre writing (the repeated applauding of Makarenko in the *Aesthetics* is just one such case) and to an equally distasteful apology for the Soviet Republic. Socialism has not achieved social reconciliation, yet to expect its literature to say so is indeed to propose and defend a reconciliation under duress.

Lukács's ontology of art, from his early essays to the 1963 *Aesthetics*, concentrates on the question of form. Without being able to trace the development of this idea, discussed in the *Aesthetics* under the headings of rhythm, geometry, proportion, and ornament, at least the main criterion for artistic form must be pointed out. The form of the work of art unites artist and recipient because form is composition that guides the reception. In aesthetic encounters, we are not free vis-à-vis the object, but we are led along a path that the artwork has mapped out for us. We can fail to understand this formal law of reception, yet such failure means not to comprehend the work in question at all. Guiding composition is an objective fact, not a suggestion. Hence, the recipient must give himself over to the "ordering, systematizing force of the work" (II, 216). It follows that there is only one truly adequate response to the work of art, namely, that which comprehends the objective form of the work in the process of its reception. While the ideal of perfect comprehension might have to remain an approximation, its postulation nevertheless entails that Lukács give up on Kant's *aesthetic idea*. For Lukács, it is not an essential element of the artwork that it can never be reached by an adequate description or interpretation and that it always invites an infinite number of such attempts. For him, art can basically be fully cognized, since its form is an objective moment of the work. As will become apparent, this position gets dangerously close to making art superfluous, a mere detour through the senses and the effects of beauty to a goal that could perceivably also be reached on the straight road of theory.

In his discussion of the epistemological function of the work of art, Lukács states that the realist artwork presents the essence of reality to the recipient. Realist art, unlike naturalist creations, cuts through the surface of reality and lays bare the organizing principles of the historical situation of the work of art, that is, the distribution of the means of production, society's more or less advanced stage of interchange with nature, and so on. Yet a problem emerges out of such conception of mimesis:[29] If we want to distinguish good realist from bad naturalist art, we must presuppose another cognitive instance that can distinguish the correct representation of the essence of reality from the incorrect representations. For Lukács, this ability results from the application of Marxist-Leninist theory, especially its moment of historical materialism. But if such a theory is capable of uncovering the historical and present truths of reality, what function other than the illustration of a theoretically gained insight could art possibly have? Lukács's theory knows of a privileged access to reality, yet this access is not artistic but theoretical. He seems forced to think of art either as an ornamental repetition of that truth that materialist theory had already provided or as secularized *biblia pauperum* (a bible for the spiritually poor) for those not educated enough to grasp the objective historical truth without visual aids. Neither position seems to do justice to the complexities of art, to which Lukács's lifelong fascination with this subject also attests.

In order to avoid such reductive tendencies in the theory of art, both Heidegger and Adorno resort to a Schellingian conception that attributes a truth value to art that cannot be had philosophically. Art again becomes the only "organon of truth," unrivaled by any theory that claims privileged access to reality. These positions and the problems that emerge from them will concern us in the next chapters.

Herbert Marcuse

In some respects, Herbert Marcuse (1898–1979) is even closer to Schiller than is Lukács. Yet unlike the latter, he never aimed at a systematic aesthetic theory, although aesthetic thought is very much at the center of his philosophical endeavors. More a philosophical essayist like Montaigne or Pascal, he sketches his ideas lightly, and the precise relation between individual elements of these thoughts on aesthetics is not always clear. Yet like Schiller, Marcuse basically struggles all his life to merge a theory of drives – in his case, not taken from Fichte but from Freud – and a classical notion of the work of art. And much like Schiller, Marcuse also finds that these two moments don't square easily, so at different stages of his development, one tends to take precedence over the other. Another way of describing the two meanings of "aesthetics" in Marcuse is as a new sensibility or a new libidinal reality principle, on the one hand, and the idealist conception of the artwork as a totality, on the other. Neither notion ever wins the upper hand for long, so that commentators who focus on only one aspect generally end up with a distorted picture.[30] To rephrase aesthetics as a concept of sensibility is yet another attempt to go back beyond Kant to Baumgarten. But for Marcuse, this aesthetic sensibility has less a cognitive than a libidinal function, dreaming up "images of a life without fear"[31] and of a nonrepressive society.

Earlier stages of Marcuse's aesthetic thought stress the sensitive aspect of aesthetics more, but they give way to an emphasis on the artwork in later writings. Marcuse goes through a brief phase during which he dismisses all traditional art as affirmative of a repressive society and as a false reconciliation in the realm of illusion. Art is seen in opposition to life and is faulted for the political passivity it produces in the individual: "But the achievement [of art] is illusory, false, fictitious: it remains within the dimension of art, a work of art; in reality, fear and frustration go on unabated (as they do, after the brief *katharsis*, in the psyche)."[32] During Marcuse's most intensive involvement with the student rebellion of the late 1960s and its attempts to develop forms of antiart as a continuation of the avant-garde call from the beginning of the century to merge art and life, he no longer believed that the artwork was a negotiation between pleasure principle and reality principle, as Freud had described it. Instead, he argued that the traditional artwork had been entirely co-opted by a falsely permissive society and, hence, had to be replaced by artistic acts capable of liberating the last reserves of libidinal energy capable of resisting the present society: "The disorderly, uncivil, farcical, artistic desublimation of culture constitutes an essential element of radical politics: of the subverting forces in transition."[33] But a few years later, Marcuse has already returned to a notion of the work of art as the actual site of the aesthetic, claiming that radical antiart must fail, because by trying to bridge the gap to reality it loses its power to negate precisely this reality.[34] Yet it is the *negative* moment of art that makes it an indispensable tool in the struggle for political liberation.

Marcuse claims that the advanced capitalist society has managed to ban the authoritative father figure and has instituted a regime of false permissiveness and "repressive tolerance." Where everything is allowed, but nothing matters and makes a difference, art is the last resort of the negative that is directed against the status quo: "In this sense, every authentic work of art would be revolutionary, i.e., subversive of perception and understanding, an indictment of the established reality, the appearance of the image of liberation."[35] These negating moments of art Marcuse also locates in works and periods of art that are labeled "decadent" by the aesthetics of socialist realism. Marcuse praises such works as Baudelaire's *Les Fleur du Mal,* with their celebration of evil as value-neutral aesthetic achievements, not for their own sake but because these poems liberate energies that can be directed against the present reality. In opposition to Lukács, for whom such literature was the final artistic expression of a dying social class, Marcuse regards it as a reservoir of libidinal energies useful for purposes of rebellion.

After Marcuse faces up to the failure of antiart as a political tool, he again locates the potential for change in the classical artwork: "Art cannot change the world, but it can contribute to changing the consciousness and drives of the men and women who could change the world."[36] Whereas Schiller, Fichte, and Freud all argue for a transhistorical nature of man's drives, Marcuse here develops the notion that art can influence the instinctual or libidinal makeup of a person. This idea still allows him to consider aesthetics as a matter both of sensibility and of art. Yet as far as art is concerned, Marcuse has reached the conclusion that only "great art" will serve as a means to achieve these changes. Much like Lukács, Marcuse thus ends up with a notion of a "transhistorical substance of art."[37] Against Lukács, however, he insists that art can never expose the basic socioeconomic structure and dynamic of a society, because only a scientific analysis can fulfill this task. Like Adorno, Marcuse holds that the traditional work of art with its emphasis on beauty contains energies of resistance: "The Beautiful belongs to the imagery of liberation."[38] But even after liberation from repression has been achieved, art will not disappear for Marcuse, because "socialism does not and cannot liberate Eros from Thanatos."[39] In other words, art remains unreconciled with *all* reality, even that of a utopia, because no reality, no matter how free from fear and how unrepressed, can overcome death. Only in art can Eros triumph over Thanatos. So it is death that assures the immortality of art and teaches us that in art "beauty returns, the 'soul' returns."[40] Such language reminds us of the young Lukács, who could have used this phrase in one of the essays of *Soul and Form.* While Lukács himself felt compelled to revoke his early writings, obviously other Marxist thinkers found useful notions in them.

Taking into consideration only the dates of the publication of central works in the twentieth-century German aesthetic tradition, one might conclude that hardly any progression from one philosophical position to another is made. Instead, it might seem as if a more or less random simultaneity of revivals or paradigms governs aesthetics after Nietzsche and the positivists. Cassirer's neo-Kantian *Essay on Man* appears in 1944; Heidegger's renewal of Schelling in 1936; Adorno's appropriation of Schelling in 1970; Lukács's Schillerian *Aesthetics* in 1963; Marcuse's essays on art around the same time. Kant would be preceded by Schelling, who in turn would be followed by Schiller. Still, these dates suggest a chronological disorder that is deceptive. If we take into account when the thoughts contained in the published works were first developed by their authors, a more well-structured narrative emerges. Cassirer developed his neo-Kantian aesthetics in the 1920s, while Lukács only returned to questions of art and the Schillerian social aspects of it in the early 1930s. Next came Heidegger's neoromantic position, followed by Adorno's rereading of Schelling. Hence, despite some overlaps, repetitions – Marcuse is a point in question – and minor irregularities, the aesthetics of the twentieth century remains strikingly close to the order of paradigmatic positions as they were developed by Kant, Schiller, Schelling, and Hegel. From the resurrection of the Kantian and Schillerian paradigms, we must now turn to the first attempt to establish a new version of Schelling's aesthetics.

9

Heidegger, Gadamer

Martin Heidegger

Martin Heidegger's (1889–1976) writings on art renew the romantic paradigm in the philosophy of art for the twentieth century. Despite all his criticism of the idealist tradition, Heidegger insists with Schelling on art as a *Wahrheitsgeschehen,* a truth-event, that is, an occasion when truth becomes conspicuous. Still, Heidegger differs from his romantic precursor in that he does not elevate art to that height where it becomes the *only* access to truth. Rather, he allows for some few alternative events in which truth reveals itself as well. Nevertheless, Heidegger agrees with Schelling insofar as both thinkers place art as an "organon of truth" *above* the propositional correctness of science and, hence, some versions of philosophy.

Heidegger begins to write about art in the 1930s. He deals with this subject in his lectures on Hölderlin and Nietzsche of the 1930s and 1940s; in 1935 he gives the lecture *"Der Ursprung des Kunstwerks"* (The origin of the work of art) in Freiburg and repeats it the following year in Zurich and Frankfurt am Main. Although this text was the most probing and systematic of his pronouncements on art, it was not published until 1950 when it appeared as the opening essay of the book *Holzwege* (Paths in the wood). In 1951 the essay *"Bauen Wohnen Denken"* (Building dwelling thinking) followed, in 1969 *"Die Kunst und der Raum"* (Art and space). A good number of essays on poetry, especially on the works of Hölderlin, Rilke, and Stefan George, as well as on the visual arts which become more important for Heidegger in the 1950s and 1960s, round out the picture.[1]

Heidegger's gesture in all his writings on art is to repudiate philosophical aesthetics. He draws the line between himself and almost all of the Western tradition of philosophy of art, especially the classical German tradition in the wake of Baumgarten and Kant. Just as Heidegger thinks of the history of philosophy after the pre-Socratics as one of *Seinsvergessenheit* (forgetfulness of being), he narrates the story of the philosophy of art as one that never came into its own. In his lectures on Nietzsche, Heidegger distinguishes six phases in the relation of philosophy and art.[2] The first phase covers the centuries of great art in ancient Greece, presumably from Homer to Euripides, and is characterized by the absence of all philosophical reflection on art. (Heidegger neglects here the pre-Socratic philosophical opposition against the poets.) For Heidegger, the philosophy of art only begins after the decline of great art and philosophy in Greece. From its inception, this philosophy sets out on the wrong track by transposing the *hyle-morphe* distinction, that is, that between matter and form, from the sphere of the production of tools to that of art. He will return to this point in his lecture on the origin of the artwork. The beginning of the modern era marks the third phase in which taste, defined as man's individualistic relationship to his surroundings, becomes the measure of all that exists. Beauty is only discussed in reference to the subject, as his perception, that is, as *aisthesis.* Heidegger argues that great art discloses "the unconditional, absolute" (83), but that in the modern age, art loses its function to represent the absolute. That is why the high point of philosophical aesthetics – phase four – namely, the age of classical German philosophy, coincides with the end of all great art. The greatness of philosophical aesthetics in Germany results from its ability to think through this end of art, as we read it most convincingly in Hegel's system. Phase five happens when the nineteenth century, above all Richard Wagner, attempts to turn art into an absolute necessity once more, but effects only art's dissolution into mere emotionality and ultimately into nothingness. While the emotional intoxication is meant to compensate for sterile and technical human existence, it fails to provide orientation for great poetry and thought. It is Nietzsche who concludes this development in the sixth and final phase by transforming aesthetics into physiology through the conception of emotional intoxication as a phenomenon of nerves and physico-electrical responses. Here, philosophical thought on art comes to an end and is consequently in need of a new beginning – by Heidegger himself.

The problematic aspect of this narrative is not so much its one-sidedness and its resulting historical inaccuracy. More problematic is that Heidegger's claim for a fresh start glosses over his affinities for the idealist tradition, especially Schelling. Some important differences notwithstanding, Heidegger is the first thinker of the twentieth century to renew Schelling's elevation of art to the most important means of cognition, yet Heidegger constistently refuses to acknowledge this debt.

Heidegger's most important contribution to the philosophy of art, the essay *The Origin of the Work of Art,* again repudiates the entirety of the philosophical tradition and then suggests a better solution to the problem in question. This means, briefly stated, that Heidegger replaces the ontological approach to art with an epistemological approach. This is a change that we must explore in some detail. We can already note, however, that the ontological dimension of art is nevertheless not only retained but also understood from this new perspective.[3]

Heidegger's opening meditations in *The Origin of the Work of Art* follow the structure of the Scholastic ontology, according to which an object is defined by reference to its *genus,* the class of object to which the individual object belongs (i.e., the work of art being a thing as in opposition to an animal or a god), and its *differtia specifica,* the unique moment that differentiates the type from the species of which it is a subgroup (i.e., the work of art being a different thing than a rock or a hammer). An artwork, Heidegger explains, is a thing. This is its *genus:* "Works of art exist as naturally as other things too" (9).[4] Hence, we must first ask what a thing is. But when asking this question, we must always keep in mind that not everything that exists is a thing: "man is no thing," neither is God (12). Therefore, we must also inquire why and how an artwork differs from other objects; that is, we must find the *differentia specifica.* This differentiation between the thing and that which exists but is no thing will be of importance for Heidegger's critique of the traditional conceptions of thingness.[5]

Heidegger distinguishes between three traditional conceptions of thingness. The first is the oldest and has determined the ontology of our grammar. When we think of propositions as the attribution of predicates to grammatical subjects, we think of grammar as a reflection of that concept of a thing that defines it as a substance plus its attributes. Yet this ontology of *sustantia* and *accidens* is too broad to be useful for the definition of a thing, because it refers not only to things but to everything that exists: "With its help we can never delineate the thing against that which exists but is not a thing" (16).

The second concept is that of the thing as an *aistheton,* that is, as the unity of a sensual manifold. A thing would then be defined as the sum of all its properties that we can perceive, that is, see, hear, smell, taste, or touch. Yet Heidegger argues that this notion is counterintuitive. In our experience of things, we do not distinguish between a sensual perception and its material carrier. We do not hear a noise in order to determine in a separate mental process that we hear an airplane. We do not taste first something sweet in order to decide next that we are eating chocolate. Rather, to separate sensual perception from the perceived object, we must distance ourselves from our quotidian experience. Such insight is always the result of an abstraction. The fact is, then, that the things themselves are closer to us than our perceptions. The thingness of a thing precedes the conscious perception of its sensual properties.

Finally, Heidegger discusses that concept of thingness that forms the basis of all aesthetic theory, namely, the notion of the thing as formed matter. Yet this differentiation of form, *morphe,* and matter, *hyle,* suffers from the same flaw as the first conception of thingness. It does not allow for a distinction between that which exists as a thing and that which does not exist as a thing, because it can be applied to pretty much anything, including man and God, two beings that are not things. Hence, all three concepts of thingness that traditional ontologies supply are not sufficient to grasp the nature of the thing. We still do not know what the thing is: "The unobtrusive thing withholds itself most stubbornly from thought" (25). The question regarding the *genus* of the work of art has therefore failed already. Without the *genus* of an object, however, the inquiry into its *differentia specifica* is impossible. Must the ontological approach to the artwork therefore be aborted altogether? Heidegger is not willing to do so because this would eliminate ontology from the discussion of art for good. But his intention, as we will see, is to reverse the order of questioning.

Instead of basing an aesthetics on an ontology, he aims to discover the thingness of things as a result of the experience of art. Ontology does not precede aesthetics; it follows it.

Instead of abandoning the ontological question, Heidegger suggests that we might learn more about the thing when we limit our discussion to those objects that we ourselves have produced. Already in *Sein und Zeit* (Being and time, 1927), he had discussed this class of things under the rubric of *Zeug,* tools.[6] A tool, however, is characterized by its unobtrusiveness, the fact that it disappears behind its use. We do not pay attention to the hammer when we hang a picture. If we do so, hitting the nail will be much harder or impossible because our intention is not directed toward the task but toward the means to accomplish it. Similarly, we only notice our shoes when they are uncomfortable, that is, flawed tools. Otherwise, these shoes only serve as tools to make our walking more efficient. So how can we ask what the nature of the tool is if we already know that "the toolness of the tool consists in its usefulness [*Dienlichkeit*]" (26)? For Heidegger, art provides an answer to this question. Only in the work of art can we learn what the nature of the tool is because here it sheds its hiddenness: "Rather it is only through the work and in the work that the toolness of the tool becomes visible" (30).

Heidegger famously demonstrates this thesis by discussing one of van Gogh's paintings of a pair of shoes. Heidegger mistakes the boots of the painter for a pair of peasant shoes and finds captured in them the world of the peasant with her toil and joy. The art historian Meyer Schapiro has pointed out that the depicted shoes, however, have never belonged to a farming woman but, rather, to the artist himself. Despite this mistaken attribution of the shoes to an owner, the basic concept seems to remain valid. Nothing forces us to conclude, as Schapiro does, that Heidegger's fanciful description contains nothing that could not have been imagined in looking at a real pair of shoes.[7] Apart from the fact that everyday objects rarely invite any flight of fancy in the first place, it is relevant to distinguish between the depicted object and its model. The mere fact that the shoes in question never belonged to a peasant does not bear in the least on the possibility that the painting in which they are shown represents them as a pair of boots worn by farmers. Hence, it remains true that we only learn about the nature of the tool from the work of art. In art, we pay attention to that which according to its nature must otherwise remain concealed. Art has the epistemological function of letting us see what cannot be seen directly. Hence, Heidegger famously defines the artwork as *"das Sich-ins-Werk-Setzen der Wahrheit des Seienden"* (the truth of being positioning itself in the work) (30). Ultimately, the ontological question has led us to an understanding of the epistemological function of the work of art, and an important shift of emphasis has occured along the way. The ontological question has not been answered but replaced: "What art is, is one of those questions that are not answered in the essay" (91). Heidegger's opposition against philosophical aesthetics results precisely from this ontological dispute. For him, philosophical aesthetics suffers from the inability to properly distinguish art from other objects. As a result, philosophical aesthetics falls into step with instrumental reason and turns art into *Bestand,* a reservoir of objects which can be placed opposite the subject, contemplated from a distance, and ultimately controlled at will.

The Truth of Art

It is not the essence of art that is of interest for Heidegger but its function, namely, to disclose the truth of being as an event:[8] "In the work, when being is here opened up into the what and how of its existence, an event of truth is at work" (30). We must therefore ask how Heidegger conceives of this truth-event in art.

Heidegger demonstrates this *Wahrheitsgeschehen,* this truth-event, by discussing a Greek temple as an artwork. The anonymity of its architect allows Heidegger to emphasize that in the philosophy of art, only the work is of importance, not the artist: "In great art, and we only talk about such art, the artist remains irrelevant in respect to the work, almost a self-destructing passage for the production of the work" (35). Heidegger distances himself clearly from the notion of genius and the work as an expression of the self. Needless to say, for him all biographical interpretations of art are not only flawed but altogether ignorant of the nature of art.

It is equally obvious for Heidegger that art must not be thought of as mimetic of reality. Especially architecture demonstrates that an artwork does not reproduce anything that exists already: "A building, a Greek temple, does not represent anything [*bildet nichts ab*]. It merely stands there in the midst of the rugged mountain valley"[9] (37). Since the temple does not represent, it follows that works of arts are not signs that point away from themselves toward that which they represent. Works do not signify; rather, they allow something to be fully present. About the statue of the god in the temple Heidegger writes: "It is no representation that would allow us to learn how the god looks, instead it is a work that lets the god himself be present and therefore *is* the god himself. The same holds true for the linguistic work" (39). Gadamer will later use the term *ästhetische Nichtunterscheidung* (aesthetic nondifferentiation) for this fact.

In his discussion of the tool, Heidegger had demonstrated that its nature is its hiddenness and that we can only understand it by detour through the work of art. This moment of disclosure is characteristic for art in general. Works of art allow something to become visible, to be present, that had hitherto remained hidden. This moment of disclosure of truth in the work Heidegger calls *world.* World, just like tools, generally remains hidden from our view. Drawing on Husserl's concept of the *Lebenswelt,* the life-world, Heidegger explains:

> World is never an object that stands before us and can be contemplated. World is always that immaterial being that governs us as long as the paths of birth and death, blessing and spell hold us outside ourselves into Being. Where the essential decisions of our history are made, are accepted and abandoned by us, mistaken and newly inquired about, there the world worlds [*da weltet die Welt*]. (41)

Hence, world is not the sum of objects but the backdrop of our life, that is, that linguistically stored knowledge about the "objective, social and subjective world" – as Habermas later differentiates, though not in the spirit of Heidegger – that provides us with interpretations and prejudices before we enter any situation.[10] But language and world always remain behind the back of those who live in it. We cannot turn them into objects for our contemplation because that would presume a perspective from outside the world. Yet such extramundane position is an impossibility. World is only disclosed to us in the work of art: "The work erects a world. The work holds the openness of the world open" (41). The Greek temple, therefore, does not merely stand in the mountain valley but organizes both the landscape and man's existence around it: "The temple through its existence grants to the things their face and to man the perspective on himself" (39).

The poet Wallace Stevens captured this organizing power of the work in a poem with the title "The Anecdote of the Jar":

> I placed a jar in Tennessee,
> And round it was, upon a hill.
> It made the slovenly wilderness
> Surround that hill.
>
> The wilderness rose up to it,
> And sprawled around, no longer wild.
> The jar was round upon the ground
> And tall and of a port in air.
>
> It took dominion everywhere.
> The jar was gray and bare.
> It did not give of bird or bush,
> Like nothing else in Tennessee.[11]

In his 1951 essay "Building Dwelling Thinking," Heidegger uses the example of a bridge to demonstrate how a work organizes the space around it and transforms it into a world.[12] In other words, art lets us see something that remains hidden from view in our quotidian life. The work allows us a new perspective on our existence and our world:

> The positioning of truth in the work pushes open the uncanny and simultaneously pushes over the familiar and that which we take for it. The truth that discloses itself in the work can never be proven and deduced from what exists so far [*das Bisherige*]. What exists so far is refuted in its exclusive reality by the work. What art founds can therefore never be compensated by the ready-at-hand [*das Vorhandene*] and the controllable [*das Verfügbare*]. The foundation is a surplus, a present. (77)

Therefore, the work not only lets us see those things that have remained hidden so far; it also makes visible the world in which these individual objects occur. Art, to repeat this point, is not mimetic. In the artwork something new comes into existence. Paul Klee famously declared in exactly the same spirit that art does not reproduce the visible, but it renders visible. A similar formulation can be found in the work of Konrad Fiedler who writes: "We will cease to want to see nature through art; rather, we will submit to art so that it teaches us to see nature."[13]

Yet this disclosure of world is not merely cognitive; it possesses an ethical dimension. In *The Origin of the Work of Art* we read: "In the proximity of the work we had suddenly been elsewhere from where we used to be." This sentence merely hints at the change that we undergo when we experience the truth of an artwork. And while the absence of an ethics in Heidegger's works has oftentimes been bemoaned, Heidegger does imply an ethical dimension of art in his lectures on Nietzsche. The argument there runs like this. Art is what pleases. What pleases, however, depends on who I am. Who I am depends on what I demand from myself. The extent of a demand, though, can only be judged from the extremes that it covers. That demand that will tell me about myself must draw the line between what I can still endure and ask of myself and that which lies beyond. Heidegger then refers to the first of Rainer Maria Rilke's *Duino Elegies* in which beauty is said to be *"nichts als des Schrecklichen Anfang, den wir noch grade ertragen"* (nothing but the beginning of terror that we still barely endure). Hence, the beauty of art is the initiator of self-transcendence, of the development of the self toward its utmost possibilities. Art, despite its own restfulness, does not let us rest but urges us to change and develop. Heidegger never fully developed this thought,[14] but it nevertheless underlies his meditations on art.

One last moment must be noted in respect to the world-disclosing function of the work of art, namely, Heidegger's privileging of language. For him, just like for Hegel, poetry holds a special status among the arts. This is not because poetry marks the transition to the philosophical concept, as Hegel had explained it, but because language must disclose being for man before he can even produce works of art. Not only does language precede art, but it first allows all of man's expressions: "Where there is no language, as in the being of stone, plant and animal, there is also no openness of being" (75). If the disclosing event of art is a gift, as Heidegger had formulated it, then language is that gift which man has received from Being and which put him in the position to then produce works of art himself that disclose a world. In the words of Hans-Georg Gadamer: "The work of *language* is the most original poetry of Being."[15]

While it is the function of the moment of *world* in the artwork to disclose, to make visible, and to allow for a new perspective, it is vital to note that this event must not be understood as a cognitive gain that could then be captured conceptually. Heidegger's position is far from such Hegelianism and remains close to the Schelling of *The*

System of Transcendental Idealism who had argued that only art grants an intellectual intuition that can never be transposed into philosophical thought. Heidegger, too, insists that art remains ultimately unknowable. Long before Adorno, he speaks of the *"Rätsel der Kunst,"* the enigma of art (83). Every work of art contains a moment that cannot be understood, that remains hidden and resists all attempts of elucidation. Heidegger calls this moment *earth:* "Earth is the essential self-concealing [*das wesenhaft Sich-Verschliessende*]" (44). Because all art contains this moment of earth, no one experience will ever come to terms with the work; no single interpretation will ever suffice.[16] The earth is the reason that Kant's *aesthetic idea,* namely, that the work of art invites endless thought, also holds true for Heidegger's philosophy of art. Yet if earth were simply that which remains hidden, we would have no knowledge of it to begin with. Therefore, earth must announce itself as hidden: "The earth is not simply the concealed, but that which announces itself as self-concealing [*was als Sichverschliessendes aufgeht*]" (54). The hiddenness of the earth is twofold: It is the reason that we can mistake something for something else, that is, that errors can occur in our judgment (Heidegger's term *Verstellen,* blockage), but it is also that which resists all cognition (*Versagen,* refusal) (54).

Especially this latter manifestation, earth as refusal to yield to cognition, has important consequences not only for art. The reason that Heidegger does not want to dismiss the ontological question in his philosophy of art is that art becomes endowed with the function of an ontological safekeeper. This is because Heidegger extends the notion of earth from the sphere of art to being in general. Earth is what resists cognition: "The earth lets every attempt to intrude upon it crash against it. It turns every calculating intrusion into destruction" (43). Art is merely the privileged site of the demonstration that technical and scientific reason are ultimately destructive. It differs in this respect from other objects – things or tools – because it *presents* itself as that which withdraws. Only in our encounters with art do we realize that every attempt to force it to disclose its secret will result in the destruction of those qualities that distinguish the work of art from a nonartistic object. By extension, art protects all things in the age of the destruction of things, of serial production, easy replaceability, and the absence of all traces of human workmanship in the object: "Therefore the work of art is an instance that protects from the general loss of things. Just as Rilke transfigures the innocence of the thing poetically in the midst of the collective disappearance of thingness by showing the thing to the angel, the thinker thinks the same loss of thingness by realizing its safe-keeping in the work of art."[17]

Heidegger himself does not refer to Rilke's *Dinggedichte* (Thing poems) in the artwork essay, but in the text *"Wozu Dichter?"* (Why Poets?) he quotes approvingly from a 1925 letter by Rilke in which the poet claims that his grandparents still knew things, whereas the present generation knows merely objects.[18] It would lead us too far astray to discuss this safekeeping function of art further, but it is certainly true that Heidegger's essay "*Das Ding*" (The thing) must be read as a continuation of the discussion that had not found its conclusion in *The Origin of the Work of Art,* as Gadamer has stated.[19] The two moments of *world* and *earth* in the work of art do not merely coexist alongside each other; their respective functions, disclosure and concealing, are engaged in a struggle: "The opposition of world and earth is a strife" (46). Strife must here be understood in the sense of *agon,* the contest that was an essential element in the Greek concept of self-perfection: "In the essential strife the opponents raise each other into the self-realization of their essence.... In the strife each carries the other beyond itself" (46). Therefore, the artwork always contains a tension, an internal kinetic energy. Only because the work of art moves can it move us. Yet there is nothing restless about the artwork either. Just as the artwork harbors both world and earth, it must be thought of as simultaneously moving and at rest. We will have to return to this thought as an interesting reversal of Kant's kinetic explanation of the aesthetic experience.

Heidegger had claimed that our encounters with art contain a moment of the uncanny because we realize that truth is not a matter of mere disclosure but also of concealing. Every truth partakes in that which remains unknown: "The essence of truth, i.e. of unconcealedness, is shot through with refusal" (53). Truth is therefore the struggle *between world* and *earth* and by no means the struggle of *world against earth.* In the work of art, we experience this struggle as beauty: "Beauty is one way in which truth appears [*west*] as unconcealedness" (55). We must take note of the indefinite article in this sentence. Heidegger does not claim that truth appears only in art, but that art is just one of its manifestations. He acknowledges other instances of truth as well and names the founding of a state, the self-sacrifice for an ideal, and philosophical thought (55). As we will see shortly, however, Heidegger explicitly excludes science from this list of truth-events.

As this comparison of art with political events might already indicate, Heidegger's notion of art is far from that of a solitary aesthetic *Erlebnis,* an experience of consumption. Rather, he continues that idealist tradition that had always regarded art as a communal event: "The safekeeping of the work does not isolate human beings in their experiences, but moves them into the belonging to the truth that happens in the work. Thus it founds the being for and with each other as the historical relation of human existence to unconcealedness [*und gründet so das Für- und Miteinandersein als das geschichtliche Ausstehen des Da-seins aus dem Bezug zur Unverborgenheit*]" (69). Hence, the experience of art is not a matter of personal taste or of withdrawn contemplation but, rather, an event that allows man to overcome his isolation. Art is not existential,[20] but it grants man the experience of society that constitutes one aspect of his world.

Art, however, is more than that experience that breaks down the barriers between men. Heidegger's conception of art is more radical than this. In his view, we do not always already live in a society in order to then produce art for certain collective purposes. Art, as much as the political founding of a state, is one of man's primary activities on which all social life is based. Without art, man would not know social life at all. Man has a history precisely because he can encounter himself and his world in the work: "Art is history in the essential sense that it founds history [*dass sie Geschichte gründet*]" (80). This founding of history Heidegger regards in the 1930s as closely connected to the historical fate of nations.[21] Later, this historical and political moment of art disappears from his texts. What remains, nevertheless, is the insistence on the communal aspect of art. In regard to the political moment of art Heidegger writes: "World is the disclosing openness of the wide paths of the simple and essential decisions in the fate of a historical people" (45).

It would be no more than a truism to state that an artwork is almost always the result of a single individual, even in the case of architecture, where the execution of the structure depends on the help of many but the conception is that of one mind. Yet this does not mean that the individual is the source of the work of art. Biographical interpretation also fails because art, especially poetry, is not the achievement of a solitary genius but, rather, must be considered the "telos of historical existence" (78). It is not the poet who speaks; rather, the language of a historical people speaks through him or her.[22] Heidegger takes this notion from the poets Friedrich Hölderlin, who thinks of the poet as a transmitter of poetic messages from the gods, and Stefan George, for whom poetry was the constitutive moment of those elitist circles that guard and transmit Western culture. Hence, there is nothing that makes this concept specific for a National Socialist aesthetics, as had been argued.[23] That it can also be used for the purposes of a fascist state, as Heidegger might very well have intended, still does not make it genuinely totalitarian. Nevertheless, the fact that Heidegger drops the political references in his writings on art in the 1950s and 1960s could be understood as a result of his disappointment with the National Socialists.

Heidegger and Idealism

By advancing art as a truth-event, Heidegger renews Schelling's paradigm of art as an "organon of truth." For the Schelling of 1800, it was a certainty that art ranked above philosophy in its potential to grant intellectual intuition of the absolute. Although he would later reverse this hierarchy and thus move closer to Hegel's position, for a brief period the notion of art as the most important means of cognition was paradigmatic. Heidegger, however, is never as clear on this question as Schelling. Repeatedly he thinks and writes about the relationship of poetry and philosophy, and in different essays he suggests different hierarchical relationships. In his late philosophical poem "Cezanne," for example, Heidegger indicates that art achieves what philosophy can only aim for. Art enters the realm of *Einfalt* (simplicity, unity), whereas thought remains tied to *Zwiefalt* (doubling, division). Heidegger here renews the idea that the sublation of signification in art lets the signified be present. Philosophy, on the other hand, does not result in a full presence.[24]

Still, this position is merely a tendency and not Heidegger's last word on the strife between poetry and philosophy. Other essays suggest at least an equality; some even tend to attribute ultimate supremacy to thought. It might be tempting to solve this problem by suggesting a division of labor between two unique, yet ultimately incomparable, activities. One could consequently think of this difficult relation in the following manner: Philosophy is a Hegelian enterprise that looks backward in time and meditates about the present as a result of past developments. Poetry, on the other hand, could be thought of as that visionary activity that opens paths into the future, as the poet Hölderlin had conceived of it. Poetry's world-disclosing moment could be seen as the opening of a space in which man's individual and communal life can take place. A rivalry between poetry and philosophy would be replaced in this conception by a division of tasks. Heidegger would have avoided both Schelling's supremacy of art as well as Hegel's displacement of art by religion and philosophy. And yet, Heidegger's thinking about art never reaches the clear separation of functions suggested here. Up to the very last pronouncements on art, he struggles to achieve a hierarchical order of art and thought that would not depend on the separation of their specific functions. Mostly, art wins out in this strife and establishes itself as that event that can fulfill its own promise, while philosophy does not know the quiet self-fulfillment of art.

Whereas the precise relation of art and philosophy remains problematic for Heidegger, this is not the case for the hierarchy of art and science. This is not the place to discuss Heidegger's notion of science, but two things must be kept in mind when thinking about scientific and aesthetic truth. The first is that Heidegger thinks of science as the historical manifestation of instrumental reason, that is, the quantifying and calculating objectification of man's life-world. Secondly, Heidegger regards scientific truth claims as one-dimensional propositions. Generally speaking, his notion of science comes closer to the positivist self-definition of the scientists of the nineteenth century than to the post-empiricist conception of science in the twentieth century. There is little need to uphold the strict opposition of art and science, as proposed by Heidegger, in an age in which those conceptions of science as advanced by Thomas Kuhn or Paul Feyerabend move science much closer to the domain of art. This new understanding of science acknowledges preconditions for its research that Heidegger had advanced in his essay on the origin of art. Hence, the notion that science depends on a previously disclosed understanding of being – a *paradigm* in the words of Kuhn[25] – today seems more acceptable to scientists as well.

Heidegger excludes science from his list of truth-events with the following explanation: "Science is no originary truth-event, but rather the expansion of an already open sphere of truth by means of appropriation and justification of that which presents itself as possible and necessary correctness in its surrounding" (62). We must note two things in this statement. Heidegger sets up an opposition between truth and correctness [*Richtigkeit*]. While truth happens in art, self-sacrifice, and the founding of a state, science merely achieves correctness. This is because scientific correctness is secondary to, even parasitic on, truth. Correct statements are not possible without a preceding truth. Art opens a sphere of orientation that must already exist before any kind of scientific question can be posed. Without a disclosed world, science is an impossibility. As Manfred Frank comments: "Truth as propositional truth is only possible under the precondition of a semantically disclosed world – and art is true in that sense that it stands on the side of this disclosure of meaning that precedes all propositions."[26] The problematic aspect of this relationship, however, is that science tends to forget about its necessary dependence on aesthetic unconcealedness. Instead of acknowledging its debt to art, science obscures it. More and more, truth becomes associated with correctness; one-dimensional propositions triumph over thought. Yet while this simplified narrative no longer holds, it has been corrected in Heidegger's sense. Science now largely acknowledges that its questions depend on something that lies outside its own sphere and precedes it.

The relation of Heidegger's philosophy of art to idealism is complex. While the proximity of his thought to the Schelling of *The System of Transcendental Idealism* is unmistakable, Heidegger positions himself in a complicated constellation of attraction and repulsion in regard to other idealists as well.[27] While it seems at first sight that his aesthetic position is thoroughly anti-Kantian, this is not quite the case when one takes a second look. True enough, Heidegger clearly breaks with Kant's subjectivist aesthetics, and he insists that art is not an *Erlebnis,* a merely subjective experience of consumption. While an ontology of art is more or less inconceivable inside the Kantian framework, Heidegger, just like the post-Kantian idealists, emphasizes the objective moment of art. This is most obvious when we think about the kinetic moment in aesthetics. Kant had argued that the aesthetic experience consists in a playful back and forth between imagination and understanding, because imagination keeps sending its material to the faculty of understanding in order to be unified under a concept. This conceptualization, however, fails, and understanding returns the material to the imagination. In this process, we joyfully become aware of the workings of these mental faculties and their interaction that is endless, yet never frustrating. Heidegger, too, finds the kinetic moment in art of importance. Yet for him this cannot be an issue of subjective response; the motion must be located in the object. Hence, he conceives of the strife of *world* and *earth* as a continuing *agon,* a movement that allows each moment to develop fully due to the resistance of the opposing other. As little as the continuing back and forth between imagination and understanding produces nervous agitation for Kant, but rather is synonymous with self-perpetuating pleasure, for Heidegger the strife of world and earth is an internal struggle within an object that seems entirely peaceful.

Yet Kant had also left the realm of purely subjective responses to art behind both by claiming a moral function for the artwork and by insisting on its importance in the process of social unity, which needs to be renewed consistently. Much like him, Heidegger also insists on the ability of the artwork to overcome solitary reception and to play a role in the constitution and maintenance of a community. While Kant argues this point by referring the necessary collective character of the aesthetic judgment, Heidegger is less clear on the precise interaction of artwork and community. As with his philosophy in general, a desideratum for a social hermeneutics seems to announce itself in this discussion of art's transindividual relevance.

Furthermore, Heidegger continues Kant's notion of the *aesthetic idea.* If the only function of a work of art were to erect a world, the meaning of this work could conceivably be transposed into philosophical concepts. But against this Hegelian transformation of the "enigma of art" into propositional truth, Heidegger advances the notion of earth. Earth guarantees the continuing enchantment of the work; it opposes all final interpretation, it protects the thing against its disappearance in total utilization, and it teaches us about the necessary limits of all cognition, especially that of a scientific nature. While Heidegger agrees with Hegel's attempts to overcome the opposition of subject and object in art, he makes it equally clear that art is not one manifestation of spirit that could be overcome by more advanced manifestations: "Art neither belongs to the accomplishments of culture nor is it a manifestation of spirit. Rather, it belongs to the *event* that allows one to determine the 'meaning of Being'" (91).

Ultimately, however, Heidegger's position comes closest to that of Schelling, for he insists on art as an event of truth, possibly even one that leaves philosophy behind. For a brief moment, Schelling was convinced of art's supremacy. Heidegger is more cautious, and at least in *The Origin of the Work of Art* acknowledges that truth can also be brought about by practices other than art. Yet the fact that art is discussed in an epistemological context and that its truth is opposed to scientific correctness is certainly beholden to Schelling. Both in the works of his student Gadamer and in that of his opponent Adorno, this insistence on the truth of art will manifest itself as well.

Hans-Georg Gadamer

Heidegger's philosophy of art contains a gesture of concealment. A debt to early Romantic aesthetics is indicated, yet never spelled out. In the works of Heidegger's student Hans-Georg Gadamer (1900–2002), we find the same repudiation of idealist aesthetics that had already covered up unacknowledged romantic sympathies and debts in the writings of his teacher. But whereas Heidegger includes much of the pre-idealist philosophy of art in his criticism of the tradition, Gadamer advocates a return to ancient philosophy as a means of overcoming the impasse created by Kantian aesthetics. Gadamer's solution to the question of how to overcome the idealist heritage is to renew the philosophy of art by transforming aesthetics into a privileged area of hermeneutics. Hermeneutics for Gadamer no longer signifies a method of interpretation, as it had for the Bible scholars of the Reformation and the European humanists, who aimed for the comprehension or restitution of an authentic text, nor a controlled reading operation to prevent misunderstanding, as for the founder of modern hermeneutics, the romantic Friedrich Schleiermacher. Instead, Gadamer develops Heidegger's "hermeneutics of facticity" into a philosophical hermeneutics, that is, a philosophy that regards understanding – seen as a process between persons or as a dialogue with oneself – as one of the most important constituting factors in man's existence and no longer as merely a tool for the comprehension of texts.[28]

Gadamer's magnum opus *Wahrheit und Methode* (Truth and method, 1960) opens its discussion of truth not with an analysis of traditional philosophical theories of truth but, rather, with a long section on art. Yet for Gadamer, art has to be defended against aesthetics, because the truth of art got lost in it: "The following investigations therefore begin with a critique of aesthetic consciousness in order to defend the experience of truth that the work of art grants us against the scientific concept of truth."[29] As the decisive turn in the history of aesthetics Gadamer pinpoints the work of Kant; his subjectivization of aesthetics, Gadamer claims, has led to the separation of aesthetics and epistemology. Against this dominant notion in aesthetics Gadamer pitches the necessity of regaining a concept of art as cognition.

He faults Kant's aesthetic theory for discrediting all notions of cognition except that of the natural sciences. Therefore, the humanities were forced to emulate the methodological operations of the natural sciences, yet the truth of their objects, mainly art, gets lost in this transformation. Gadamer argues that no methodology exists that could be applied in order to disclose the truth of art and to understand a work correctly.

The reverse side of Kant's antiepistemic approach to aesthetics is his subjectivization of man's encounter with art. Art is no longer defined as a specific kind of object but, rather, as that which elicits an aesthetic judgment. More important than the work is now the subjective response to it: The experience replaces the work. But to discredit the importance of the work entails its separation from the social, historical, and religious world of its production. The aesthetic experience fails to connect to the world of the work. Therefore, a hermeneutic philosophy of art must reintegrate the work into the totality of its existence in order to overcome the isolating aesthetic experience. Such reintegration into its world will also restitute the work's cognitive function. Hence, Gadamer can claim: "Art is cognition and the experience of the work of art grants this cognition."[30]

In order to overcome the subject–object division in the aesthetic experience, Gadamer does not rely on a Hegelian metaphysics of spirit. Instead, he suggests an ontological approach to art that de-essentializes the artwork without ceasing to consider it as a transhistorical point of reference, an object of "hermeneutical identity."[31] Gadamer takes up those interpretations of art that consider it a form of play. In his version of aesthetics, the work of art is seen as a game that bridges the gap between work and recipient because a game lacks existence without players who play it. Similarly, art can be understood neither as the work outside the situation of its reception nor as the subjective experience of aesthetic pleasure that disregards its source. The artwork only comes into true existence in the moment of its reception. Here it gains its identity as much as it grants a renewed identity to viewer and reader. Taking up Husserl's notion of horizon, Gadamer describes this process of mediation between work and viewer as one of *Horizontverschmelzung*, the melting together of horizons. In the process of the reception of a historical work, neither the work nor the recipient remains the same. Past and present together form a new totality that explains both the continuing vividness of the work and its power to affect the life of the viewer, listener, or reader. Art does not leave the lives of its recipients unchanged, but it exerts a transformative power. And yet, the recipients remain subjects in the humanist sense as well. Art for Gadamer never turns into a play without players, an event without human beings, as for example Derrida's notion of *jeu* suggests.

While *Truth and Method* does not explain how Gadamer conceives of the transformative power of art, later essays take up this question. One of the most provocative of these texts presents a new conception of mimesis, the concept that had figured large in Lukács's aesthetics and would do so, too, in Adorno's writings. By taking up an ancient notion of mimesis, Gadamer provides art with a practical function that encompasses the individual and the social sphere. For this, he turns away from Plato's understanding of mimesis and replaces it with that of the Pythagoreans. In their view, mimesis is not the imitation of an existing object but, rather, the threefold experience of order, namely, the order of the world, of musical harmony, and of a well-balanced soul.[32] Hence, Gadamer writes:

> To attest order – this to me seems to have always been valid insofar as every work of art, even in our world that changes more and more into uniformity and seriality, attests to the mental power of order that constitutes the reality of our life. In the work of art happens in an exemplary manner what we all do in existing: constant construction of world. It stands in the midst of a disintegrating world of the familiar as a guarantee of order, and maybe all forces of protection on which all culture rests rely on that which we encounter

in an exemplary manner in the doing of the artist and in the experience of art: that we always bring back to order what disintegrates.[33]

Art provides order in a disorderly, chaotic world. This order is not merely cognitive but also moral. Although this is not the place to discuss the complex interaction of cognitive and moral order, there can be little doubt that Gadamer's notion of mimesis supports a view of art that considers it a necessity in the constitution of a just community.[34]

In order to demonstrate how art can disclose truth, Gadamer resorts to Plato's theory of art, but only to reverse it. Whereas Plato had charged artworks with being ontologically flawed representations of ideas, even further removed from the eternal essence of the object than their materially existing counterparts, Gadamer argues for a *superior* status of art. It is art that truly contains the essence of the object, not an immaterial idea. In the artwork we do not face a lack of ontological significance but, rather, an increase of true existence and, hence, of cognizability: "Works of art have an ontologically superior status."[35]

Art allows a process of cognition to take place. Processes of cognition, of learning, and of comprehension, however, are the genuine subject of hermeneutics as the theory of understanding. Hence, Gadamer concludes that art as an event of cognition falls into the domain of hermeneutics. Instead of perpetuating aesthetics as a subjectivist endeavor, it must give way to an encompassing theory of understanding, namely, philosophical hermeneutics: "Hermeneutic consciousness achieves a scope wider than that of aesthetic consciousness. *Aesthetics must be dissolved into hermeneutics.*"[36]

Gadamer shares with Heidegger the emphasis on the truth of art that is a heritage from Schelling's romantic aesthetics. Yet while Heidegger never makes the final decision regarding philosophy's potential to disclose truth as art does, Gadamer establishes a hierarchy. For him, the work of art transmits a kind of knowledge that philosophy lacks: "We do not read philosophical texts like a poem that knows everything. We rather read a philosophical text as one that will also not know, but whose author has inquired and thought for longer."[37]

Another way of putting the same idea is by stating that philosophical knowledge cannot find closure, whereas art has always reached its telos. Yet philosophical texts have the same capacity to bridge the gap of time and to become fully present for us.[38] Their presence, though, is an invitation to think and hence to question, if questioning is, as Heidegger famously put it, the piety of thought. Our encounters with art, to be sure, must also begin with a question so that the dialogue between us and the work can be opened up. But once we have listened to the answer of the work, we find ourselves included in the restfulness of art. And although Gadamer would probably not claim that we encounter the absolute in these priviledged moments, the effects of Schelling's intellectual intuition and Gadamer's shared truth of the work seem very much alike.

10

Adorno

Art and Society

In Theodor W. Adorno's (1903–1969) philosophy, we find much the same gesture as in Heidegger when it comes to the inheritance of classical German philosophy. While Adorno sets himself in a position of both opposing and continuing idealism, he tends to gloss over his debts to early romantic aesthetics. Although Schelling is mentioned with approval several times in *Ästhetische Theorie* (Aesthetic theory, 1970), Adorno is very shy in spelling out his reliance on the philosophy of art of the former as an "organon of truth." Instead, throughout his philosophical and critical writings, Adorno's struggle with Hegel occupies a place in the foreground.[1] His 1966 *Negative Dialectics* is written with the aim of inheriting, as well as dismantling, Hegel's legacy. Here, Adorno attempts to prove that the dialectical model with its synthesis as reconciliation always produces a totality that does injustice to those moments that necessarily escape the concept. Hegelian dialectics reduces all individuality to something that can be subsumed under a concept to be then integrated into a general movement. Against this idealist heritage Adorno pitches his own conception of philosophy: "Philosophy's true interest at this historical moment lies where Hegel, agreeing with tradition, demonstrated his disinterest: with the conceptless, singular and specific."[2] Adorno terms this singularity that remains irreconcilable with conceptual thought the nonidentical, a term that resurrects Kant's noncognizable thing-in-itself against Hegel's totalizing dialectics, and that also plays a prominent role in Adorno's theory of art. That a striking parallel exists between Adorno's notion of the nonidentical and Heidegger's notion of Being shall only be remarked in passing.[3]

Against the systematic philosophy of the idealists, Adorno mobilizes the romantic notion of systematic antisystematicity. For him, the idealist system is a symptom of the desire to model spirit after appetite, to devour everything external and turn it into the substance of the self: "The system is stomach become spirit, anger the signature of all idealism" (Neg. Dial., 34). While systematic thought participates in the oppression of its moments, the fragment that hints at a totality but never aims to achieve it is considered the only viable alternative: "Only the fragment as the form of philosophy would bring into their own the monads that were conceptualized in an illusionary way by idealism" (Neg. Dial., 39). This position bestows new philosophical dignity on the essay, which combines a circumscribed incidence as the catalyst for writing with speculative thought.[4]

Philosophical analyses of art and questions of aesthetics are very much at the center of Adorno's work. Starting with his 1933 *Habilitationsschrift* (the second dissertation required by the German academic system for all university teachers) on Kierkegaard's aesthetics, at least half of his publications deal with questions of art. In 1949 he published *Philosophie der neuen Musik* (Philosophy of new music); in 1952 *Versuch über Wagner* (Essay on Wagner); in 1956 *Dissonanzen: Musik in der verwalteten Welt* (Dissonances: Music in the administered world); from 1957 to 1974 *Noten zur Literatur I–IV* (Notes on literature); in 1960 *Mahler: Eine musikalische Physignomik* (Mahler: A musical physiognomy); in 1967 *Ohne Leitbild: Parva Ästhetica* (Without ideal: Parva Aesthetica); and finally in 1970 *Ästhetische Theorie* (Aesthetic theory). The list is incomplete; more monographs on music and essays carry Adorno's name. His legacy to philosophical aesthetics, however, can be found mainly in the posthumous *Aesthetic Theory.* Just like Lukács's *Aesthetics,* Adorno's magnum opus on the theory of art is a collection of meditations on central concepts of classical aesthetics. These are intimately interwoven reflections, yet they are not clearly structured. Adorno's basic maneuver is to take up the notion of paradigmatic aesthetics and unfold their negativity. The meaning of this strategy will become apparent in the course of our discussion.

Adorno's critique of idealism and his renewal of romantic aesthetics were undertaken from a very specific vantage point. As a member of the *Institut für Sozialforschung,* center of the Frankfurt School, he attempted to formulate a critical theory of society. Max Horkheimer, head of the institute, had formulated in his famous essay "Traditional and Critical Theory" that the latter is concerned with the abolition of social injustice. Philosophically, this means, following Marx's diagnosis, that at the heart of idealism lies unacknowledged materialism.[5] Yet the problem for Adorno, Horkheimer, and the other members of the Frankfurt School was to adhere to a strain of neo-Marxist thought at a time when society had become total – roughly meaning lacking critical oppositional elements – because of the integration of the proletariat. While Horkheimer tended more and more toward a nihilistic position that was only appeased slightly late in his life by a turn toward metaphysics, Adorno always relied on art as the last factor of resistance against a total society.

Adorno's theory of art is based on an analysis of society and art after the eighteenth century. It is important to make this fact explicit, because his aesthetics rest on several presuppositions that are not spelled out, yet they carry several consequences that Adorno prefers to ignore. Moreover, just like the Frankfurt School's analysis of society, Adorno's own theory does not rely on empirical historical analyses but is based on a "theory of history of ontological status."[6] Very briefly summarized, Adorno's historical presuppositions for his theory of art are the following.

Adorno holds that society has broken the promise of Enlightenment because it has not overcome its inner antagonisms, merely appeased them. This appeasement has led to the integration of all oppositional forces into society, which has become total. On a political level, this societal co-opting was most successful with the integration of the proletariat into the bourgeoisie. For the critical theorists, however, philosophy itself has also not opposed this tendency toward a total society, but has both inaugurated and mimicked it. In their devastating analysis of contemporary society *Dialektik der Aufklärung* (Dialectics of Enlightenment, 1944), Horkheimer and Adorno argue that a total society has even eliminated all oppositional conceptual thought.[7] Such diagnosis, however, poses the problem of all-encompassing statements regarding self-referentiality: How can philosophy escape the embrace of total society in order to view it from the outside and make statements about it that can claim to be true? Isn't philosophy itself, including the critical kind, part of totality? While the answers to this puzzle change in the course of the development of the Frankfurt School – one favorite was always the *performativer Widerspruch,* the performative opposition that turns critique into a gesture (in philosophical logic, the term refers to a proposition that is self-contradictory due to its self-referentiality) – for Adorno art has always carried the hope of escaping from an airtight totality.[8] Since critical theory is in constant danger of falling back into ideology itself, it cannot guarantee a secure ground for the project that motivates the members of the institute, namely, to abolish social injustice. Yet in art, Adorno locates the potential formerly attributed to philosophy both to show reality as it is and to remind us of a better reality. At the very basis of art we therefore find two interconnected functions: the presentation of reality in all its shortcomings and its critique with a better society in mind.

Still, not all products that lay claim to art fulfill this double function. Total society also attempts to co-opt art and rid it of its moment of opposition to the status quo. For this purpose, it has set up what Adorno and Horkheimer call the culture industry. This industry, in which Hollywood looms large, creates pseudoartistic products to fulfill the public's need for entertainment without any danger of arousing ideas or desires that challenge the present conformity. While the encounter with American popular culture in their exile was a strong influence on Adorno's and Horkheimer's theory of cultural industry, it was also developed in opposition to Walter Benjamin's theory of the postauratic artwork. Before we turn to Adorno's aesthetic theory itself, we must therefore take a detour through Benjamin's theses on the reproducibility of art and Adorno's subsequent critique of the culture industry.

Benjamin and the Culture Industry

In his essay *Das Kunstwerk im Zeitalter seiner technischen Reproduzierbarkeit* (The artwork in the age of its mechanical reproducibility, 1936), Walter Benjamin (1892–1940) narrates the history of the work of art from its ritualistic function via its display function to the present era of technical reproduction. Two elements change in this long process: On the one hand, the work of art loses its concrete historical place and function – what Benjamin calls its aura; on the other hand, man's sense perception and, hence, his relation to art changes as much.

Initially, Benjamin argues, the work of art could not be separated from its magical and cultic function. The "here and now of the original," that is, the aura that Benjamin had defined as "the singular appearance of a distance, no matter how close," is characterized in its cultic stage by the unapproachable distance of the holy.[9] When the work of art loses its function in the cult, it becomes an object of display and a secular type of veneration. Although Benjamin offers hardly an explanation for this historical process,[10] he nevertheless goes on to claim that the social function of art changed from ritual to politics.

Only the technical reproduction of art in photography and sound film has completed this process in which the aura of the artwork slowly evaporates. Not only do traditional artworks lose their "here and now" due to their photographic or auditory reproduction; mechanically produced works of art no longer even possess an aura. This is a process that for Benjamin carries a twofold meaning, one negative, the other positive. Because the traditional artwork allows later recipients to encounter the history of the work and, hence, to encounter previous ages, the loss of the aura involves the loss of historical experience. On the other hand, Benjamin hopes for a wider participation in art's promise of a better life, because the works are accessible by a wider audience in reproduction.

Moreover, Benjamin even suggests – without following the logic of his own argument – that maybe traditional works of art are not even necessary for the public at large, since the new technical works will fit the needs of the masses much more. In order to make his argument, Benjamin has recourse to his thesis about the historical malleability of sense perception. He celebrates film for being the ideal means for a modern collective audience to train their eye in a new mode of perception, that is, one that is characterized by disjoined moments and a rapid succession of impulses. Such patterning must be learned, as life in the city demands the adaptation to an ever-increasing speed of life. The cutting technique of film forces the same experience of shock and distraction on its viewer as life in the production hall or on the street of a metropolis. As Heidegger had talked about the *Stoss,* the push that the viewer receives from art, Benjamin venerates the shock. Yet while Heidegger refers to traditional works, Benjamin restricts the shock experience to film. Needless to say, such encounter with a work of art no longer takes place as a mode of contemplation. Instead, perception is unfocused, distracted, and passive: "Contemplation [*Versenkung*] that had become a training for antisocial behavior in the decay of the bourgeoisie is opposed by distraction as a form of social behavior" (502). It is hard to see how any meaning other than a rather superficial one can be attributed to the term "social" in this statement, but Benjamin goes even further in his praise for the renewing qualities of film. By means of a changed perception, movies manage to turn around the relationship of the masses to modernist art so that reactionary disapproval is replaced by progressive acceptance.

Should we understand him to say here that those who have been trained through movie watching will suddenly comprehend twelve-tone compositions and cubist painting? Benjamin may not be as naïve as that, but it is difficult to discern how we are meant to read this assertion. Again, Benjamin merely proclaims a fact and abstains from argument. Altogether unmotivated and unconvincing is his attempt to connect these theses to a political agenda, namely, the communist politicization of art that takes a stand against the fascist aesthetization of politics. And yet, the claim for a socially progressive function for movies and the argument in favor of changed perceptive habits of the audience constituted a challenge to Adorno, who always oriented himself to works of art in the traditional sense, even in their modernist form. Adorno's main argument against Benjamin's positive valuation of the loss of aura in contemporary art is that with its aura, art also loses its truth-claim. While the aura might be tied up with societal mechanisms of control, as Habermas later emphasized,[11] it nevertheless also harbors those historical forces that withstood integration and remained nonidentical. To give up on the traditional notion of the work of art and its reception means to further the totalizing impetus.

It is important to realize that for Adorno, the mass culture of the twentieth century as we encounter it in the culture industry is not a modern version of folk art. Rather, we are dealing with industrially produced and carefully calculated artifacts. They are not works of art by any means; instead, they must be seen as commodities calculated to fulfill the present needs of the masses.[12] These needs, however, are not genuine but are themselves products of the culture industry. The audience is meant to amuse itself, but this amusement is nothing but the elimination of critical thought: "*Vergnügtsein heißt Einverstanden-sein*" – amusement means agreement.[13]

Amusement is precisely that kind of distracted consumption that Benjamin hailed as the only appropriate perception of art. In his essay "Über den Fetischcharakter in der Musik und die Regression des Hörens" (About the fetish character in music and the regression of listening), Adorno argues vehemently against this position. Distracted viewing or listening no longer allows for a sense of the totality of the work to develop. Instead, the focus of attention turns to disjointed individual stimuli – for example, in music to memorable themes in a symphony. Such shortening of the attention span and the inability to mentally construct a whole leads to infantilization. Distracted listeners "are infantile: their primitivism is not that of the undeveloped, but of the man forced into regression."[14] Such infantilization, though, carries with it serious political implications. The culture industry "disables the development of autonomous, judicious individuals capable of independent decisions. Yet those would be the prerequisites for a democratic society that can only unfold and sustain itself through enlightened persons [*in Mündigen*]."[15] The consumption of the products of the culture industry, therefore, does nothing less than erode the basis of democracy. Benjamin's theory of distracted consumption cannot be distinguished in its consequences from the purposes of the producers of mass entertainment.

While Adorno has the better arguments on his side in his quarrel with Benjamin, there are also problems that emerge from his rejection of popular culture. It is not so much because there might be some individual products that do not fit the mold of the theory; the problem lies more with Adorno's unwillingness to examine individual works for their merits. As with his critique of jazz music,[16] his apodictic pronouncements repeatedly seem to result from a theoretical conviction based on insufficient evidence.[17] Yet if art is hailed for its potential to surpass the truth-claims of theory, as it is in Adorno's appropriation of Schelling, a theoretical prejudice that no longer allows for a detailed examination of the work in question poses a threat to the aesthetic theory at large. As will become apparent, this problem resurfaces in Adorno's conception of art as it opposes the cultural industry.

Society and the Form of Art

Art, in contrast to the commercial products of the culture industry, has a double character for Adorno: It is both "autonomous and fait social."[18] This seemingly contradictory interplay of dependence on and freedom from society produces perpetual conflicts of the two spheres (340), a conflict within the work of art that is responsible for the work's paradoxical character as movement in rest. Like Heidegger, Adorno transposes Kant's kinetic aesthetics from the mental faculties of the subject onto the work of art, although he insists that art is neither subjective nor objective, but dialectical.

To call the artwork a fait social does not mean to subscribe to a simple Marxist notion in which the cultural superstructure is determined by the economic base. Rather, Adorno takes recourse to Leibniz's metaphysics. The work of art is an effect of the social because it is a "monad: center of force and thing at once. Works of art are closed off against each other, blind, but in their concealedness [*Verschlossenheit*] they represent what is outside" (268). Artistic monads are able to mirror social reality because the same rules underlie the work of art as society: "The configuration of elements of works of art into a whole obeys immanent laws that are related to those of the society out there" (350). Adorno bases his discussion of artistic form on this very principle taken from rationalist metaphysics, although the explanatory force of this theory might not really surpass that of orthodox Marxism. Art, however, is not only inescapably linked to the forces of society; it also is free from all present laws and forces at the same time. Art's truth rests mainly on this second moment, not on its truthful replication of what exists: "True is only what does not fit into this world" (93). Art resists all attempts to be co-opted by society; it negates the present state of affairs and keeps alive the hope for a better life in a better world. It does not do so, though, by painting a utopia that is to be achieved; rather, art's utopia consists in its "No" to the present. With Stendhal, Adorno terms this feature of art its *promesse de bonheur,* its promise of happiness.

Adorno declares that in a total society, the antagonisms are not resolved but merely glossed over. In the work of art, however, the antagonisms of reality manifest themselves in the form of the work: "The unsolved antagonisms of reality return again in the works of art as the immanent problems of their form. This, not the influx of concrete moments, defines the relation of art to society" (16). Form is, therefore, both the coherence of the artwork and simultaneously the manifestation of struggling forces within it. But unlike the synthesis of idealist dialectics, the form of the artwork is a synthesis without being a totality; Adorno never tires of reversing Hegel's famous dictum by stating that the total is the false. Art achieves – although not entirely without traces of domination – a synthesis that lets nonidentical moments be. Likewise, the coherence of the work is not unity; it remains open. Adorno characterizes the form of the work of art:

> It is the noncoercive synthesis of the multifarious that nevertheless retains it as what it is, in its divergence and its contradictions, and is thus truly an unfolding of truth. Posited unity as one that is posited always suspends itself; it is essential for it to interrupt itself through what is other to it; its coherence [*Stimmigkeit*] is not to cohere. (216)

And yet no work of art entirely escapes that moment of control that form exerts over the individual moment. All art also carries part of the guilt that haunts society characterized by injustice. Hence, Adorno can proclaim that "form is amoral" (217).

For Adorno, art can be valued according to its effort to escape the totality of form. The less a work aims at unity and the more it allows the disparate elements to remain unreconciled, the greater the work. Truly great art, Adorno declares, always explodes its unity: "Art of the highest order pushes beyond form as totality toward fragmentation" (221). Form, in other words, is merely a precarious balance of the individual moments, none of which are meant to give up their independence for the sake of the whole. Or, as Adorno phrases it with Hegel, art searches for the identity of the identical and the nonidentical. Because this search never reaches its goal, form must not be considered a product but a process.

Adorno's conception of form as an interplay of constructive synthesis and fragmentation is derived from his analyses of modernist works. In fact, the notion of the work itself is characterized for Adorno by the aesthetic products of the modernist period. Thus, he rejects the classical notion of the artwork both as a closed totality and as the radical dissembling of the work in happenings and performance art. As so often, he formulates paradoxically: "The only works that count today are those that are no longer works."[19]

While Adorno would be hard put to demonstrate his theory of fragmentation with regard to masterpieces from all ages and artistic genres, the thesis allows him to argue for art's potential to safeguard the nonidentical. In *Negative Dialectics*, philosophical theory had been faulted for subsuming everything under its systematic totality, but the form of the artwork can grant independence to its moments while incorporating them into a larger unit. In a total society, the nonidentical finds its haven in art. Yet art does not offer a real reconciliation of the nonidentical and the totality. This reconciliation could only occur within a society that had abolished injustice. The reconciliation that art offers is appearance [*Schein*]: "Works of art are appearance [*Schein*] because they grant a type of second, modified existence to that which they cannot be themselves. They are an apparition [*Erscheinung*] because those nonexisting elements within them for which they exist achieve by means of aesthetic realization an existence, no matter how fragmentary" (167). Adorno uses the theological term "apparition" in order to emphasize the intrusion of something transcendental that denounces reality as it is and announces a better existence that is yet to become. Directed partly against Benjamin, the notion of apparition insists on the auratic moment of art, yet it restricts it to a brief moment.[20]

Form, then, is the dialectics of a constructive process, a synthesis, and nonidentical moments. These enter into art not by a process of selection and incorporation, because such cognitive mechanisms would require previous subsumation under concepts and, hence, the destruction of the nonidentical. Instead, the artist takes recourse to a precognitive mode of behavior in order to open a passage for the nonidentical into the work. This aesthetic interaction with the object, which permits the appearance of the latter in the work without being subjected to a process of generalization, Adorno calls *mimesis.* Like Lukács, Adorno takes up one of the central notions of classical aesthetics, but only to reverse its traditional meaning. Adorno defines mimesis as "the nonconceptual affinity of the subject's product to its other, to that which it had not posited" (86 f.). From this somewhat cryptic formulation, a critique of the traditional concept of mimesis emerges.

The Platonic tradition, in particular, had considered artistic mimesis with some skepticism, since it was merely a reduplication of material objects that were, in turn, already flawed approximations to their ideas. Adorno now declares such mimesis, that is, the duplication of the world in art, problematic because it bestows a dignity on the status quo that is unmerited. Such mimesis sanctions the powers that be: "Insofar as art was also mimesis [*Abbild*], its coherence has approved of the mimicked object as a necessity, no matter how tragically it fared or how much it was denunciated."[21] Hence, Adorno agrees with Plato that mimesis as the artistic reproduction of reality must be shunned, because the existing reality does not deserve this kind of attention. Where Plato argues from a metaphysical point of view that advances a noncorporeal world as the reality worth our attention, Adorno pitches the utopia of a reconciled society against the status quo in order to discredit mimesis, understood as reproduction. His own concept, although never fully formulated, considers mimesis to be an archaic relation to the object that is closer to magic rituals than to technical skill. Just as ugliness is the return of the archaic in art, mimesis, too, signifies a primordial moment that breaks into civilization. Art must contain ugliness because reality is cruel; it must be mimetic to remind us that the violence we exert against each other and on the object shall be overcome. But whereas the ugly is linked up with cruelty, mimesis is a reconciliatory embrace. Oftentimes, Adorno uses the term *Anschmiegung* as a description for the mimetic process as it should be, a kind of cuddling up to the object that has tender and protective associations. Such behavior is ruled by the letting-be of the object; mimesis becomes the anticipation of a society reconciled with itself and with nature. Art must contain ugliness because reality is cruel; likewise, it must be mimetic to remind us that the violence we exert against each other and on the object shall be overcome.

Adorno is purposefully yet nevertheless disappointingly vague when it comes to the mimetic process. It is hard to see which faculties are supposed to be involved in this preconceptual, archaic relation to the object and how such mimesis enters into the work of art. Still, Adorno insists that mimesis is not an emotional or physical response to the world but a form of cognition. More precisely, artistic mimesis complements conceptual cognition through the incorporation of that which escapes the concept. Because of its mimetic moment, art is "a form of cognition and hence 'rational' itself" (87).[22]

The Truth of Art

Adorno emphatically sides with Schelling against Kant regarding the question of aesthetic truth. Not only does art offer cognition, but it also offers such cognition where the philosophical concept falls short. Adorno declares that Kant's theory of disinterested pleasure is a humiliation of spirit because it reduces spirit to the contemplation and admiration of the pleasurable aesthetic object without any consideration for its truth content.[23] Yet art must be interrogated about its truth: "All aesthetic questions terminate in those regarding the truth content of the works of art: is that which a work in its specific form carries with it true in terms of objective spirit?" (498). Also, art is by no means disinterested. If only in a mediated sense, every great work, due to its twofold nature as autonomous entity and fait social, contains within it the longing for happiness.

Although Adorno subscribes to Schelling's view of art as a means of cognition that surpasses those of theory, he nevertheless holds that the cognitive content of the work requires conceptual interpretation. The adequate interpretation of a work of art, though, cannot be supplied by the historical sciences of art, such as philology, art history, or musicology; rather, the only sufficient explication of art must be philosophical. An artwork may contain a truth that is singular to it, but it is in need of an interpreter. The truth it contains requires translation into philosophical language: "Therefore art requires philosophy that interprets it in order to say what the former cannot say while it can only be said in art by not saying it" (113).[24] Referring back to the interplay of Kantian faculties, A. Wellmer comments: "As much as a moment of blindness adheres to aesthetic intuition, a moment of emptiness adheres to the mediation of philosophical thought."[25] It is not quite clear how Adorno imagines safeguarding the truth content of art in its translation into philosophy, since even the critical theory that has given up on the totalizing synthesis is always in danger of regressing into ideology. Still, he insists on the sublation of aesthetic experience into thought: "genuine aesthetic experience must become philosophy or it will not be at all" (197).

Nevertheless, it would be a mistake to think of this transposition of the aesthetic experience into philosophy as a process of conceptualization. The nonidentical moment in art, its mimetic *Anschmiegung*, can never be eliminated from the realm of aesthetics. Art is a form of rationality that criticizes that which is only rational. Much like Heidegger with his theory of the interplay of world and earth, Adorno situates the work of art between its elusiveness to thought and its philosophical interpretation. While interpretation of art is mandatory, its result is never sufficient. The advantage that art has over conceptual thought is not eliminated in the interpretation: "The enigmatic character [of art] survives the interpretation that demands an answer" (189). Even after the interpretation, the work of art remains a riddle. Despite his opposition to Kant, this notion yet again resurrects the concept of the *aesthetic idea.* Because all great works remain enigmatic, they always require further elucidation and new attempts to comprehend their truth. Although without philosophy art cannot be understood at all, philosophy is not sufficient to completely understand it.

In still another aspect Adorno harks back to Kant. Like the latter, Adorno does not restrict the aesthetic experience to art as had been customary after Hegel. Instead, he includes natural beauty in aesthetics. The beauty of nature manifests itself as that which escapes technical reason and the reduction of nature to the status of resource for production in a capitalist society. Hence, it becomes a different name for the nonidentical: "Natural beauty is the trace of the nonidentical within the objects under the spell of universal identity" (114).[26] Attempts to formulate an aesthetics of ecology have taken up this conception, which can be utilized to combine an aesthetic attitude with an ethics of respect. Although Adorno himself would be skeptical regarding the chances for such a new ethos because for him no right attitude toward the object can emerge within a wrong society, he must nevertheless be credited for reintroducing natural beauty into aesthetics after its long absence.

Adorno is skeptical in general about the possibility of attributing specific political functions to art. Once art becomes engaged in concrete social struggles, it becomes propaganda or, even worse, a commodity. Diametrically opposed to the position of Lukács and also to

Sartre's concept of an engaged literature, Adorno's notion of the political in art does not manifest itself in the content. Any concrete political agenda undermines the precarious balance of synthesis and mimesis by affixing a distinct position to the work. Once art tells precisely how life and society should be, it has stopped being enigmatic. Therefore, the political element in art must reside in its form. Adorno posits that art takes an opposition to the present society, not by specifically contradicting any of its moments but through its mere existence. Because art refuses to be useful and because it only follows its own internal logic, "it criticizes society through its existence only. . . . Nothing that is pure and constructed according to its immanent law exists without silently criticizing, without denouncing the humiliation by an existence that moves ever closer to the total society of commodity exchange" (335).

While art critiques explicit societal shortcomings, it abstains from painting the picture of a better polity. Adorno refuses to attribute any picture-book utopia to works of art: "The consolation of great artworks rests less in what they say and more in the fact that they exist despite the status quo. The most desolate carry hope with the greatest possibility."[27] For Adorno, the fact that art exists tells us that society should not exist as it is. Theologically speaking, art is a sign of the fallen condition. At the end of history, either as a theological parusia or in a completely reconciled communist world, art will therefore no longer be. All art carries within it the desire for its own sublation, its disappearance within a life that no longer needs it. The sadness of art, to which we will turn momentarily, is also due to the fact that its essence is tainted by a desire for self-overcoming. While art defends life against a society in which the Thanatos drive becomes ever more pronounced, deep within it, it harbors the same desire for its own abolition.

Art cannot escape its aporetic situation; it must remain independent from any political agenda, and at the same time, it has to retain a social nexus if it does not want to become a harmless pastime. Hence, it perpetually struggles between engagement and entertainment, and its existence is threatened by both moments. This seemingly inescapable dilemma for Adorno mirrors the state of society that has become total and attempts to "swallow everything that occurs" (353). Therefore, art can only be political by completely refusing to participate in all matters social – it must negate communication. Yet it is precisely from this renunciation of communication that art's political uselessness results:

Today, the acute reason for the social uselessness of artworks that do not cede to crude propaganda is that they must rid themselves of all communicative means which might bring them closer to the population so that they can resist the total system of communication. Artworks only have a practical function at most through a hardly quantifiable change of consciousness, not because they harangue." (360)

Still, a certain tension is undeniable between Adorno's adherence to Schelling's paradigm of art as an organon of truth and his thesis regarding the refusal to communicate. While it is not necessary to think of communication in terms of conceptual language, it seems to be essential for a truth content to radiate from the work to the recipient. If he considers hermetic works to be paradigmatic for art, Adorno must explain how the truth-claim can be upheld.

Again art's role is defined negatively: It must resist total society. All constructive efforts would be co-opted; hence, art's obligation is to anarchism. Whereas Gadamer had hailed art for its potential to aid order in a world threatening to fall apart, Adorno wants to mobilize it against a world characterized by deathly rigidity: "The task of art today is to bring chaos into the order."[28] Hence, the effect of artworks is the dissolution of previous conceptions of world and self. Like Gadamer, Adorno emphasizes that a work must disappoint expectations; like Benjamin and Heidegger, he considers the encounter with great art to be a shock for the recipient. Art allows the subject to overcome his or her own limitations and restrictions: "Shock [*Erschütterung*], in opposition to the usual sense of the concept, is no particular satisfaction of the self, not related to pleasure. Rather, it is a moment of liquidation of the self that becomes aware of its own limits and finality through this shock" (364). Unlike Benjamin, however, Adorno regards the shock not as occurring in distraction but as the result of contemplative effort: "The self, in order to see even the slightest bit beyond the prison that it itself is, does not need distraction, but the highest concentration" (364). In a vision of the work's form, its construction into a unity, the self loses itself and something objective breaks into the subjective consciousness. Truth occurs after the highest effort has given way to an egoless objectivity – a notion that resembles Zen practices.

Just as encounters with great art break down the subjectivity of the recipient, great art also transcends all subjective efforts of the artist. In respect to lyric poetry Adorno declares: "The highest lyrical products are those in which the subject resonates in language without residue of matter until language itself speaks."[29] Sounding initially much like Heidegger, Adorno quickly establishes the distance between them by arguing that for him, the great poem contains a reconciliation of self and language, whereas for Heidegger, it is the manifestation of the sacrifice of the self to Being: "The moment of selflessness in which the subject submerges into language is not its sacrifice to Being. It is not that of violence, not even of violence against the subject, but that of reconciliation: language only speaks once it no longer speaks as alien to the subject, but rather as its own voice" (57).

The objective moment of art that we experience once our preconceived notions of it have been suspended Adorno defines as the truth of history. Schiller had also argued that artworks preserve the memory of humankind. For him, they are reminders of man's potential to achieve the outstanding, whereas for Adorno, they transmit to later generations the story of suffering. Just like man's own history, the history of art is one of anguish and affliction. Therefore, the character of all great art is that of darkness, joylessness, and dissonance. These moments are constant in the history of art, not specific to any historical period. The history of art cannot be written as a withdrawal of the harmonious and its replacement by dissonance. Nor is dissonance a musical phenomenon only. Rather, it is that which disrupts the seemingly harmonious totality of all great art and, thus, allows the antagonistic forces contained therein to become visible. In Michelangelo, Rembrandt, or the late Beethoven, dissonance triumphs over harmony (168). Art gives expression to suffering; it does not transmit joy. As the truth of existence is pain, art must be true to it: "Expression of art is mimetic as the expression of all creatures is torment" (169).

Given this painful nature of art, no encounter with it can be characterized by pleasure. To understand art means to shun all pretensions to the delight that it might give. Whoever avers to get joy from a work of art makes himself known as an ignoramus. Moreover, for Adorno, it is an ethical imperative not to enjoy art if one does not want to aid the powers that be: "In the false world all ἡδονή is false" (26). Admiration for the truth of a great work takes the place of pleasure.

Adorno's aesthetic theory privileges art from the mid–eighteenth century onward, and he even tends to make modernist works paradigmatic. This leads to the problem that modernist form experiments, such as dissonance, rupture, and hermetic communication structures, are projected backward onto works with a different genesis and appeal. It can certainly be a matter of debate if such retrospective interpretation yields aesthetically interesting results, partly because Adorno himself limits himself to a minimum of examples in his concrete analyses and returns time and again to the late Beethoven as his main proof. There can be little doubt, however, about the inadequacy of this theory to comprehend preautonomous art. Adorno's categories become absurd when he claims: "The autonomous Beethoven is more metaphysical than Bach's ordo, hence more true."[30] If the truth of art depends on how well its form captures the antagonisms of society, and Adorno attributes to Bach the capability to do just this in an exemplary fashion,[31] then this valuation lacks all basis and calls into question the usage of "truth."

In addition, from Adorno's favoring of modernist art emerges a doubtful tendency to be prescriptive regarding contemporary aesthetic production. In an apodictic manner, Adorno declares all representative painting to be an impossibility and states that only nonfigurative art can resist society's efforts at integration. Even a portrait of Che Guevara is more acceptable to the establishment than any abstract canvas (316). Not only is such a statement at best problematic,[32] but Adorno also contradicts himself when he declares that absolute painting is always in danger of becoming harmless and indistinguishable from wallpaper (51). Still, he insists that today's art must be abstract because it must mirror societal relations that have become abstract themselves.

These lapses in judgment and self-contradictions indicate that there is a tendency in Adorno to let the theory dominate the actual aesthetic experience. Oftentimes, preconceived notions of art's nature and proper function seem to determine the interpretation of the work itself. Under such conditions, however, it is hard to uphold the claim that art possesses a truth that philosophy cannot grasp on its own. Rather, the already established philosophical position seems repeatedly to determine what kind of truth art is expected to reveal.[33]

Adorno aims to renew Schelling's aesthetic theory, but in the course of the adaptation of this paradigm to his own philosophical framework, he reduces it to a dark shadow of its former self. After he has reduced the practical function of art to that of saying "No" to the status quo, Adorno also restricts the epistemic role of art. Despite his insistence that art discloses a truth that escapes the philosophical concept, this truth, too, is restricted to negation. Art's only positive moment is its nonparticipation in anything negative, that is, its abstention from all practice. Its *promesse de bonheur* is not to tire of saying that things as they are now are not to be like this. Art's truth is dark; it has none of the features of fulfillment that Schelling's Neoplatonic encounter with the absolute had contained. Even the anticipation of a reconciled society is burdened by the thought that art will disappear once such a society becomes reality. At the beginning of the nineteenth century, truth, art, and joy were linked in Schelling's aesthetic paradigm; by the middle of the twentieth century, Adorno's reworking of this paradigm interdicts all pleasure, except the cognitive pleasure of knowing the truth about society, restricted to those few capable of deciphering art's dark message.

Conclusion

Our narrative of the German aesthetic tradition has reached the present. Yet we have come to no conclusion, if by conclusion we mean closure, the end of an intentional development and a telos to be reached. We end our story, because to continue it would mean to step into the realm of prediction. Hegel is right when he says that philosophy awakens only at the end of a day to look back, to wonder, to sort out, and to find a logic in events that escape the immediacy of the present.

The current stage of aesthetics is one of revivalism. Yet while all of the twentieth-century aesthetic positions revived previous notions, there was hardly a time when almost *all* paradigmatic theories were taken up *simultaneously*. Today, however, some philosophers return to Baumgarten in order to replace aesthetics as a philosophy of art with the original notion of aesthetics as sense perception. Those, for example, who champion an ecological aesthetics argue for such a shift in the conception of aesthetics as a discipline. Others aim to restrict the notion of aesthetics to art, yet warn of a philosophical overburdening of art. These thinkers see the post-Kantian development in aesthetics as a wrong turn toward the cognitive. For them, to place demands upon art, like to grant access to the absolute and to contain truth unavailable through philosophy, does art no favor. Rather, art needs to be freed from the heterogeneous claims that philosophy heaps upon it. Still others take the opposite stance and celebrate the early romantic philosophers for being the ones to challenge the coherence theory of truth from an aesthetic perspective. Art, however, retains its connection to cognition rather emphatically in this view. A fourth group focuses on Hegel's pronouncement regarding the end of art and deduces that art has now reached the stage where it no longer is under any obligations with regard to period style, medium, subject matter, and so forth and has therefore finally reached a stage of a joyous anything goes. Finally, the anti-idealism of Nietzsche especially is renewed in much poststructuralist thought. Foucault's notion of aesthetics, as well as that of his German and American followers, revives the attempt to broaden aesthetics to enable it to give answers to traditional philosophical enigmas like self-consciousness, cognition, and the nature of the polity.

Some questions emerge when we consider the multiplicity of positions, all attempting to continue aesthetic philosophy. First, it seems that one needs to determine if aesthetics is to deal predominantly or even exclusively with art – and generally, that means the great works of art from the tradition – or if aesthetics should be regarded as an inquiry into sense perception. In the second case, aesthetics can continue to deal with art but is by no means restricted to it. All other cultural products – television, movies, fashion, diets, design, pop music, and so on – as well as nature itself are as good or better as objects of analysis than great artworks. In consequence, empirical psychology, anthropology, sociology, cultural studies, and other fields could be incorporated into aesthetics. In fact, aesthetics would largely cease to be a philosophical discipline. While this prospect might be of interest to some, even to some philosophers, it tends to sell out philosophical thought to current cultural trends.

Or, to take the opposite view, is aesthetics still to become truly autonomous and shed the guidance of philosophy? Maybe the experience of art – and this position presupposes a restriction of aesthetics to art, because no other product can be truly autonomous – can only fully unfold once it has freed itself from all philosophical expectations as well. This would mean to leave the question regarding the absolute to metaphysics, the question regarding truth to epistemology, the question regarding the foundations of a community to practical politics, and hence, to leave art to itself at last. Yet it is difficult to see what would remain to be said for philosophical aesthetics once it had described the experience of art. Is an elaboration on Kant's subjective aesthetics all that remains to be accomplished? Would not true aesthetic autonomy even mean to eventually leave all philosophical reflection behind? Would not philosophy ultimately be condemned to silent admiration only?

When two alternatives seem equally unattractive, it could be that the question to which these positions give answer is wrong. Both aesthetics, the one that wants to return to Baumgarten's theory of sense perception and the one that aims to grant true autonomy to the aesthetic experience for the first time, regard the autonomy of art as a given. Yet it might be that the multifaceted and somewhat confused state of contemporary aesthetics is due to the fact that the era of autonomous art has ended, motivating especially the turn away from art to sense perception in aesthetics. Not to be misunderstood, certainly art has by no means lost its present autonomy. But it can hardly be doubted that art neither accepts nor experiences any restrictions at all these days. It can choose to be political if it wants, but it can equally well opt not to be. It can quote historical styles, yet it can also aim to be original and free from citations. Such freedom of art, however, seems problematic, both for art itself and for its philosophical reflection. For the artists themselves, Thomas Mann has expressed this difficulty in his novel *Doktor Faustus.* The dilemma of his protagonist Adrian Leverkühn is precisely that art no longer belongs anywhere, yet it cannot overcome its longing to belong. In order to create nevertheless, Leverkühn sells his soul to the devil. In the end, though, no saving grace interferes with his fate; death overcomes life and renders the works meaningless.

If this is the plight of art today, it should not be a surprise to find aesthetics in the contradictory state it is in. Philosophical aesthetics can only find its function when art itself has found its role beyond autonomy once more. Yet this role cannot be prescribed by politics, philosophy, or theology. Art can only give up its freedom of its own free will. That art encounters no invitations from anywhere to sacrifice its autonomy, however, is a sad fact to acknowledge. An art, though, that would tie itself to something other than itself, to something that merits the sacrifice of autonomy, would under one perspective look a lot like that romantic art that Hegel had considered as overcome by religion and eventually by philosophy. Rather than being a *Kunstreligion* in which the gods and their sculptural representation collapse into one, the notion of romantic art rests on art's acknowledgment of a metaphysical truth that lies beyond its own sphere, but to which it is nevertheless obliged, because it has its very foundation in this ground. Such a conception still seems to be a realistic option today, but its possibility must be elucidated elsewhere.

Notes

Chapter 1. Baumgarten, Mendelssohn

1 For an interesting account of the philosophical issues that were at stake in the decade immediately following the publication of the first *Critique,* cf. Frederick C. Beiser, *The Fate of Reason: German Philosophy from Kant to Fichte* (Cambridge, Mass.: Harvard University Press, 1987).

2 For an account that argues against any break between the rationalist metaphysics and Baumgarten's aesthetics, cf. Horst Michael Schmidt, *Sinnlichkeit und Verstand: Zur philosophischen und poetologischen Begründung von Erfahrung und Urteil in der deutschen Aufklärung (Leibniz, Wolff, Gottsched, Bodmer und Breitinger, Baumgarten)* (Munich: Fink, 1982), Chapter 4.

3 Herbert Marcuse argues from a socioanalytic perspective that this devaluation of epistemic sensibility was brought about by the association of sensibility as cognitive means and as appetite: "But the senses are not exclusively, not even primarily, organs of cognition. Their cognitive function is confused with their appetitive function (sensuality); they are erotogenic, and they are governed by the pleasure principle. From this fusion of the cognitive and appetitive functions derives the confused, inferior, passive character of sense-cognition which makes it unsuitable for the reality principle unless subjected to and formed by the conceptual activity of the intellect, of reason" (*Eros and Civilization.* [Boston: Beacon Press, 1966], p. 183 f.). Consequently, Marcuse claims Baumgarten as one precursor for his project of nonrepressive sublimation in which art safeguards the pleasure of the senses against their domination by the reality principle.

4 The most elaborate version can be found in *Meditationes de Cognitione, Veritate et Ideis* (Meditations on cognition, truth and ideas) of 1684.

Another sketch is provided in §24 of *Discours de Métaphysique* (Discourse on metaphysics). The most fundamental distinction between obscure and clear cognition is also taken up in §289 of *Essais de theodicée sur la bonté de Dieu, la liberté de l'homme et l'origine du mal* (Essay on the goodness of God, the freedom of man and the origin of evil).

5 *Discours de Métaphysique*, §24.

6 New Haven and London: Yale University Press, 1997, p. 4.

7 At least this famous first paragraph shall be quoted in the original Latin here: "Aesthetica (theoria liberalium artium, gnoseologia inferior, ars pulchre cogitandi, ars analogi rationis) est scientia cognitionis sensitivae." In Alexander Gottlieb Baumgarten, *Theoretische Ästhetik: Die grundlegenden Abschnitte aus der "Aesthetica" (1750/1758)*, Latin/German text edited and translated by Hans Rudolf Schweizer (Hamburg: Meiner, 1983), p. 3. It might be added that a complete translation of the *Aesthetica* into German does not yet exist.

8 See Ursula Franke, *Kunst als Erkenntnis: Die Rolle der Sinnlichkeit in der Ästhetik des Alexander Gottlieb Baumgarten*, Studia Leibnitiana Supplementa, Vol. 9 (Wiesbaden: Franz Steiner, 1972), p. 39. Franke's dissertation still remains one of the best commentaries on Baumgarten's aesthetics.

9 "Kollegium über die Ästhetik," in Alexander Gottlieb Baumgarten, *Texte zur Grundlegung der Ästhetik*, Latin/German text edited and translated by Hans Rudolf Schweizer (Hamburg: Meiner, 1983), p. 80.

10 All quotations from Mendelssohn refer to his *Gesammelte Schriften* (Berlin: Akademie-Ausgabe, 1929). The writings on aesthetics can be found in the first two volumes.

11 See Julius H. Schoeps, *Moses Mendelssohn* (Königstein: Jüdischer Verlag, 1979).

12 Cf. *Geschichte der Kunst des Altertums*, in *Winckelmanns Werke* (Berlin and Weimar: Aufbau, 1982), p. 196.

13 E. H. Gombrich demonstrates that Vasari's definition of "Gothic" is not the result of a morphological study, but rather due to the application of a stereotypical listing of architectural flaws that Vasari takes over from Vitruvius. The condemnation of the Gothic, however, becomes dogmatic only when in Northern Europe the Classical is pitched against regional architecture so that "Gothic"comes to signify the bad taste of the Middle Ages that was overcome by the Italian resurrection of Antique principles of art. *Norm and Form: Studies in the Art of the Renaissance* (London: Phaidon, 1966).

14 *Hamburger Ausgabe* (Munich: Deutscher Taschenbuch Verlag, 1988), vol. 12, p. 11.

15 *A Philosophical Enquiry into the Origin of our Ideas of the Sublime and Beautiful*, Part III, Section 6 (Oxford: Oxford University Press, 1990), p. 97.

16 Cf. Klaus-Werner Segreff, *Moses Mendelssohn und die Aufklärungsästhetik im 18. Jahrhundert* (Bonn: Bouvier, 1984), pp. 97 ff.

Chapter 2. Kant

1 Brigitte Scheer comments on this notion of esoteric mimesis in *Einführung in die philosophische Ästhetik* (Darmstadt: Primus, 1997), p. 21.

2 Odo Marquard attempts a somewhat idiosynchratic explanation of the rise of philosophical aesthetics in the eighteenth century. He argues that aesthetics is the outcome of the frustration with scientific reason that cannot comprehend the totality of reality (Kant's thing in itself remains unknowable) and the frustration with practical reason that thinks the concept of the good independent of its concrete existence. Thus, the turn toward aesthetics mediates between abstract scientific reason and concrete historical reason that has not yet been achieved by philosophical thought. *Aesthetica und Anaesthetica: Philosophische Überlegungen* (Paderborn: Schöningh, 1989), pp. 21–31.

3 *Werke in drei Bänden* (Munich: Hanser, 1982), vol. 3, p. 20.

4 The philosopher who sees this radical split between art and truth as detrimental for the history of aesthetics is Hans-Georg Gadamer. Cf. *Wahrheit und Methode,* 6th ed. (Tübingen: Mohr and Siebeck, 1990), pp. 48–107.

5 Otto Pöggeler, *Die Frage nach der Kunst: Von Hegel zu Heidegger* (Munich and Freiburg: K. Alber, 1984), pp. 215. In all fairness it has to be pointed out, however, that Kant included more references to concrete works of art in his 1764 *Beobachtungen über das Gefühl des Schönen und Erhabenen* (Observations about the sensation of the beautiful and sublime). Here, Kant mentions such antique literary figues as Homer, Virgil, and Ovid, as well as Milton, Klopstock, and the painter Hogarth. Similarly, in his *Anthropology,* Kant mentions a fair number of contemporary writers, such as Sterne, Fielding, Richardson, and others, as well as painters from different ages. For a study on Kant's reception in the history of art, see Mark A. Cheetham's *Kant, Art and Art History: Moments of Discipline* (Cambridge: Cambridge University Press, 2001).

6 For a detailed account of Kant's third *Critique* in English, cf. Paul Guyer's *Kant and the Claims of Taste,* 2d ed. (Cambridge: Cambridge University Press, 1997). Equally important are his two other volumes, *Essays in Kant's Aesthetics* (Chicago: University of Chicago Press, 1982) and *Kant and the Experience of Freedom* (Cambridge: Cambridge University Press, 1993). For discussions of many of the problems of Kant's aesthetic theory, see the excellent volume edited by Herman Parret: *Kants Ästhetik. Kant's Aesthetics. L'esthétique de Kant* (Berlin and New York: de Gruyter, 1998).

7 Winfried Menninghaus argues in his book *In Praise of Nonsense: Kant and Bluebeard* (Stanford, Calif.: Stanford University Press, 1999), that a direct

line can be drawn from Kant's notion of free beauty in art to the notion of the arabesque and the poetry of nonsense of the early Romantics. To me, this argument overemphasizes the antihermeneutic moments in the third *Critique*, yet certain parallels in argumentation exist without a doubt.

8 Kant relativizes this position in his 1798 *Anthropologie in pragmatischer Hinsicht* (Anthropology in the pragmatic respect). Here, he argues that an a priori judgment of taste exists, and he labels this aesthetic judgment *vernünftelnd,* roughly meaning moving in the direction of a nonsensual judgment. Yet even with respect to the regular aesthetic judgment, Kant now claims that it is both a judgment of taste and a judgment of understanding, although the purity of the latter suffers in it (§64). These highly complex problems merit further discussion, but this has to be done in a separate study.

9 Karl Philipp Moritz, "Versuch einer Vereinigung aller schönen Künste und Wissenschaften unter dem Begriff des *in sich selbst Vollendeten,*" *Beiträge zur Ästhetik* (Mainz: Dieterich'sche Verlagsbuchhandlung, 1989), pp. 7–18. Quotation is on p. 12.

10 Ernst Cassirer points out that there is a tradition of the moment of disinterested pleasure that ranges from Plotinus to Moses Mendelssohn and Karl Philipp Moritz. *Kant's Life and Thought* (New Haven, Conn.: Yale University Press, 1981), p. 326. See also Chapter 1 in this volume and the discussion of *Billigungsvermögen* in Mendelssohn.

Heinz Paetzold has attempted to read disinterested pleasure as a paradigm for a noninstrumental way of the subject to relate to objects. He sees in this an anticipation of Heidegger's theory of art. Paetzold also suggests that there is a utopian element in the free play of imagination and understanding that hints at a successful existence in which sensuality and rationality are reconciled. Aesthetic perception therefore contains the possibility of a different society. I think that this reading stretches Kant beyond his limits, but it is an interesting recent attempt to reread the aesthetic tradition from a more or less neo-Marxist point of view. *Ästhetik des deutschen Idealismus* (Wiesbaden: Steiner, 1983).

11 Manfred Frank has suggested that the relevance of this moment of Kant's theory for the philosophers of discourse ethics, primarily J. Habermas and K.-O. Apel, is due to the strong emphasis on the universalizability of a subjective judgment. While there are certainly connections here, I doubt that especially Apel's insistence on rational ultimate explanation can be seen as taking very many cues from Kant's commonality of feeling. Ultimate explanations rely heavily on conceptualization, albeit a counterfactual one. *Einführung in die frühromantische Ästhetik* (Frankfurt am Main: Suhrkamp, 1989), pp. 68 ff.

12 Peter Bürger suggested that the aesthetic idea does not have to be restricted to works of art, but that it also accounts for historical personalities, etc. *Zur Kritik der idealistischen Ästhetik,* 2d ed. (Frankfurt am Main: Suhrkamp, 1990). While this is certainly worth considering, it becomes unclear which kind of objects could contain aesthetic ideas and which could not. Once the first step beyond the work of art is taken, there is little reason not to argue that basically everything might become subject to an infinite number of interesting interpretations. This position is generally held by such neopragmatists as Richard Rorty, Stanley Fish, and others. For the negation of any ontologically special status of art, see, for example, Fish's *Is There a Text in This Class?* (Cambridge, Mass.: Harvard University Press, 1980), as well as Rorty's "The Pragmatist's Progress," in Umberto Eco with Richard Rorty, Jonathan Culler, and Christine Brooke-Rose, *Interpretation and Overinterpretation,* edited by Stefan Collini (Cambridge: Cambridge University Press, 1992), pp. 89–108.

13 Winfried Menninghaus, *In Praise of Nonsense,* especially pp. 15–31.

14 At times, artists and theoreticians have fantasized about a perceptive innocence that would lead to aesthetic appreciation free from all concepts. Such seeing or listening, it is then assumed, would very much resemble that of animals. This fantasy is obviously a far cry from Kant, who would regard it as neither desirable nor possible. For an account of this position, see Arthur Danto's "Animals as Art Historians: Reflections on the Innocent Eye," in *Beyond the Brillo Box: The Visual Arts in Post-Historical Perspective* (Berkeley: University of California Press, 1992), pp. 14–31.

15 In his book *Kant and Fine Art* (Oxford: Oxford University Press, 1986), Salim Kemal challenges this reading by claiming a superiority of art over nature because of its link to morality (p. 15 and passim). Although this argument certainly calls into question the rigidity of Kant's hierarchy, I doubt that it carries enough weight to actually reverse it.

16 *Werke in einem Band* (Berlin and Weimar: Aufbau, 1982), p. 150.

17 In recent years, the Italian proponent of "weak thought," Gianni Vattimo, argued that part of the aesthetic pleasure results from the subject's recognition of its own membership in a group. This recognition together with taste is what defines the aesthetic function. "Death or Decline of Art," in *The End of Modernity* (Baltimore: Johns Hopkins University Press, 1991).

18 Generally speaking, Kant argues against habitual morality, a notion that Hegel treats under the heading of *Sittlichkeit.* In his 1798 *Anthropologie in pragmatischer Hinsicht* (Anthropology in pragmatic respect), he states clearly: "Virtue is that moral strength that lies in obedience to one's duty without ever becoming a habit, but that must rather emerge always anew and original from one's mental disposition [*Denkungsart*]" (§10). A few paragraphs later, however, Kant argues that social role playing can be

helpful in turning merely pretended virtues into habitual ones (§12). It seems that a certain tension regarding the desirability of morality based on habit continues to exist in Kant.

19 Nelson Goodman argues that Kant's emphasis on the beautiful causes his entire aesthetic theory to become unbalanced, since there are many instances in which art is not beautiful. *Languages of Art: An Approach to the Theory of Symbols* (Indianapolis and New York: Bobbs-Merrill, 1968). I briefly address this concern later in the context of pleasure. For an argument similar to mine, see Mary A. McCloskey, *Kants's Aesthetics* (London: Macmillan Press, 1987), Chapters 2 and 4.

Chapter 3. Schiller

1 All of Schiller's later writings on aesthetics are collected in Volume 2 of the *Werke in drei Bänden* (Munich: Hanser, 1966).

2 In his book *The Aesthetic State: A Quest in Modern German Thought* (Berkeley: University of California Press, 1989), Josef Chytry focuses on what he believes is the utopian moment of an aesthetically ordained state in German thought from classicism to the twentieth century. Unfortunately, he greatly underestimates the metaphysical quest that motivated the inquiries of Schiller, as well as Hölderlin, Schelling, and Hegel (and, ex negativo, Heidegger). The great emphasis placed on the aspect of practical philosophy – especially in Romantic and Idealist philosophy only one of the many reflexes of the metaphysical basis of the system – therefore leads to a distorted view of this philosophical tradition.

3 *Kallias oder Über die Schönheit*, p. 352.

4 In a letter to his friend Körner of December 21, 1792, Schiller states: "I believe to have found the objective concept of beauty that eo ipso qualifies for an objective principle of taste and that Kant doubts." Quoted from Jürgen Bolten, ed., *Schillers Briefe über die ästhetische Erziehung* (Frankfurt am Main: Suhrkamp, 1984), p. 99. See also the letter to Fischenich of February 11, 1793.

5 Lukács makes this point repeatedly in his writings. One good summary of his views on Schiller's aesthetics is the 1935 essay "Zur Ästhetik Schillers" in his book *Beiträge zur Geschichte der Ästhetik* (Berlin: Aufbau, 1956). Still, despite complimenting Schiller on his historical sense, Lukács nevertheless faults him for failing to develop a "thoroughly concrete historical position," because Schiller deduces his historical categories from his categories of reason and, hence, postulates the priority of consciousness over being. For the Marxist Lukács, this general problem of idealism can only be corrected by the materialism of Marxism-Leninism.

6 Generally, in the nineteenth century, Schiller was regarded as a Kantian who attempted to solve some of Kant's unresolved issues, whereas in the twentieth century, he was considered a precursor of Hegel. For a brief recapitulation of this turnabout in the reception, cf. Michael J. Böhler, "Die Bedeutung Schillers für Hegels Ästhetik," in *PMLA* 87 (1972): 182–91.

7 Jürgen Habermas plays down this moment by claiming that all aesthetic education in Schiller refers to the community, not to the individual. While certainly true for the stated intentions in the beginning of the *Aesthetic Letters,* the twenty-seventh letter undercuts this position, as will be discussed at the end of this chapter. *Der philosophische Diskurs der Moderne* (Frankfurt am Main: Suhrkamp, 1984), p. 59.

8 Trans. G. M. A. Grube (Indianapolis: Hackett, 1974). Translation altered. See also Plato's *Protagoras,* p. 326, as well as *Nomoi* II, pp. 653–6, and VII, pp. 797–816.

9 J. Bolten, Schillers Briefe, 41. In his famous poem *Das Lied von der Glocke* (The song of the bell), Schiller echoes these criticisms of both the Enlightenment and revolution. Against the Enlightenment educators he argues: "*Weh denen, die dem Ewigblinden / Des Lichtes Himmelsfackel leihn! / Sie strahlt ihm nicht, sie kann nur zünden / Und äschert Städt und Länder ein.*" (Woe upon those who lend the torch of heaven to the eternally blind. It does not enlighten him, it only enflames and burns down cities and countries.) And against the revolutionaries: "*Wenn sich die Völker selbst befrein, / Da kann die Wohlfahrt nicht gedein.*" (When the peoples free themselves, welfare cannot prosper.)

10 Without this philosophical understanding of freedom, an interpretation of Schiller's aesthetics is bound to remain superficial. Fredric Jameson, for example, regards freedom merely in the twofold sense of an integration of personality on the psychic level and the political freedom of the (bourgeois) individual on the societal level. This limitation of the comprehension of the concept of freedom then leads to the claim that Schiller's *Aesthetic Letters* is not an aesthetic but, rather, a political system in which the experience of art is considered the utopian anticipation of revolution. It hardly comes as a surprise that such a restricted reading of the text leads to the faulty conclusion that art's synthesis is "little more than costume drama and a meditation on the lessons of antiquity." *Marxism and Form* (Princeton, N.J.: Princeton University Press, 1971), p. 94.

11 For a very insightful interpretation of this aspect of Schiller's aesthetics, cf. Dieter Henrich, "Beauty and Freedom: Schiller's Struggle with Kant's Aesthetics," in Ted Cohen and Paul Guyer, eds., *Essays in Kant's Aesthetics* (Chicago: Chicago University Press, 1982), pp. 237–57.

12 Plotinus, *The Enneads*, trans. Stephen MacKenna (London: Penguin, 1991), pp. 49 f.

13 Karl Philipp Moritz, "Versuch einer Vereinigung aller schönen Künste und Wissenschaften unter dem Begriff des *in sich selbst Vollendeten*," *Beiträge zur Ästhetik* (Mainz: Dieterich'sche Verlagsbuchhandlung, 1989), pp. 7–18. Quotation is on p. 11.

14 *Werke in drei Bänden*, vol. 1, pp. 701–18. Quotation is on p. 709.

15 Cf. Dieter Henrich, "Der Begriff der Schönheit in Schillers Ästhetik," in *Zeitschrift für philosophische Forschung* 6 (1957): 527–47. Also compare Manfred Frank, *Einführung in die frühromantische Ästhetik* (Frankfurt am Main: Suhrkamp, 1989), pp. 104–20.

16 Friedrich Hölderlin, *Sämtliche Werke und Briefe* (Munich: Hanser, 1970), vol. 1, p. 522.

17 Ibid., p. 744.

18 In fact, matters are a bit more complicated than this. As with many of Schiller's philosophical terms, definition remains vague and the same term is often used to denote different concepts. As Manfred Frank (*Einführung in die frühromantische Ästhetik*, p. 118) has pointed out, the term freedom is used by Schiller in four different senses. However, the relevant sense for the present discussion is the one we refer to here.

19 For a good account of the relation of Schiller and Fichte in these respects, see Wilhelm Hogrebe, "Fichte und Schiller: Eine Skizze," in J. Bolten, Schillers Briefe, pp. 276–89.

20 *Werke*, vol. 3, p. 473.

21 Fichte. *Gesamtausgabe* I (Stuttgart: Frommann, 1981), vol. 6, pp. 333–61. Quotation is on p. 348.

22 *Wahrheit und Methode*, p. 89.

23 In his discussion of the naïve and the sentimental, Georg Lukács comes to the same conclusion: "But the deepest contradiction of Schiller's conception is that between historical and aesthetic understanding of his own basic concepts." "Schillers Theorie der modernen Literatur," in *Goethe und seine Zeit* (Bern: A. Francke, 1947), pp. 78–109. Quotation is on p. 106.

Chapter 4. Schelling

1 *Schelling: Die Kunst in der Philosophie*, Vol. 1: *Schellings Begründung von Natur und Geschichte* (Pfullingen: Neske, 1966), p. 10. Jähnig also underestimates Schelling's contributions to philosophy other than aesthetics when he claims in his foreword that the actual achievement of Schelling is the final part of the *System of Transcendental Idealism*, and that therefore this is what the name Schelling stands for.

2 Friedrich Schlegel, *Kritische Ausgabe.* (KA) (Paderborn, Munich, Vienna, and Darmstadt: Schöningh and Wissenschaftliche Buchgesellschaft, 1958 ff.). The fragments are quoted according to volume, page, and number of the individual fragment.

3 The dictum comes from the *Nachgelassene Schriften* and is quoted in the introduction (xi) to the *Vorlesungen über Ästhetik* (Lectures on aesthetics, 1819) by K. W. L. Heyse. A reprint of the original 1828 edition appeared in 1969 (Darmstadt: Wissenschaftliche Buchgesellschaft).

4 Stuttgart: Reclam, 1968, p. 83.

5 *Eine Einführung in Schellings Philosophie* (Frankfurt am Main: Suhrkamp, 1985), p. 11. My reading of Schelling owes much to the writings of Manfred Frank, who has done a lot to rekindle a philosophical interest in this thinker and the Romantic philosophers in general. In fact, my own engagement with aesthetics began in a more serious manner as a student in his lecture class on the aesthetics of early Romanticism; these lectures were consequently published as *Einführung in die frühromantische Ästhetik.* Despite this debt, we differ in our valuation of the importance that contemporary philosophy should attribute to the Romantic paradigm.

6 "Über einige Beziehungen zwischen Ästhetik und Therapeutik in der Philosophie des neunzehnten Jahrhunderts," in Manfred Frank and Gerhard Kurz, eds., *Materialien zu Schellings philosophischen Anfängen* (Frankfurt am Main: Suhrkamp, 1975), pp. 341–77. Quotation is on p. 371.

7 Cf. Lorenz Dittmann, "Schellings Philosophie der Bildenden Kunst," in H. Baur, L. Dittmann, et al., eds., *Kunstgeschichte und Kunsttheorie im 19. Jahrhundert* (Berlin: de Gruyter, 1963), pp. 38–82. The quotation from Schelling can be found on p. 79.

8 *System des transzendentalen Idealismus* (Hamburg: Meiner, 1992). The page numbers in parentheses do not refer to this edition, however, but to the original edition of 1800.

9 Cf. Walter Schulz, Introduction to *System des transzendentalen Idealismus* (Hamburg: Meiner, 1992), pp. ix–xlvi. This reference is on p. xi.

10 *Schriften,* Vol. 2: *Das philosophische Werk I* (Stuttgart: Kohlhammer, 1960), p. 413.

11 *Grosse Stuttgarter Ausgabe,* Vol. IV, Book 1 (Stuttgart: Kohlhammer, 1960), pp. 216–17.

12 Cf. Henrich's important article "Hölderlin über Urteil und Sein: Eine Studie zur Entstehungsgeschichte des Idealismus," *Hölderlin Jahrbuch* 14 (Tübingen: Mohr and Siebeck), (1965–6), pp. 73–96. Quotation is on p. 79. For a more detailed account, cf. Henrich's *Der Grund im Bewusstsein: Untersuchungen zu Hölderlins Denken (1794–1795)* (Stuttgart: Klett-Cotta, 1992), pp. 40–112.

13 *Zweite Einleitung in die Wissenschaftslehre (1797)*. J. G. Fichte, *Werke, Vol. 1: Schriften zur Wissenschaftslehre* (Frankfurt am Main: Deutscher Klassiker Verlag, 1997), §5, p. 145.

14 Andrew Bowie argues for a close proximity of Schelling's aesthetics to linguistic philosophy, since he considers both as subverting the notion of representation. It cannot be said what the absolute really is – the work of art only shows the absolute, yet does not make it knowable. *Schelling and Modern European Philosophy: An Introduction* (London and New York: Routledge, 1993), p. 183 f. Bowie's notion of representation is the one much criticized in recent philosophy as presuming a full presence of the represented. My use of the term, however, refers back to the original legal meaning of the term to which Gadamer has alerted us, namely, as a situational mediation between the absent that is represented and the stand-in that is present. In turn, the representing element itself is characterized by a curious mixture of presence – its physical and mental identity – and absence – the irrelevance of this identity that is meant to disappear behind the represented.

15 Walter Schulz, Introduction to *System des transzendentalen Idealismus*, p. xv.

16 For a detailed discussion of Hölderlin's role as the pathbreaker for both Schelling and Hegel, cf. Panajotis Kondylis's dissertation, titled *Die Entstehung der Dialektik: Eine Analyse der geistigen Entwicklung von Hölderlin, Schelling und Hegel bis 1802* (Stuttgart: Klett-Cotta, 1979).

17 "Hölderlin über Urteil und Sein," p. 82.

18 *Gedanken über die Nachahmung der griechischen Werke in der Malerei und Bildhauerkunst*, in *Werke*, pp. 1–35. Quotation is on p. 17.

19 Cf. Manfred Frank, *Der kommende Gott: Vorlesungen über die Neue Mythologie* (Frankfurt am Main: Suhrkamp, 1982).

20 Hölderlin, *Grosse Stuttgarter Ausgabe*, Vol. IV, Book 1, pp. 297–9.

21 *Schriften*, Vol. 3: *Das philosophische Werk II* (Stuttgart: Kohlhammer, 1960), pp. 507–24. Quotation is on p. 519.

22 Friedrich Schlegel, *Schriften zur Kunst und Literatur* (Munich: Hanser, 1970), p. 305.

23 Cf. Hans Michael Baumgartner and Harald Korten, *Friedrich Wilhelm Joseph Schelling* (Munich: Beck, 1996), p. 99.

24 Cf. Schelling's letters to A. W. Schlegel of Sept. 3, 1802, and Oct. 4 and 21, 1802, in F. W. J. Schelling, *Texte zur Philosophie der Kunst* (Stuttgart: Reclam, 1982), pp. 134–8.

25 *Sämtliche Werke*, Vol. 5 (Stuttgart and Augsburg: J. G. Cotta, 1859).

26 Cf. Werner Beierwaltes, Introduction to F. W. J. Schelling, *Texte zur Philosophie der Kunst*, p. 24.

27 *Über das Verhältnis der bilden den Künste zu der Natur* (RN), *Sämtliche Werke*, vol. 7, pp. 289–329.

28 For Lessing, this notion would be detrimental. In his *Laokoon* he argued: "Only that is fruitful which leaves room to play for the imagination. The more we see, the more we have to contribute in thought. The more we contribute in thought, the more we must believe to see. In the entire process of an affect no moment lacks this advantage more than its epitome. Above it nothing exists, and to show the acme to the eye means to tie the wings of imagination." *Werke in drei Bänden*, vol. 3, p. 27.

29 *Erwin: Vier Gespräche über das Schöne und die Kunst* (Munich: Fink, 1970), reprint of the 1907 edition, p. 387.

30 Cf. W. Beierwaltes, Introduction, 23.

31 *Werke in drei Bänden*, vol. 3, p. 245.

32 *Vorlesungen über die Methode des akademischen Studiums* (LM), *Sämtliche Werke*, Vol. 5.

33 Frank, *Einführung in die frühromantische Ästhetik*, pp. 199 f.

34 Berlin: Paul Cassirer, 1920, pp. 87 f.

35 "Die Theorie der romantischen Ironie," in *Studien zur Romantik und zur idealistischen Philosophie* (Paderborn: Schöningh, 1988), pp. 46–65, especially p. 58.

36 *Vorlesungen über die Ästhetik I*, Vol. 13 of *Werke*, edited by E. Moldenhauer and Karl Markus Michel (Frankfurt am Main: Suhrkamp, 1970), p. 95.

37 For an account that positions F. Schlegel's concept of irony much closer to Hegel's quest for the absolute, see R. Bubner's "Zur dialektischen Bedeutung romantischer Ironie," in *Innovationen des Idealismus* (Göttingen: Vandenhoeck und Ruprecht, 1995), pp. 152–63. Bubner argues that Schlegel's irony mediates between Fichte's notion of the absolute ego as a beginning for all philosophy and Hegel's notion of the absolute as an objective telos. In his reading of Schlegel, irony keeps awake the desire to leave all particular achievements behind in order to advance to the absolute and its philosophical conception.

38 *The Concept of Irony with Continual Reference to Socrates*, trans. Howard and Edna Hong, vol. 2 in *Works* (Princeton, N.J.: Princeton University Press, 1989), pp. 275 f.

39 *Einführung in die frühromantische Ästhetik*, p. 335.

Chapter 5. Hegel

1 Paradigmatic for this view is Helmut Kuhn's "Die Vollendung der klassischen deutschen Ästhetik durch Hegel," in *Schriften zur Ästhetik* (Munich: Kösel, 1966), pp. 15–144.

2 Cf. E. H. Gombrich, "Hegel und die Kunstgeschichte," in *Neue Rundschau* 2(1977): 202–19, especially p. 203 f.

3 For a brief introduction to Hegel's aesthetic theory in English, see William Desmond's *Art and the Absolute: A Study of Hegel's Aesthetics* (Albany: State University of New York Press, 1986). Desmond presents a clear outline of the basic issues, although the book mostly abstains from critical engagement with its material.

4 *Grundrisse der Kritik der politischen Ökonomie* (Rohentwurf, 1857–8) (Berlin: Dietz, 1953), p. 31.

5 Especially Annemarie Gethmann-Siefert has argued forcefully for a necessary revision of Hegel's aesthetics in the light of the newly published original lecture notes. See, e.g., "Schöne Kunst und Prosa des Lebens: Hegels Rehabilitierung des ästhetischen Genusses," in Christoph Jamme, ed., *Kunst und Geschichte im Zeitalter Hegels* (Hamburg: Meiner, 1996), pp. 115–50, and "Einleitung: Gestalt und Wirkung von Hegels Ästhetik," in G. W. F. Hegel: *Vorlesungen über die Philosophie der Kunst* (Hamburg: Meiner, 1998), pp. xv–ccxxiv. This volume contains H. G. Hotho's lecture notes from 1823. For another version of the aesthetics lectures, see the combined notes of Wilhelm von Ascheberg and W. Sax van Terborg from 1820–1 that were edited by Helmut Schneider. G. W. F. Hegel: *Vorlesungen über Ästhetik* (Frankfurt am Main: Peter Lang, 1995).

6 Cf. Dieter Henrich's essay "Hegel und Hölderlin," in *Hegel im Kontext* (Frankfurt am Main: Suhrkamp, 1971), pp. 9–40. For the above context, especially p. 27.

7 Cf. Vittorio Hösle, *Hegels System: Der Idealismus der Subjektivität und das Problem der Intersubjektivität,* Vol. 2: *Philosophie der Natur und des Geistes* (Hamburg: Meiner, 1987), p. 594.

8 Cf. Immanuel Kant's famous definition of laughter in the *Critique of Judgment*: "Laughter is an affect due to the sudden resolution of an intense expectation into nothing" (§53, Commentary).

9 Cf. Horst Althaus, *Hegel und Die heroischen Jahre der Philosophie* (Munich: Hanser, 1992), p. 423.

10 Hegel's texts – unless otherwise indicated – are quoted according to the edition of the complete works that were edited by Eva Moldenhauer and Karl Markus Michel (Frankfurt am Main: Suhrkamp, 1970). The first number refers to the volume, the second to the page.

11 The chapter on natural beauty (13. 157–77) is very likely the result of an undue elaboration by Hotho.

12 The position of the *Encyclopedia of Philosophical Sciences* is less critical of Schelling and the Romantic genius. Cf. §560 (10. 369).

13 In the first part of the *Encyclopedia* as well as in the *Logic,* essence [*Wesen*] in turn is defined as the appearance [*Schein*] of being [*Sein*] (8. 231). The intricacies of Hegel's terminology, however, cannot be discussed in the present context.

14 It seems very likely that Hegel himself never used this phrase, but that it was coined by Hotho. As far as the edited lecture notes allow us to tell, Hegel spoke of the "ideal of the beautiful" instead.

15 *Hegel* (Cambridge: Cambridge University Press, 1975), p. 470.

16 *Wahrheit und Methode* (Tübingen: Mohr and Siebeck, 1990), pp. 375 ff.

17 Peter Szondi, "Antike und Moderne in der Ästhetik der Goethezeit," in *Poetik und Geschichtsphilosophie I* (Frankfurt am Main: Suhrkamp, 1974), pp. 11–266.

18 Hösle, *Hegels System*, vol. 2, pp. 620 ff.

19 Ibid., pp. 637 f.

20 This thesis was echoed in the twentieth century by the art historian Hans Sedlmayr in his controversial book *Der Verlust der Mitte.* For Sedlmayr, the decline of modern art is the symptom of a larger societal malaise – quite contrary to Hegel's optimistic view of the modern state as the telos of development. For a good comparison between Sedlmayr and Hegel, see Dieter Jähnig, "Hegel und die These vom 'Verlust der Mitte,' " in A. M. Koktanek, ed., *Spengler-Studien* (Munich: Beck, 1965), pp. 147–76.

21 Cf. Hans-Georg Gadamer, "Die Stellung der Poesie im System der Hegelschen Ästhetik und die Frage des Vergangenheitscharakters der Kunst," in *Kunst als Aussage* (Tübingen: Mohr and Siebeck, 1993), pp. 221–31. In the same volume, see also the essay "Ende der Kunst? Von Hegels Lehre vom Vergangenheitscharakter der Kunst bis zur Anti-Kunst von heute," pp. 206–20.

22 Charles Taylor makes this observation (*Hegel*, 479). For Hegel himself, however, the argument that reality "defeated" the concept would hardly be permissible. To the charge that reality did not line up with the concept, Hegel was known to answer: So much the worse for reality. In this context, see also Heidegger's criticism of the empirical argument. "Der Ursprung des Kunstwerks," in *Holzwege* (Frankfurt am Main: Klostermann, 1980), pp. 1–72, p. 66.

23 Cf. Annemarie Gethmann-Siefert, "Schöne Kunst und Prosa des Lebens," p. 118.

24 Also compare Willi Oelmüller, "Der Satz vom Ende der Kunst," in *Die unbefriedigte Aufklärung: Beiträge zu einer Philosophie der Moderne von Lessing, Kant und Hegel* (Frankfurt am Main: Suhrkamp, 1969); Karsten Harries, "Hegel on the Future of Art," in *The Review of Metaphysics* (1974): 677–96; Curtis L. Carter, "A Reexamination of the 'Death of Art' Interpretation of Hegel's Aesthetics," in Lawrence S. Stepelevich, ed., *Selected Essays on G. W. F. Hegel* (Atlantic Highlands, N.J.: Humanities Press, 1993), pp. 11–26. Other essays on this question and other problems of Hegel's aesthetics can be found in the volume edited by William Maker: *Hegel and Aesthetics* (Albany: State University of New York Press, 2000).

25 Arnold Gehlen, *Zeit-Bilder: Zur Soziologie und Ästhetik der modernen Malerei,* 3d enlarged ed. (Frankfurt am Main: Klostermann, 1986), p. 206.

26 Ernst Bloch comments on this aspect of Hegel's aesthetics as follows: "Art in Hegel never appears as disinterested contemplation in respect to the pure form of imagination of its objects, but it appears in its end as content of fulfillment in which man who contemplates it does no longer need a restlessness of interest during this contemplation. This is the polis that Hegel found in art, a marvelous Athens of all times and latitudes." *Subjekt-Objekt: Erläuterungen zu Hegel* (Frankfurt am Main: Suhrkamp, 1985), p. 289.

27 *Hegels System,* vol. 2, p. 611.

28 As this term indicates, the study of ugliness and its theory has turned into its own subfield of aesthetics. Thus, the literature on it is too numerous to even list the "classics" of the field. A good first orientation can be obtained by turning to the entries on ugliness in the outstanding encyclopedia from the disciplines of philosophy, art and literary history, and rhetoric. Cf. Ursula Franke, "Das Hässliche," *Historisches Wörterbuch der Philosophie*; Carsten Zelle, "Das Hässliche," *Historisches Wörterbuch der Rhetorik*; Jerome Stolniz, "Ugliness," *The Encyclopedia of Philosophy*.

29 Althaus, *Hegel,* p. 424.

30 For a discussion of the sublime and the comical as moments of the beautiful, compare Friedrich Theodor Vischer's 1837 *Über das Erhabene und Komische* (On the sublime and comical) (Frankfurt am Main: Suhrkamp, 1967). Unlike for Kant or Schiller, the sublime for Vischer is not a concept on par with the beautiful, but a manifestation of the latter.

Chapter 6. Schopenhauer

1 Many of the inconsistencies of Schopenhauer's aesthetics are explored carefully in Barbara Neymeyr's dissertation *Ästhetische Autonomie als Abnormität: Kritische Analysen zu Schopenhauers Ästhetik im Horizont seiner Willensmetaphysik* (Berlin and New York: de Gruyter, 1996). For a basic, albeit uncritical, introduction in English, see the chapter "Art and Ideas" in Christopher Janaway's *Schopenhauer* (Oxford: Oxford University Press, 1994).

2 A good summary of Schopenhauer's simplification of Kant's epistemology can be found in Ulrich Pothast, *Die eigentlich metaphysische Tätigkeit: Über Schopenhauers Ästhetik und ihre Anwendung durch Samuel Beckett* (Frankfurt am Main: Suhrkamp, 1982). Pothast points out Schopenhauer's lack of arguments for the ideal existence of time and space and the absence of the metaphysical and transcendental deduction of the categories, as

well as some other tight spots in his reduction of Kant's epistemology to the principle of sufficient reason. See especially p. 18.

3 *Die Welt als Wille und Vorstellung* (WWR) (Stuttgart: Reclam, 1987) vol. 1, p. 35.

4 See Walter Schulz, "Die problematische Stellung der Kunst in Schopenhauers Philosophie," in Jürgen Brummack et al., eds., *Literaturwissenschaft und Geistesgeschichte: FS für Richard Brinkmann* (Tübingen: Niemeyer, 1981), pp. 403–15, especially p. 403.

5 See Walter Schulz: "Schopenhauer und Nietzsche: Gemeinsamkeiten und Differenzen," in Wolfgang Schirmacher, ed., *Schopenhauer, Nietzsche und die Kunst* (Vienna: Passagen, 1991), 21–34, especially p. 22. For a celebration of this position as a liberation of the unconscious that had been violated by conceptual thought in Kant, see Nick Land's essay "Art as Insurrection: The Question of Aesthetics in Kant, Schopenhauer, and Nietzsche." The piece is philosophically not very convincing but constitutes a typical postmodern attempt to downplay rationality, and thus it provides a good example for the thesis that Lukács might have been wrong with his accusations against Schopenhauer in his *The Destruction of Reason,* yet that his criticism could hold for some Schopenhauer advocates. In Keith Ansell-Peterson, ed., *Nietzsche and Modern German Thought* (London and New York: Routledge, 1991), pp. 240–56.

6 See Jochen Schmidt, *Die Geschichte des Genie-Gedankens in der deutschen Literatur, Philosophie und Politik 1750–1945* (Darmstadt: Wissenschaftliche Buchgesellschaft, 1985) vol. 1, especially pp. 471 f.

7 Paul Guyer has put his finger on this spot very perceptively in his essay "Pleasure and Knowledge in Schopenhauer's Aesthetics," in Dale Jaquette, ed., *Schopenhauer, Philosophy and the Arts* (Cambridge: Cambridge University Press, 1996), pp. 109–32, especially pp. 116f. I follow him in his argumentation.

8 See Schopenhauer's 1821 essay "Über das Interessante," in A. Schopenhauer, *Sämtliche Werke* (Munich: Piper, 1923), vol. 6, pp. 379–89, especially p. 381.

9 For this discussion, see also Ulrich Pothast, *Die eigentlich metaphysische Tätigkeit*, pp. 69 ff.

10 Schopenhauer, "Zur Metaphysik des Schönen und der Ästhetik," in *Sämtliche Werke,* vol. 2, pp. 453–93, especially p. 457.

11 For a detailed discussion of this theory of genius, see Jochen Schmidt, *Die Geschichte des Genie-Gedankens.*

12 See Arthur Hübscher, "Der Philosoph der Romantik," *Schopenhauer-Jahrbuch* 34 (1951–2): 1–17.

13 Ulrich Pothast, *Die eigentlich metaphysische Tätigkeit,* p. 81.

14 Günther K. Lehmann also finds it puzzling that Schopenhauer's metaphysical aesthetics of quietude and silence finds its most adequate

expression in music as the art of sound. *Ästhetik der Utopie* (Stuttgart: Neske, 1995), p. 45.

15 Schopenhauer, "Zur Metaphysik des Schönen und der Ästhetik, " p. 473.

16 See also Brigitte Scheer, *Einführung in die philosophische Ästhetik* (Darmstadt: Primus, 1997), p. 152.

17 This discussion is taken up from an aesthetic perspective in Arnold Gehlen's excellent yet still underrated work *Zeit-Bilder: Zur Soziologie und Ästhetik der Modernen Malerei* (Frankfurt am Main: Klostermann, 1986).

18 A. Schopenhauer, *Aphorismen zur Lebensweisheit* (Munich: Goldmann, 1978), p. 159.

19 For a Marxist critique of this position, see Hans-Dieter Bahr, *Das gefesselte Engagement: Zur Ideologie der kontemplativen Ästhetik Schopenhauers* (Bonn: Bouvier, 1970).

Chapter 7. Kierkegaard, Nietzsche

1 *Kierkegaard: Konstruktion des Ästhetischen* (Frankfurt am Main: Suhrkamp, 1962), p. 17.

2 Gerhard vom Hofe, "Kunst als Grenze: Hegels Theorem des 'unglücklichen Bewusstseins' und die ästhetische Erfahrung bei Kierkegaard," in Herbert Anton, ed., *Invaliden des Apoll: Motive und Mythen des Dichterleids* (Munich: Fink, 1982), pp. 11–34, especially p. 15.

3 S. Kierkegaard, *Either/Or*, 2 vols. (Princeton, N.J.: Princeton University Press, 1959).

4 S. Kierkegaard, *The Sickness Unto Death: A Christian Psychological Exposition for Upbuilding and Awakening,* trans. H. and E. Hong (Princeton, N.J.: Princeton University Press, 1980), p. 77.

5 See also Josef Früchtl's *Ästhetische Erfahrung und moralisches Urteil: Eine Rehabilitierung* (Frankfurt am Main: Suhrkamp, 1996), p. 140.

6 G. vom Hofe, "Kunst als Grenze," p. 21.

7 Karsten Harries argues this point convincingly in his book *The Meaning of Modern Art: A Philosophical Investigation* (Evanston, Ill.: Northwestern University Press, 1968), p. 53.

8 Ibid., p. 54.

9 Nietzsche's writings are quoted according to the *Kritische Studienausgabe* (KSA) of the collected works in 15 volumes, edited by Colli and Montinari and published by Deutscher Taschenbuch Verlag and de Gruyter (Munich, Berlin, and New York, 1988). The numbers in brackets refer to the sections, rather than to the pages, so that the quotations can be easily found in any German or English edition.

10 KSA, vol. 1, pp. 551–77. See especially p. 561.

11 Michel Foucault, *The Order of Things: An Archaeology of the Human Sciences* (New York: Vintage, 1994), p. 387.

12 It shouldn't be necessary to point out that this view of Euripides is hardly fair or historically accurate. A good summary in English of the main arguments against Nietzsche's position can be found in Martha Nussbaum's essay, "The Transfiguration of Intoxication: Nietzsche, Schopenhauer, and Dionysus," where additional literature is quoted. In Salim Kemal, ed., *Nietzsche, Philosophy, and the Arts* (Cambridge: Cambridge University Press, 1998), pp. 36–69. For a rich and detailed study of Nietzsche's views on tragedy, see M. S. Silk and J. P. Stern, *Nietzsche on Tragedy* (Cambridge: Cambridge University Press, 1981). Also of some interest is John Sallis's *Crossings: Nietzsche and the Space of Tragedy* (Chicago: University of Chicago Press, 1991). Nicholas Martin in his *Nietzsche and Schiller: Untimely Aesthetics* (Oxford: Clarendon Press, 1996) investigates the influence of Schiller's *Aesthetic Letters* on Nietzsche's early aesthetics, arguing on p. 9 that both are "aesthetic prescriptions for a diseased culture."

13 Jochen Schmidt even argues that more important than the opposition Apollo–Dionysus is that of Dionysus and Socrates, that is, that between the genuine life and scientific civilization. See *Die Geschichte des Genie-Gedankens,* p. 149. Another tension, namely, that between "radical epistemological scepticism" and the "possibility of normative discourse" to which art is meant to provide a possible solution, is explored by Matthew Rampley in his book *Nietzsche, Aesthetics, and Modernity* (Cambridge: Cambridge University Press, 2000).

14 KSA, vol. 1, pp. 515–32; quotation is on p. 516.

15 "Das griechische Musikdrama," 528.

16 KSA 6; 1876, 23 [159].

17 *Götzen-Dämmerung,* section "Streifzüge eines Unzeitgemässen: 10," KSA 6.

18 Heidegger made this point in his lectures on Nietzsche from the 1930s that were published in a revised form in 1961. *Nietzsche* (Frankfurt am Main: Klostermann, 1996), p. 108. A carefully argued account of Nietzsche's charges against Kant that are actually meant to prove Schopenhauer wrong can be found in Urs Heftrich's article "Nietzsches Auseinandersetzung mit der 'Kritik der Urteilskraft,' " *Nietzsche-Studien* 20 (1991): 238–66.

19 KSA 10; 1883, 7 [18].

20 KSA 13; 1888, 14 [117].

21 *Der philosophische Diskurs der Moderne* (Frankfurt am Main: Suhrkamp, 1985), p. 118. Regarding Nietzsche's aesthetization of ontology and ethics, see also Alan Megill's *Prophets of Extremity,* Part I: "Friedrich Nietzsche as Aestheticist" (Berkeley: University of California Press, 1985).

22 *Die fröhliche Wissenschaft,* §107, KSA 3.
23 Ibid., §299.
24 *Nietzsche: Life as Literature* (Cambridge, Mass.: Harvard University Press, 1985).
25 *Nietzsche contra Wagner,* section "Wo ich Einwände mache," KSA 6.
26 1886, 7 [7], KSA 12.
27 "Über Wahrheit und Lüge im aussermoralischen Sinne," KSA 1, 880.
28 *Also sprach Zarathustra* II, section "Von den Dichtern," KSA 4, 164.
29 *Jenseits von Gut und Böse,* KSA 5, 192.
30 The issue of Nietzsche's perspectivism is rather problematic and would warrant detailed discussion. In his study *Nietzsche: Life as Literature,* Alexander Nehamas argues on p. 49: "Perspectivism . . . is not equivalent to relativism. But perspectivism does imply that no particular point of view is priviledged in the sense that it affords those who occupy it a better picture of the world as it really is than all others. Some perspectives are, and can be shown to be, better than others." Also compare his essay "Nietzsche, Modernity, Aestheticism," in Bernd Magnus and Kathleen Higgins's volume *The Cambridge Companion to Nietzsche* (Cambridge: Cambridge University Press, 1996), pp. 223–51. An excellent discussion of various interpretations of perspectivism, as well as a critique of Nehamas's reading, can be found in Maudemarie Clark's *Nietzsche on Truth and Philosophy* (Cambridge: Cambridge University Press, 1990). She writes on p. 158: "the perspectival character of knowledge is perfectly compatible with some interpretations being true, and it introduces no paradoxes of self-reference. Perspectivism is, or course, a perspectival truth, but this does not imply that any competing claim is also true."
31 *Nietzsche,* p. 219. For similar arguments, see also A. Nehamas's *Nietzsche: Life as Literature,* pp. 8 et passim, as well as Allan Megill's article "Nietzsche as Aestheticist," *Philosophy and Literature* 5, no. 2 (1981): 204–25.
32 See Hans-Georg Gadamer, *Wahrheit und Methode,* 6th ed. (Tübingen: Mohr and Siebeck, 1990), p. 41.
33 See Hans-Georg Gadamer, "Der Kunstbegriff im Wandel," in *Hermeneutische Entwürfe* (Tübingen: Mohr and Siebeck, 2000), pp. 145–60.
34 *Die fröhliche Wissenschaft,* §39, vol. 3.
35 Habermas, *Der philosophische Diskurs der Moderne,* p. 121.
36 Section "Streifzüge eines Unzeitgemässen," §20, vol. 6.
37 Fragment from 1883, KSA 10, 7 [154].

Chapter 8. Cassirer, Lukács

1 *An Essay on Man: An Introduction to a Philosophy of Human Culture* (New Haven, Conn.: Yale University Press, 1944), pp. 147, 168.

2 See also Emery E. George's essay "Ernst Cassirer and Neo-Kantian Aesthetics: A Holistic Approach to the Problems of Language and Art," in R. W. Bailey, L. Matejka, and P. Steiner, eds., *The Sign: Semiotics around the World* (Ann Arbor: Michigan Slavic Publications, 1978), pp. 132–45.

3 E. Cassirer, "Language and Art II," in *Symbol, Myth, and Culture: Essays and Lectures 1935–1945* (New Haven, Conn.: Yale University Press, 1979), pp. 166–95. Quotation is on p. 195.

4 *An Essay on Man,* p. 148.

5 Ibid., pp. 144–5.

6 For an account that positions Cassirer much closer to the constructionist and aesthetic camp of language philosophy, see Hazard Adams's article "Thinking Cassirer," in *Criticism* 25, no. 3 (1983): 181–95.

7 *An Essay on Man,* p. 148. Also of interest in regard to this question is Cassirer's 1943 lecture "The Educational Value of Art," in *Symbol, Myth, and Culture: Essays and Lectures 1935–1945,* pp. 196–215.

8 "The Educational Value of Art," p. 211.

9 "Language and Art I," *Symbol, Myth, and Culture: Essays and Lectures 1935–1945,* pp. 145–65. Quotation is on p. 157.

10 *An Essay on Man,* p. 164.

11 "Zur Ästhetik Schillers," *Beiträge zur Geschichte der Ästhetik* (Berlin: Aufbau, 1956), pp. 96 and 16, respectively.

12 "Zur Ästhetik Schillers," p. 77.

13 See Sebastian Kleinschmidt's thoughtful article "Georg Lukács und die Wertabstufungen in der Kunst," *Sinn und Form* 1(1985): 638–54. Reference is on p. 651. Obviously, here and elsewhere Lukács harks back to Aristotelian concepts, as can be easily seen with respect to his discussions of mimesis and catharsis. Yet a thorough discussion of Aristotelianism in Lukács is still lacking. Pierre van Rutten's article "L'aristotelisme dans l'esthétique de Lukács" (*Georg Lukács et la théorie littéraire contemporaine* [Montreal: Association des professeurs de français des universités et collèges canadiens, 1983], pp. 99–114) points out a number of references to Aristotle throughout the writings of Lukács, but abstains from a philosophical discussion. Moreover, van Rutten seems to lack a thorough understanding of Aristotle as when he writes on p. 106: "Lukács reconnait qu'Aristote est très proche du positivisme matérialiste." Of course, everything depends on one's understanding of proximity, yet a full-blown material positivism can hardly be attributed to the Stagirite.

14 A good and brief summary of Lukács's main writings on aesthetic realism can be found in Stuart Sim's *Georg Lukács* (Hertfordshire: Harvester Wheatsheaf, 1994). Unfortunately, the aesthetic theory itself is left out in this volume.

15 The French structuralist Marxist Lucien Goldmann considered *Soul and Forms* to be the result of a more curious mixture, namely, that of phenomenological structuralism and tragic Kantianism. "The Aesthetics of the Young Lukács," *New Hungarian Quarterly* 47 (1972): 129–35. Reference is on p. 129.

16 In Frank Benseler and Werner Jung, eds., *Lukács 1996: Jahrbuch der Internationalen Georg-Lukács-Gesellschaft* (Bern: Peter Lang, 1997), pp. 13–26. The text was originally written in Hungarian and appeared for the first time in German translation in this volume.

17 While I agree with Dennis Crow's assessment that the central contribution of *Soul and Forms* lies in the criticism of nihilism and aesthetic individualism, I disagree with his view that Lukács offers no vision of transcendence of this culture and that life therefore has to remain stuck in tragic and frustrated individualism. "Form and the Unification of Aesthetics and Ethics in Lukács' *Soul and Forms*," *New German Critique* 15 (1978): 159–77. Reference is on p. 176.

18 For an example, see the article "Literatur und Kunst als Überbau," *Beiträge zur Geschichte der Ästhetik*, pp. 404–27.

19 Rüdiger Bubner seems right in his judgments that the 1963 *Aesthetics* is verbose and that it neither presents a substantially new concept of realism nor formulates an established concept more convincingly. Yet it is still one of the better places to study Lukács's ideas in a larger context. "Hegel's Aesthetics: Yesterday and Today," in Warren Steinkraus and Kenneth Schmitz, eds., *Art and Logic in Hegel's Philosophy* (Atlantic Highlands, N.J.: Humanities Press and Sussex: Harvester Press, 1980), pp. 15–33.

20 See Jürgen von Kempski's article "Zur Ästhetik von Georg Lukács," *Neue Rundschau* (1965): 109–20; reference is on p. 118. For the opposite, yet hardly convincing opinion, see Agnes Heller's "Lukács' Aesthetics," *New Hungarian Quarterly* 24 (1966): 84–94. Reference is on p. 93.

21 While Lukács never wrote this third part of his aesthetic theory, his friend Arnold Hauser in 1953 published the impressive *Sozialgeschichte der Kunst und Literatur* (Social history of art and literature) (Munich: Beck, 1990) that was much to Lukács's liking.

22 *The Aesthetic Dimension: Toward a Critique of Marxist Aesthetics* (Boston: Beacon Press, 1978). The text appeared in German in 1977 as *Die Permanenz der Kunst: Wider eine bestimmte Marxistische Ästhetik* and was subsequently translated and revised by the author and his wife Erica Sherover. Quotation is on p. 1 f.

23 Therefore, the literary critic Fredric Jameson seems wrong when he claims that "Lukács' work may be seen as a continuous and lifelong meditation on narrative." (*Marxism and Form*, [Princeton, N.J.: Princeton University Press, 1971] p. 163.) While the role of narrative figures large

in Lukács's studies, the more fundamental category is that of mimesis, which finds its application not only in literature but also in music, painting, and so on.

24 The 1963 *Aesthetics* is here quoted in the shortened version in four volumes that Lukács asked his student Ferenc Fehér to prepare for publication. The Roman numeral refers to the volume, the Arabic numeral to the page. *Ästhetik* I–IV (Darmstadt and Neuwied: Luchterhand, 1972).

25 In more of a Marxist jargon, this thought is phrased in "Literatur und Kunst als Überbau" on p. 419 as follows: "Every superstructure does not only reflect reality, but takes an active stance for or against the old or the new base, and when the superstructure gives up this active role it stops being the superstructure. Applied to the theory of art this means that all literature and art also are an activity, a vote [*Stellungnahme*] for or against a base."

26 Georg Lukács, "Es geht um den Realismus," in *Werke*, Vol. 4: *Probleme des Realismus I: Essays über Realismus* (Neuwied and Berlin: Luchterhand, 1971), pp. 313–43. Quotations are on pp. 318, 21.

27 Kleinschmidt, "Georg Lukács und die Wertabstufungen in der Kunst," pp. 650 f.

28 "Erpresste Versöhnung," in *Gesammelte Schriften*, Vol. 2: *Noten zur Literatur* (Frankfurt am Main: Suhrkamp, 1977), pp. 251–80. Quotation is on p. 263.

29 In this discussion I follow Rüdiger Bubner's important article "Über einige Bedingungen gegenwärtiger Ästhetik," *Neue Hefte für Philosophie* 5 (1973): 38–73.

30 The tendency in overemphasizing one moment usually favors the first over the second. Two examples are Fredric Jameson's essay "Marcuse and Schiller" in *Marxism and Form* and the chapter on Marcuse in Heinz Paetzold's *Neomarxistische Ästhetik II: Adorno-Marcuse* (Düsseldorf: Pädagogischer Verlag Schwan, 1974).

31 Herbert Marcuse, *One-Dimensional Man: Studies in the Ideology of Advanced Industrial Society* (Boston: Beacon Press, 1966), pp. 238 f.

32 *An Essay on Liberation* (Boston: Beacon Press, 1969), p. 44.

33 Ibid., p. 48.

34 Herbert Marcuse, *Counterrevolution and Revolt* (Boston: Beacon Press, 1972), p. 101.

35 Herbert Marcuse, *The Aesthetic Dimension*, p. xi.

36 Ibid., pp. 32 f.

37 Ibid., p. xii.

38 Ibid., p. 65.

39 Ibid., p. 72.

40 *Counterrevolution and Revolt*, p. 117.

Chapter 9. Heidegger, Gadamer

1 For a biographical account of Heidegger's involvement with the visual arts, see Heinrich Wiegand Petzet's book *Auf einen Stern zugehen: Begegnungen mit Martin Heidegger 1929–1976* (Frankfurt am Main: Societäts-Verlag, 1983), pp. 141–67. Especially Heidegger's early interest in the Worpswede artist colony is not well known. Also noteworthy is Heidegger's reported statement of the late 1950s in which he claims, after having studied the works of Paul Klee, that art is changing and that this might necessitate a second part of the *Origin of the Work of Art.* The fact that he never attempted to write such a sequel suggests that modern phenomena in art can also be comprehended within the framework that Heidegger provides in his 1936 lecture. For an attempt to trace influences of painters, sculptors, and poets on Heidegger's philosophy at large, see Gerhard Faden's *Der Schein der Kunst: Zu Heideggers Kritik der Ästhetik* (Würzburg: Könighausen und Neumann, 1986).

2 *Nietzsche* (Frankfurt am Main: Klostermann, 1996), vol. 1, pp. 77 ff.

3 O. Pöggeler goes so far as to argue that "the essay *The Origin of the Work of Art* does not present a philosophy of art"; rather, it must be read as an elaboration on the ontological meditations of *Being and Time.* I will show that these two moments do not only not exclude each other but are dependent upon one another (Otto Pöggeler, *Der Denkweg Martin Heideggers* [Pfullingen: Neske, 1963], p. 207).

4 Heidegger's essay is quoted from the 1960 Reclam edition for which Hans-Georg Gadamer wrote an introduction, "Zur Einführung" (Stuttgart: Reclam, 1997).

5 For a close reading of Heidegger's essay, see Friedrich-Wilhelm von Herrmann's *Heideggers Philosophie der Kunst: Eine systematische Interpretation der Holzwege Abhandlung "Der Ursprung des Kunstwerks"* (Frankfurt am Main: Klostermann, 1980). Hermann's detailed elucidation of the text, however helpful, abstains from any attempt to explicate the genesis of Heidegger's thought by reference to the philosophical tradition.

6 *Sein und Zeit,* 16th ed. (Tübingen: Niemeyer, 1986), §22.

7 "The Still Life as a Personal Object – A Note on Heidegger and van Gogh," in *Theory and Philosophy of Art: Style, Artist, and Society* (New York: George Braziller, 1994), pp. 135–43.

8 Therefore, it strikes me as a misguided interpretation to claim, as Sandra Lee Bartky does: "Like so many aestheticians before him, what Heidegger seeks to uncover is the essence of art." "Heidegger's Philosophy of Art," in Thomas Sheehan, ed., *Heidegger: The Man and the Thinker* (Chicago: Precedent Publishing, 1981), pp. 257–74. Quotation is on p. 257.

9 For a discussion of Heidegger's view on architecture, see my article "Hegel, Heidegger und die Architektur" in *Weimarer Beiträge* 3 (2001): 433–46.

10 *Theorie des kommunikativen Handelns* (Frankfurt am Main: Suhrkamp, 1995), vol. 2, pp. 182 ff.

11 I owe this reference to Richard Rorty, who quoted the poem in one of his lectures.

12 While *The Origin of the Work of Art* regards only two forces, namely world and earth, at work in the work, the later essay views art as the site of the *Geviert* (fourfold) of heaven and earth, man and gods. See Walter Biemel's *Heidegger* (Reinbeck: Rowohlt, 1973), p. 97.

13 K. Fiedler, *Über die Beurteilung von Werken der Bildenden Kunst*, p. 97, quoted in A. Gehlen, *Zeit-Bilder*, p. 62.

14 *Nietzsche*, vol. 2, pp. 111 ff.

15 "Zur Einführung," 114.

16 Walter Biemel takes this term much too literally when he connects it to the concept of *physis* and writes in his discussion of the Greek temple: "The earth is meant to appear as earth, i.e. as sea, rock, sky, olive trees and everything else that belongs to it" (*Heidegger*, 84). Also, George Steiner misunderstands Heidegger when he argues that the moment of *earth* in art refers to the absence of the signified object, while *world* refers to the presence of the signifier: "In the great work of art, hiddenness and exhibition – the absence of the object itself and its intense presence via the artist's representation – are in eternal conflict." (*Martin Heidegger* [Chicago: University of Chicago Press, 1991], p. 135.) Heidegger does not have the absence of the signified object in mind but, rather, the absence of the possibility of any definite interpretation.

17 Gadamer, "Zur Einführung," p. 112.

18 *Holzwege* (Frankfurt am Main: Klostermann, 1980), pp. 265–316, quotation on p. 287.

19 M. Heidegger, "Das Ding," in *Vorträge und Aufsätze* (Pfullingen: Neske, 1954), pp. 157–80.

20 Sandra Lee Bartky mistakenly opposes scientific and existential aesthetic truth. Heidegger's philosophy of art, however, is not an individualist account but a collective one. "Heidegger's Philosophy of Art," p. 271.

21 It is somewhat difficult to comprehend how O. Pöggeler can argue that Heidegger's aesthetic analysis was advanced in lieu of a political one: "Heidegger undertook the analysis of the artwork when he refused himself the analysis of the state due to the political circumstances." (*Philosophie und Politik bei Heidegger*, 2d ed. [Munich and Freiburg: K. Alber, 1974], p. 122.) To read Heidegger's essay on the artwork as an expression of political romanticism, i.e., the flight from the polity, seems to cleanse it of

its political implications, which certainly contain moments that oppose the totalitarian regime.

22 Richard Rorty certainly cannot point to *The Origin of the Work of Art* when he argues that Heidegger's philosophy of art centers around self-creation: "So to say that Dasein is guilty is to say that it speaks somebody else's language, and so lives in a world it never made – a world which, just for this reason, is not its *Heim*." *Contingency, Irony, and Solidarity* (Cambridge: Cambridge University Press, 1989), p. 109. But even the later Heidegger does not subscribe to an individualist aesthetics. While Heidegger does not continue to claim that art has a national and political function, he never loses sight of its communal moment. On the notions of language and *Heim* or *Heimat* in Heidegger, see my essay "*Heimat* in Heidegger and Gadamer," *Philosophy and Literature* 24, no. 2 (2000): 312–26.

23 Philippe Lacoue-Labarthe, *Heidegger, Art and Politics: The Fiction of the Political,* trans. Chris Turner (Oxford: Basil Blackwell, 1990).

24 M. Heidegger, "Cezanne," *Jahresgabe* der Heidegger-Gesellschaft 1991. Text version of 1974.

25 *The Structure of Scientific Revolutions,* 2d enlarged ed. (Chicago: University of Chicago Press, 1970).

26 *Einführung in die frühromantische Ästhetik,* p. 26.

27 See the essays in the volume edited by Tom Rockmore: *Heidegger, German Idealism and Neo-Kantianism* (New York: Humanity Books, 2000). Unfortunately, the question of aesthetics receives marginal attention at best in this collection. Even Heidegger's relation to Schelling is discussed in respect to mysticism and Schelling's *Freiheitsschrift,* not to the 1800 *System of Transcendental Idealism* (Douglas Hedley, "Schelling and Heidegger: The Mythical Legacy and Romantic Affinities," pp. 141–56).

28 For this and the following, see also my monograph *Hans-Georg Gadamer* (Munich: Beck, 1999). In respect to art, especially pp. 35–50 and 78–93.

29 Wahrheit und Methode (Tübingen: Mohr and Siebeck, 1990), p. 3.

30 Ibid., p. 103.

31 It is somewhat difficult, yet not necessarily impossible, to square these two notions. Generally, the problem has been discussed in the context of Gadamer's concept of classical art that is meant to constitute the ideal combination of transhistorical validity and nonessential existence. For a critique of such a possibility, see Hans Robert Jauss's *Literaturgeschichte als Provokation* (Frankfurt am Main: Suhrkamp, 1970), p. 186, as well as Peter Christian Lang's *Hermeneutik, Ideologiekritik, Ästhetik: Über Gadamer und Adorno sowie Fragen einer aktuellen Ästhetik* (Königstein: Forum Academicum in der Verlagsqruppe Athenäum, Hain, Scriptor, Hanstein, 1981), p. 24. In defense of Gadamer, Georgia Warnke's *Gadamer:*

Hermeneutics, Tradition and Reason (Stanford, Calif.: Stanford University Press, 1987), p. 189. Also Hammermeister, *Hans-Georg Gadamer,* p. 113.

32 "Kunst und Nachahmung" in *Gesammelte Werke,* vol. 8, pp. 25–36.

33 Ibid., p. 36.

34 Mary Deveraux in her article "Can Art Save Us? A Meditation of Gadamer," in *Philosophy and Literature* 15 (1991): 59–73, argues against the notion that art always supports order. In his response, Kenneth Buckman attempts to strengthen Gadamer's position ("Gadamer on Art, Morality, and Authority," in *Philosophy and Literature* 21 [1997]: 144–50). Both Deveraux and Buckman, however, do not realize that Gadamer localizes order neither in the structure of the work nor in the activity of the artist, but in the situation of reception.

35 Jean Grondin, ed., *Hans-Georg Gadamer Lesebuch* (Munich: Fink, 1997), p. 182.

36 *Wahrheit und Methode,* p. 170.

37 "Hermeneutik auf der Spur," in *Gesammelte Werke,* vol. 10, pp. 148–74. Quotation is on p. 173.

38 "Philosophie und Literatur," in *Gesammelte Werke,* vol. 8, pp. 240–57.

Chapter 10. Adorno

1 The reception of his aesthetic theory follows him along this path. Peter Uwe Hohendahl writes on p. 197 of his book *Prismatic Thought: Theodor W. Adorno* (Lincoln: University of Nebraska Press, 1990): "Adorno's theory of the artwork openly and explicity harks back to German idealism, especially to the theories of Kant and Hegel." While this is certainly true, the Romantics, primarily Schelling, are of at least equal importance, although the latter is never even mentioned by Hohendahl. And while Christoph Menke on p. 249 of his study *The Sovereignity of Art: Aesthetic Negativity in Adorno and Derrida* (Cambridge, Mass.: MIT Press, 1998) acknowledges "remnants of the romantic model," he, too, prefers to play them down in order to emphasize Adorno's self-reflexive position that is aware of the dangers of the aesthetic experience of negativity "for the interplay of the dimensions of reason." Since this book is available in English translation, I quote the translation here and further down the German original.

2 *Negative Dialektik,* 9th ed. (Frankfurt am Main: Suhrkamp, 1997), pp. 19f.

3 See also R. Bubner, "Adornos Negative Dialektik," in J. Habermas and L. von Friedeburg, eds., *Adorno-Konferenz 1983* (Frankfurt am Main: Suhrkamp, 1983), pp. 35–40.

4 "Der Essay als Form," in *Noten zur Literatur,* 7th ed. (Frankfurt am Main: Suhrkampt, 1998), pp. 9–33. For some other parallels between Adorno

and early Romanticism, especially in regard to the theory of subjectivity, see Jochen Hörisch's article "Herrscherwort, Geld und geltende Sätze: Adornos Aktualisierung der Frühromantik und ihre Affinität zur poststrukturalistischen Kritik des Subjekts," in Burkhard Lindner and W. Martin Lüdke, eds., *Konstruktion der Moderne: Materialien zur ästhetischen Theorie Theodor W. Adornos* (Frankfurt am Main: Suhrkamp, 1980), pp. 397–414.

5 Max Horkheimer, "Traditionelle und kritische Theorie," in *Traditionelle und kritische Theorie: Fünf Aufsätze* (Frankfurt am Main: Fischer, 1992).

6 Rüdiger Bubner, "Kann Theorie ästhetisch werden? Zum Hauptmotiv der Philosophie Adornos," in *Konstruktion der Moderne,* pp. 108–37. Quotation is on p. 114.

7 Max Horkheimer and Theodor W. Adorno, *Dialektik der Aufklärung* (Frankfurt am Main: Fischer, 1971), p. 2.

8 See Christoph Menke-Eggers, *Die Souveränität der Kunst: Ästhetische Erfahrung nach Adorno und Derrida* (Frankfurt am Main: Atheäum, 1988), p. 12: "The concept of aesthetic negativity is the key to understanding the double function of modern art for Adorno: It is aesthetic discourse next to other discourses and simultaneously a subversion of the reason of all discourses." Menke-Eggers does not see the basic duplicity of art in its nature as both autonomous and socially determined, but rather in the tension between modern artistic autonomy *pari passu* with other discourses and Romantic aesthetic superiority over all expressions of rationality.

9 Walter Benjamin, *Gesammelte Schriften* I, Book 2 (Frankfurt am Main: Suhrkamp, 1991). I am quoting from the third version of the essay, pp. 471–508. Quotations are on pp. 479 ff.

10 Jürgen Habermas, "Zwischen Kunst und Politik: Eine Auseinandersetzung mit Walter Benjamin," *Merkur* 9 (1972): 856–69. Reference is on p. 858.

11 Ibid., p. 859.

12 "Résumé über Kulturindustrie," in *Ohne Leitbild. Gesammelte Schriften* 10, Book 1 (Frankfurt am Main: Suhrkamp, 1977), pp. 337–45. Reference is on p. 338. Compare also *Dialektik der Aufklärung,* p. 108.

13 *Dialektik der Aufklärung,* p. 130.

14 "Über den Fetischcharakter in der Musik," in *Dissonanzen,* in *Gesammelte Schriften* 14 (Frankfurt am Main: Suhrkamp, 1991) pp. 14–50. Quotation is on p. 34.

15 "Résumé über Kulturindustrie," p. 345.

16 "Zeitlose Mode: Zum Jazz" in *Prismen,* in *Gesammelte Schriften* 10, Book 1, pp. 123–37.

17 Wolfgang Sandner, in his article "Popularmusik als somatisches Stimulans: Adornos Kritik der 'leichten Musik,' " argues convincingly that Adorno has a rather simplified notion of jazz music and uses the term oftentimes to refer to commercial dance hall music. In Otto Kolleritsch, ed., *Adorno und die Musik* (Graz: Universal Edition, 1979), pp. 125–32.
18 *Ästhetische Theorie* (Frankfurt am Main: Suhrkamp, 1992), p. 16.
19 *Philosophie der neuen Musik* (Frankfurt am Main: Suhrkamp, 1991), p. 37.
20 See also Karol Sauerland, *Einführung in die Ästhetik Adornos* (Berlin and New York: de Gruyter, 1979), pp. 54 ff.
21 "Die Kunst und die Künste," in *Ohne Leitbild, Parva Aesthetica, Gesammelte Schriften* 10 , Book 1, pp. 432–49. Quotation is on p. 450.
22 Josef Früchtl's dissertation *Mimesis: Konstellation eines Zentralbegriffs bei Adorno* traces the many implications of this concept in Adorno's philosophy. A good overview of the complexity of this notion is provided by the graphic representation on p. 276. (Würzburg: Könighausen und Neumann, 1986).
23 *Negative Dialektik*, p. 387.
24 Compare *Negative Dialektik*, p. 25.
25 "Wahrheit, Schein, Versöhnung: Adornos ästhetische Rettung der Moderne," in *Adorno-Konferenz 1983*, pp. 138–76. Quotation is on p. 143.
26 See also Günter Figal's dissertation, *Theodor W. Adorno: Das Naturschöne als spekulative Gedankenfigur* (Bonn: Bouvier, 1977).
27 *Minima Moralia: Reflexionen aus dem beschädigten Leben*, 20th ed. (Frankfurt am Main: Suhrkamp, 1991), p. 299.
28 Ibid., p. 298.
29 "Rede über Lyrik und Gesellschaft," *Noten zur Literatur*, pp. 49–68. Quotation is on p. 56.
30 *Negative Dialektik*, p. 389. Adorno repeats the statement in *Ästhetische Theorie*, p. 317.
31 "Bach gegen seine Liebhaber verteidigt," in *Prismen*, in *Gesammelte Schriften* 10, Book 1, pp. 138–51.
32 See also Rolf Wiggershaus, 2d ed., *Adorno* (Munich: Beck, 1998), p. 121.
33 See also Rüdiger Bubner, "Kann Theorie ästhetisch werden? Zum Hauptmotiv der Philosophie Adornos," p. 129.

Bibliography

Adams, Hazard. "Thinking Cassirer." *Criticism* 25, no. 3 (1983): 181–95.

Adorno, Theodor W. *Kierkegaard: Konstruktion des Ästhetischen.* Frankfurt am Main: Suhrkamp, 1962.

Gesammelte Schriften. 13. vols. Frankfurt am Main: Suhrkamp, 1977.

Minima Moralia: Reflexionen aus dem beschädigten Leben. 20th ed. Frankfurt am Main: Suhrkamp, 1991.

Philosophie der neuen Musik. Frankfurt am Main: Suhrkamp, 1991.

Ästhetische Theorie. Frankfurt am Main: Suhrkamp, 1992.

Negative Dialektik. 9th ed. Frankfurt am Main: Suhrkamp, 1997.

Noten zur Literatur. 7th ed. Frankfurt am Main: Suhrkamp, 1998.

Althaus, Horst. *Hegel und die heroischen Jahre der Philosophie.* Munich: Hanser, 1992.

Ansell-Peterson, Keith, ed. *Nietzsche and Modern German Thought.* London and New York: Routledge, 1991.

Anton, Herbert, ed. *Invaliden des Apoll: Motive und Mythen des Dichterleids.* Munich: Fink, 1982.

Bahr, Hans-Dieter. *Das gefesselte Engagement: Zur Ideologie der kontemplativen Ästhetik Schopenhauers.* Bonn: Bouvier, 1970.

Bailey, R. W., L. Matejka, and P. Steiner, eds. *The Sign: Semiotics around the World.* Ann Arbor: Michigan Slavic Publications, 1978.

Bartky, Sandra Lee. "Heidegger's Philosophy of Art." In Thomas Sheehan, ed. *Heidegger: The Man and the Thinker.* Chicago: Precedent Publishing, 1981, pp. 257–74.

Baumgarten, Alexander Gottlieb. *Theoretische Ästhetik: Die grundlegenden Abschnitte aus der "Aesthetica" (1750/1758).* Hamburg: Meiner, 1983.

Baumgartner, Hans Michael, and Harald Korten. *Friedrich Wilhelm Joseph Schelling.* Munich: Beck, 1996.

Baur, H., L. Dittmann, et al. eds. *Kunstgeschichte und Kunsttheorie im 19. Jahrhundert.* Berlin: de Gruyter, 1963.

Behler, Ernst. *Studien zur Romantik und zur idealistischen Philosophie.* Paderborn: Schöningh, 1988.

Beierwaltes, Werner. "Einleitung." In F. W. J. Schelling. *Texte zur Theorie der Kunst.* Stuttgart: Reclam, 1982, pp. 3–35.

Beiser, Frederick C. *The Fate of Reason: German Philosophy from Kant to Fichte.* Cambridge, Mass.: Harvard University Press, 1987.

Benjamin, Walter. *Gesammelte Schriften.* 7 vols. Frankfurt am Main: Suhrkamp, 1991.

Benseler, Frank, and Werner Jung, eds. *Lukács 1996: Jahrbuch der Internationalen Georg-Lukács-Gesellschaft.* Bern: Peter Lang, 1997.

Bernstein, J. M. *The Fate of Art: Aesthetic Alienation from Kant to Derrida and Adorno.* University Park, Pa.: Penn State University Press, 1992.

Biemel, Walter. *Heidegger.* Reinbeck: Rowohlt, 1973.

Bloch, Ernst. *Subjekt-Objekt: Erläuterungen zu Hegel.* Frankfurt am Main: Suhrkamp, 1985.

Böhler, Michael J. "Die Bedeutung Schillers für Hegels Ästhetik." *PMLA* 87 (1972): 182–91.

Bolten, Jürgen, ed. *Schillers Briefe über die ästhetische Erziehung.* Frankfurt am Main: Suhrkamp, 1984.

Bowie, Andrew. *Schelling and Modern European Philosophy: An Introduction.* London and New York: Routledge, 1993.

Brummack, Jürgen et al., eds. *Literaturwissenschaft und Geistesgeschichte: FS für Richard Brinkmann.* Tübingen: Niemeyer, 1981.

Bubner, Rüdiger. "Über einige Bedingungen gegenwärtiger Ästhetik." *Neue Hefte für Philosophie* 5 (1973): 38–73.

"Hegel's Aesthetics: Yesterday and Today." In Warren Steinkraus and Kenneth Schmitz, eds. *Art and Logic in Hegel's Philosophy.* Atlantic Highlands, N.J.: Humanities Press and Sussex: Harvester Press, 1980, pp. 15–33.

"Kann Theorie ästhetisch werden? Zum Hauptmotiv der Philosophie Adornos." In Burkhard Lindner and W. Martin Lüdke, eds., *Konstruktion der Moderne: Materialien zur ästhetischen Theorie Theodor W. Adornos.* Frankfurt am Main: Suhrkamp, 1980, pp. 108–37.

"Adornos Negative Dialektik." In J. Habermas and L. von Friedeburg, eds. *Adorno-Konferenz 1983.* Frankfurt am Main: Suhrkamp, 1983, pp. 35–40.

Innovationen des Idealismus. Göttingen: Vandenhoeck und Ruprecht, 1995.

Buckman, Kenneth. "Gadamer on Art, Morality, and Authority." *Philosophy and Literature* 21 (1997): 144–50.

Bungay, Stephen. *Beauty and Truth: A Study of Hegel's Aesthetics.* Oxford: Oxford University Press, 1984.

Bürger, Peter. *Zur Kritik der idealistischen Ästhetik.* Frankfurt am Main: Suhrkamp, 1990.

Burke, Edmund. *A Philosophical Enquiry into the Origin of our Ideas of the Sublime and Beautiful.* Oxford: Oxford University Press, 1990.

Carter, Curtis L. "A Reexamination of the 'Death of Art' Interpretation of Hegel's Aesthetics." In Lawrence S. Stepelevich, ed. *Selected Essays on G. W. F. Hegel.* Atlantic Highlands, N.J.: Humanities Press, 1993, pp. 11–26.

Cassirer, Ernst. *An Essay on Man: An Introduction to a Philosophy of Human Culture.* New Haven, Conn.: Yale University Press, 1944.

Symbol, Myth, and Culture: Essays and Lectures 1935–1945. New Haven, Conn.: Yale University Press, 1979.

Kant's Life and Thought. New Haven, Conn.: Yale University Press, 1981.

Castiglione, Baldassare. *The Book of the Courtier.* London: Penguin, 1976.

Cheetham, Mark A. *Kant, Art and Art History: Moments of Discipline.* Cambridge: Cambridge University Press, 2001.

Chytry, Josef. *The Aesthetic State: A Quest in Modern German Thought.* Berkeley: University of California Press, 1989.

Clark, Maudemarie. *Nietzsche on Truth and Philosophy.* Cambridge: Cambridge University Press, 1990.

Cohen, Ted, and Paul Guyer, eds. *Essays in Kant's Aesthetics.* Chicago: Chicago University Press, 1982.

Crow, Dennis. "Form and the Unification of Aesthetics and Ethics in Lukács' *Soul and Forms.*" *New German Critique* 15 (1978): 159–77.

Danto, Arthur. *Beyond the Brillo Box: The Visual Arts in Post-Historical Perspective.* Berkeley: University of California Press, 1992.

Desmond, William. *Art and the Absolute: A Study of Hegel's Aesthetics.* Albany: State University of New York Press, 1986.

Deveraux, Mary. "Can Art Save Us? A Meditation of Gadamer." *Philosophy and Literature* 15 (1991): 59–73.

Dittmann, Lorenz. "Schellings Philosophie der Bildenden Kunst." In H. Baur, L. Dittmann, et al., eds. *Kunstgeschichte und Kunsttheorie im 19. Jahrhundert.* Berlin: de Guyer, 1963, pp. 38–82.

Eco, Umberto, with Richard Rorty, Jonathan Culler, and Christine Brook-Rose. *Interpretation and Overinterpretation,* ed. Stefan Collini. Cambridge: Cambridge University Press, 1992.

Faden, Gerhard. *Der Schein der Kunst: Zu Heideggers Kritik der Ästhetik.* Würzburg: Könighausen und Neumann, 1986.

Fichte, Johann Gottlieb. *Gesamtausgabe.* 36 vols. Stuttgart: Frommann, 1981.

Werke. 2 vols. Frankfurt am Main: Deutscher Klassiker Verlag, 1997.

Figal, Günter. *Theodor W. Adorno: Das Naturschöne als spekulative Gedankenfigur.* Bonn: Bouvier, 1977.

Fish, Stanley. *Is There a Text in This Class?* Cambridge, Mass.: Harvard University Press, 1980.

Foucault, Michel. *The Order of Things: An Archaeology of the Human Sciences.* New York: Vintage, 1994.

Frank, Manfred. *Der kommende Gott: Vorlesungen über die Neue Mythologie.* Frankfurt am Main: Suhrkamp, 1982.

Eine Einführung in Schellings Philosophie. Frankfurt am Main: Suhrkamp, 1985.

Einführung in die frühromantische Ästhetik. Frankfurt am Main: Suhrkamp, 1989.

Frank, Manfred, and Gerhard Kurz, eds. *Materialien zu Schellings philosophischen Anfängen.* Frankfurt am Main: Suhrkamp, 1975.

Franke, Ursula. "Das Hässliche." In *Historisches Wörterbuch der Philosophie.* Darmstadt: Wissenschaftliche Buchgesellschaft, 1971.

Kunst als Erkenntnis: Die Rolle der Sinnlichkeit in der Ästhetik des Alexander Gottlieb Baumgarten. Wiesbaden: Franz Steiner, 1972.

Früchtl, Josef. *Mimesis: Konstellation eines Zentralbegriffs bei Adorno.* Würzburg: Könighausen und Neumann, 1986.

Ästhetische Erfahrung und moralisches Urteil: Eine Rehabilitierung. Frankfurt am Main: Suhrkamp, 1996.

Gadamer, Hans-Georg. "Zur Einführung." Introduction in Martin Heidegger. *Der Ursprung des Kunstwerks.* Stuttgart: Reclam, 1960, pp. 93–114.

Wahrheit und Methode. 6th ed. Tübingen: Mohr and Siebeck, 1990.

Kunst als Aussage. Tübingen: Mohr and Siebeck, 1993.

Hermeneutische Entwürfe. Tübingen: Mohr and Siebeck, 2000.

Gehlen, Arnold. *Zeit-Bilder: Zur Soziologie und Ästhetik der modernen Malerei.* 3d enlarged ed. Frankfurt am Main: Klostermann, 1986.

George, Emery E. "Ernst Cassirer and Neo-Kantian Aesthetics: A Holistic Approach to the Problems of Language and Art." In R. W. Bailey, L. Matejka, and P. Steiner, eds. *The Sign: Semiotics around the World.* Ann Arbor: Michigan Slavic Productions, 1978, pp. 132–45.

Gethmann-Siefert, Annemarie. "Schöne Kunst und Prosa des Lebens: Hegels Rehabilitierung des ästhetischen Genusses." In Christopher Jamme, ed. *Kunst und Geschichte im Zeitalter Hegels.* Hamburg: Meiner, 1996, pp. 115–50.

"Einleitung: Gestalt und Wirkung von Hegels Ästhetik." In G. W. F. Hegel. *Vorlesungen über die Philosophie der Kunst.* Hamburg: Meiner, 1998, pp. xv–ccxxiv.

Goethe, Johann Wolfgang. *Werke.* 14 vols. (Hamburger Ausgabe). Munich: Deutscher Taschenbuch Verlag, 1988.

Goldmann, Lucien. "The Aesthetics of the Young Lukács." *New Hungarian Quarterly* 47 (1972): 129–35.

Gombrich, E. H. *Norm and Form: Studies in the Art of the Renaissance.* London: Phaidon, 1966.

"Hegel und die Kunstgeschichte." *Neue Rundschau* 2 (1977): 202–19.

Goodman, Nelson. *Languages of Art: An Approach to the Theory of Symbols.* Indianapolis and New York: Bobbs-Merrill, 1968.

Grondin, Jean, ed. *Gadamer Lesebuch.* Munich: Fink, 1997.

Guyer, Paul. *Essays in Kant's Aesthetics.* Chicago: Chicago University Press, 1982.

Kant and the Experience of Freedom. Cambridge: Cambridge University Press, 1993.

"Pleasure and Knowledge in Schopenhauer's Aesthetics." In D. Jaquette, ed. *Schopenhauer, Philosophy, and the Arts.* Cambridge: Cambridge University Press, 1996, pp. 109–32.

Kant and the Claims of Taste. Cambridge: Cambridge University Press, 1997.

Habermas, Jürgen. "Zwischen Kunst und Politik: Eine Auseinandersetzung mit Walter Benjamin." *Merkur* 9 (1972): 856–69.

Der philosophische Diskurs der Moderne. Frankfurt am Main: Suhrkamp, 1985.

Theorie des kommunikativen Handelns. 2 vols. Frankfurt am Main: Suhrkamp, 1995.
Habermas, J. and L. von Friedeburg, eds. *Adorno-Konferenz 1983.* Frankfurt am Main: Suhrkamp, 1983.
Hamann, Johann Georg. *Sokratische Denkwürdigkeiten: Aesthetica in nuce.* Stuttgart: Reclam, 1968.
Hammermeister, Kai. *Hans-Georg Gadamer.* Munich: Beck, 1999.
"*Heimat* in Heidegger and Gadamer." *Philosophy and Literature* 24, no. 2 (2000): 312–26.
"Hegel, Heidegger und die Architektur." *Weimarer Beiträge* 3 (2001): 433–46.
Harries, Karsten. *The Meaning of Modern Art: A Philosophical Investigation.* Evanston, Ill.: Northwestern University Press, 1968.
"Hegel on the Future of Art." *The Review of Metaphysics* (1974): 677–96.
Hauser, Arnold. *Sozialgeschichte der Kunst und Literatur.* Munich: Beck, 1990.
Hedley, Douglas. "Schelling and Heidegger: The Mythical Legacy and Romantic Affinities." In Tom Rockmore, ed. *Heidegger, German Idealism and Neo-Kantianism.* New York: Humanity Books, 2000, pp. 141–56.
Heftrich, Ulrich. "Nietzsches Auseinandersetzung mit der 'Kritik der Urteilskraft.' " *Nietzsche-Studien* 20 (1991): 238–66.
Hegel, G. W. F. *Werke.* 20 vols. Frankfurt am Main: Suhrkamp, 1970.
Vorlesungen über Ästhetik. Frankfurt am Main: Peter Lang, 1995.
Vorlesungen über die Philosophie der Kunst. Hamburg: Meiner, 1998.
Heidegger, Martin. *Vorträge und Aufsätze.* Pfullingen: Neske, 1954.
Holzwege. Frankfurt am Main: Klostermann, 1980.
Sein und Zeit. 16th ed. Tübingen: Niemeyer, 1986.
"Cezanne." *Jahresgabe* der Heidegger-Gesellschaft 1991.
Nietzsche. 2 vols. Frankfurt am Main: Klostermann, 1996.
Der Ursprung des Kunstwerks. Stuttgart: Reclam, 1997.
Heller, Agnes. "Lukács' Aesthetics." *New Hungarian Quarterly* 24 (1966): 84–94.
Henrich, Dieter. "Der Begriff des Schönen in Schillers Ästhetik." *Zeitschrift für philosophische Forschung* 6 (1957): 527–47.
"Hölderlin über Urteil und Sein: Eine Studie zur Entwicklungsgeschichte des Idealismus." *Hölderlin Jahrbuch* 14 (1965–6): 73–96.
Hegel im Kontext. Frankfurt am Main: Suhrkamp, 1971.
"Beauty and Freedom: Schiller's Struggle with Kant's Aesthetics." In Ted Cohen and Paul Guyer, eds. *Essays in Kant's Aesthetics.* Chicago: Chicago University Press, 1982, pp. 237–57.
Der Grund im Bewusstsein: Untersuchungen zu Hölderlins Denken (1794–1795). Stuttgart: Klett-Cotta, 1992.
Herrmann, Friedrich-Wilhem von. *Heideggers Philosophie der Kunst: Eine systematische Interpretation der Holzwege Abhandlung "Der Ursprung des Kunstwerks."* Frankfurt am Main: Klostermann, 1980.
Heyse, K. W. L. *Vorlesungen über Ästhetik.* Darmstadt: Wissenschaftliche Buchgesellschaft, 1969.
Hofe, Gerhard vom. "Kunst als Grenze: Hegels Theorem des 'unglücklichen Bewusstseins' und die ästhetische Erfahrung bei Kierkegaard." In Herbert

Anton, ed. *Invaliden des Apoll: Motive und Mythen des Dichterleids.* Munich: Fink, 1982.

Hogarth, William. *The Analysis of Beauty.* New Haven, Conn.: Yale University Press, 1997.

Hogrebe, Wilhelm. "Fichte und Schiller: Eine Skizze." In J. Bolten, ed. *Schillers Briefe über die ästhetische Erziehung.* Frankfurt am Main: Suhrkamp, 1984.

Hohendahl, Peter Uwe. *Prismatic Thought: Theodor W. Adorno.* Lincoln: University of Nebraska Press, 1990.

Hölderlin, Friedrich. *Grosse Stuttgarter Ausgabe.* 8 vols. Stuttgart: Kohlhammer, 1960.

Sämtliche Werke und Briefe. 2 vols. Munich: Hanser, 1970.

Hörisch, Jochen. "Herrscherwort, Geld und geltende Sätze: Adornos Aktualisierung der Frühromantik und ihre Affinität zur poststrukturalistischen Kritik des Subjekts." In Burkhard Lindner and W. Martin Lüdke, eds. *Konstruktion der Moderne: Materialien zur ästhetischen Theorie Theodor W. Adornos.* Frankfurt am Main: Suhrkamp, 1980, pp. 397–414.

Horkheimer, Max. *Traditionelle und kritische Theorie: Fünf Aufsätze.* Frankfurt am Main: Fischer, 1992.

Horkheimer, Max, and Theodor W. Adorno. *Dialektik der Aufklärung.* Frankfurt am Main: Fischer, 1971.

Hösle, Vittorio. *Hegels System: Der Idealismus der Subjektivität und das Problem der Intersubjektivität.* 2 vols. Hamburg: Meiner, 1987.

Hübscher, Arthur. "Der Philosoph der Romantik." *Schopenhauer-Jahrbuch* 34 (1951–2): 1–17.

Jähnig. Dieter. "Hegel und die These vom 'Verlust der Mitte.'" In A. M. Koktanek, ed. *Spengler-Studien.* Munich: Beck, 1965, pp. 147–76.

Schelling: Die Kunst in der Philosophie. Vol. 1: *Schellings Begründung von Natur und Geschichte.* Pfullingen: Neske, 1966.

Jameson, Frederic. *Marxism and Form.* Princeton, N.J.: Princeton University Press, 1971.

Janaway, Christopher. *Schopenhauer.* Oxford: Oxford University Press, 1994.

Jaquette, Dale, ed. *Schopenhauer, Philosophy, and the Arts.* Cambridge: Cambridge University Press, 1996.

Jauss, Hans Robert. *Literaturgeschichte als Provokation.* Frankfurt am Main: Suhrkamp, 1970.

Kant, Immanuel. *Werke* (Theorie-Werkausgabe). 12 vols. Frankfurt am Main: Suhrkamp, 1993.

Kemal, Salim. *Kant and Fine Arts.* Oxford: Oxford University Press, 1986.

Kemal, Salim, ed. *Nietzsche, Philosophy, and the Arts.* Cambridge: Cambridge University Press, 1998.

Kempski, Jürgen von. "Zur Ästhetik von Georg Lukács." *Neue Rundschau* (1965): 109–20.

Kierkegaard, Søren, *Works.* 26 vols. Princeton, N. J.: Princeton University Press, 1978 ff.

Kleinschmidt, Sebastian. "Georg Lukács und die Wertabstufungen in der Kunst." *Sinn und Form* 1 (1985): 638–54.

Knox, Israel. *The Aesthetic Theories of Kant, Hegel and Schopenhauer.* New York: Humanities Press, 1958.
Koktanek, A. M., ed. *Spengler-Studien.* Munich: Beck, 1965.
Kolleritsch, Otto, ed. *Adorno und die Musik.* Graz: Universal Edition, 1979.
Kondylis, Panajotis. *Die Entstehung der Dialektik: Eine Analyse der geistigen Entwicklung von Hölderlin, Schelling und Hegel bis 1802.* Stuttgart: Klett-Cotta, 1979.
Krukowski, Lucian. *Aesthetic Legacies.* Philadelphia: Temple University Press, 1992.
Kuhn, Helmut. *Schriften zur Ästhetik.* Munich: Kösel, 1966.
Kuhn, Thomas. *The Structure of Scientific Revolutions.* 2d enlarged ed. Chicago: University of Chicago Press, 1970.
Lacoue-Labarthe, Philippe. *Heidegger, Art and Politics: The Fiction of the Political.* Trans. Chris Turner. Oxford: Basil Blackwell, 1990.
Land, Nick. "Art as Insurrection: The Question of Aesthetics in Kant, Schopenhauer, and Nietzsche." In Keith Ansell-Peterson, ed., *Nietzsche and Modern German Thought* (London and New York: Routledge, 1991), pp. 240–56.
Lang, Peter Christian. *Hermeneutik, Ideologiekritik, Ästhetik: Über Gadamer und Adorno sowie Fragen einer aktuellen Ästhetik.* Königstein: Forum Academicum in der Verlagsgruppe Athenäum, Hain, Scriptor, Hanstein, 1981.
Lehmann, Günther K. *Ästhetik der Utopie.* Stuttgart: Neske, 1995.
Leibniz, Gottfried Wilhelm. *Philosophische Schriften.* Frankfurt am Main: Suhrkamp, 1996.
Lessing, Gotthold Ephraim. *Werke in drei Bänden.* Munich: Hanser, 1982.
Lindner, Burkhard, and Martin W. Lüdke, eds. *Konstruktion der Moderne: Materialien zur ästhetischen Theorie Theodor W. Adornos.* Frankfurt am Main: Suhrkamp, 1980.
Longinus. *Vom Erhabenen.* Griechisch-Deutsch. Trans. Otto Schönberger. Stuttgart: Reclam, 1988.
Lukács, Georg. *Die Theorie des Romans.* Berlin: Paul Cassirer, 1920.
Goethe und seine Zeit. Bern: A. Francke, 1947.
Beiträge zur Geschichte der Ästhetik. Berlin: Aufbau, 1956.
Probleme des Realismus I: Essays über Realismus. Neuwied and Berlin: Luchterhand, 1971.
Ästhetik. 4 vols. Darmstadt and Neuwied: Luchterhand, 1972.
"Ästhetische Kultur." In F. Benseler and W. Jung, eds. *Lukács 1996: Jahrbuch der Internationalen Georg-Lukács-Gesellschaft.* Bern: Peter Lang, 1997, pp. 13–26.
Magnus, Bernd, and Kathleen Higgins, eds. *The Cambridge Companion to Nietzsche.* Cambridge: Cambridge University Press, 1996.
Maker, William, ed. *Hegel and Aesthetics.* Albany: State University of New York Press, 2000.
Marcuse, Herbert. *Eros and Civilization.* Boston: Beacon Press, 1966.
One-Dimensional Man: Studies in the Ideology of Advanced Industrial Society. Boston: Beacon Press, 1966.
An Essay on Liberation. Boston: Beacon Press, 1969.

Counterrevolution and Revolt. Boston: Beacon Press, 1972.
The Aesthetic Dimension: Toward a Critique of Marxist Aesthetics. Boston: Beacon Press, 1978.
Marquard, Odo. "Über einige Beziehungen zwischen Ästhetik und Therapeutik in der Philosophie des neunzehnten Jahrhunderts." In Manfred Frank and Gerhard Kurz, eds., *Materialien zu Schellings philosophischen Anfängen.* Frankfurt am Main: Suhrkamp, 1975, pp. 341–77.
Aesthetica und Anaesthetica: Philosophische Überlegungen. Paderborn: Schöningh, 1989.
Martin, Nicholas. *Nietzsche and Schiller: Untimely Aesthetics.* Oxford: Clarendon Press, 1996.
Marx, Karl. *Grundrisse der Kritik der politischen Ökonomie.* Berlin: Dietz, 1953.
McCloskey, Mary A. *Kant's Aesthetics.* London: Macmillan Press, 1987.
Megill, Alan. "Nietzsche as Aestheticist." *Philosophy and Literature* 5, no. 2 (1981): 204–25.
Prophets of Extremity. Berkeley: University of California Press, 1985.
Mendelssohn, Moses. *Gesammelte Schriften.* 16 vols. Berlin: Akademie-Ausgabe, 1929.
Menke, Christoph. *Die Souveränität der Kunst: Ästhetische Erfahrung nach Adorno und Derrida.* Frankfurt am Main: Athenäum, 1988. English: *The Sovereignity of Art: Aesthetic Negativity in Adorno and Derrida.* Cambridge, Mass.: MIT Press, 1998.
Menninghaus, Winfried. *In Praise of Nonsense: Kant and Bluebeard.* Stanford, Calif.: Stanford University Press, 1999.
Moritz, Karl Philipp. *Beiträge zur Ästhetik.* Mainz: Dieterich'sche Verlagsbuchhandlung, 1989.
Nehamas, Alexander. *Nietzsche: Life as Literature.* Cambridge, Mass.: Harvard University Press, 1985.
"Nietzsche, Modernity, Aestheticism." In Bernd Magnus and Kathleen Higgins, eds., *The Cambridge Campanion to Nietzsche.* Cambridge: Cambridge University Press, 1996, pp. 223–51.
Neymeyr, Barbara, *Ästhetische Autonomie als Abnormität: Kritische Analysen zu Schopenhauers Ästhetik im Horizont seiner Willensmetaphysik.* Berlin and New York: de Gruyter, 1996.
Nicholson, Shierry Weber. *Exact Imagination, Late Work: On Adorno's Aesthetics.* Cambridge, Mass.: MIT Press, 1997.
Nietzsche, Friedrich. *Kritische Studienausgabe.* 15 vols. Munich, Berlin, and New York: Deutscher Taschenbuch Verlag and de Gruyter, 1988.
Novalis. *Schriften.* 6 vols. Stuttgart, Berlin, and Cologne: Kohlhammer, 1960.
Nussbaum, Martha. "The Transfiguration of Intoxication: Nietzsche, Schopenhauer, and Dionysus." In Salim Kemal, ed. *Nietzsche, Philosophy, and the Arts.* Cambridge: Cambridge University Press, 1998, pp. 36–69.
Oelmüller, Willi. *Die unbefriedigte Aufklärung: Beiträge zu einer Philosophie der Moderne von Lessing, Kant und Hegel.* Frankfurt am Main: Suhrkamp, 1969.
Paetzold, Heinz. *Neomarxistische Ästhetik II: Adorno-Marcuse.* Düsseldorf: Pädagogischer Verlag Schwan, 1974.

Ästhetik des deutschen Idealismus. Wiesbaden: Steiner, 1983.

Parret, Herman, ed. *Kants Ästhetik. Kant's Aesthetics. L'esthétique de Kant.* Berlin and New York: de Gruyter, 1998.

Petzet, Heinrich Wiegand. *Auf einen Stern zugehen: Begegnungen mit Martin Heidegger 1929–1976.* Frankfurt am Main: Societäts-Verlag, 1983.

Pillow, Kirk. *Sublime Understanding: Aesthetic Reflection in Kant and Hegel.* Cambridge, Mass.: MIT Press, 2000.

Plato. *The Republic.* Trans. G. M. A. Grube. Indianapolis: Hackett, 1974.

Plotinus, *The Enneads.* Trans. Stephen Mackenna. London: Penguin, 1991.

Pöggeler, Otto. *Der Denkweg Martin Heideggers.* Pfullingen: Neske, 1963.

Philosophie und Politik bei Heidegger. 2d ed. Munich and Freiburg: K. Alber, 1974.

Die Frage nach der Kunst: Von Hegel zu Heidegger. Munich and Freiburg: K. Alber, 1984.

Pothast, Ulrich. *Die eigentlich metaphysische Tätigkeit: Über Schopenhauers Ästhetik und ihre Anwendung durch Samuel Beckett.* Frankfurt am Main: Suhrkamp, 1982.

Rampley, Matthew. *Nietzsche, Aesthetics, and Modernity.* Cambridge: Cambridge University Press, 2000.

Rockmore, Tom, ed. *Heidegger, German Idealism and Neo-Kantianism.* New York: Humanity Books, 2000.

Rorty, Richard. *Contingency, Irony, and Solidarity.* Cambridge: Cambridge University Press, 1989.

"The Pragmatist's Progress." In Umberto Eco, with Richard Rorty, Jonathan Culler, and Christine Brooke-Rose. *Interpretation and Overinterpretation,* ed. Stefan Collini. Cambridge: Cambridge University Press, 1992, pp. 89–108.

Rutten, Pierre van. "L'aristotelisme dans l'esthétique de Lukács." In *Georg Lukács et la théorie littéraire contemporaine.* Montreal: Association des professeurs de français des universités et collège canadiens, 1983, pp. 99–114.

Sallis, John. *Crossings: Nietzsche and the Space of Tragedy.* Chicago: University of Chicago Press, 1991.

Sandner, Wolfgang. "Popularmusik als somatische Stimulanz: Adornos Kritik der 'leichten Musik.'" In Otto Kolleritsch, ed., *Adorno und die Musik.* Graz: Universal Edition, 1979, pp. 125–32.

Sauerland, Karol. *Einführung in die Ästhetik Adornos.* Berlin and New York: de Gruyter, 1979.

Savile, Anthony. *Kantian Aesthetics Pursued.* Edinburgh: Edinburgh University Press, 1993.

Scheer, Brigitte. *Einführung in die philosophische Ästhetik.* Darmstadt: Primus, 1997.

Schelling, Friedrich Wilhem Joseph. *Sämtliche Werke.* 10 vols. Stuttgart and Augsburg: J. G. Cotta, 1856–61.

Texte zur Philosophie der Kunst. Stuttgart: Reclam, 1982.

Ausgewählte Schriften. 6 vols. Frankfurt am Main: Suhrkamp, 1985.

System des transzendentalen Idealismus. Hamburg: Meiner, 1992.

Schiller, Friedrich, *Werke in drei Bänden.* Munich: Hanser, 1966.

Schirmacher, Wolfgang, ed. *Schopenhauer, Nietzsche und die Kunst.* Vienna: Passagen, 1991.

Schlegel, Friedrich. *Kritische Ausgabe.* 35 vols. Paderborn, Munich, Vienna, and Darmstadt: Schöningh and Wissenschaftliche Buchgesellschaft, 1958 ff.

Schriften zur Kunst und Literatur. Munich: Hanser, 1970.

Schmidt, Horst Michael. *Sinnlichkeit und Verstand: Zur philosophischen und poetologischen Begründung von Erfahrung und Urteil in der deutschen Aufklärung (Leibniz, Wolff, Gottsched, Bodmer und Breitinger, Baumgarten).* Munich: Fink, 1982.

Schmidt, Jochen. *Die Geschichte des Genie-Gedankens in der deutschen Literatur, Philosophie und Politik, 1750–1945.* 2 vols. Darmstadt: Wissenschaftliche Buchgesellschaft, 1985.

Schoeps, Julius A. *Moses Mendelssohn.* Königstein: Jüdischer Verlag, 1979.

Schopenhauer, Arthur. *Sämtliche Werke.* 7 vols. Munich: Piper, 1923.

Aphorismen zur Lebensweisheit. Munich: Goldmann, 1978.

Die Welt als Wille und Vorstellung. 2 vols. Stuttgart: Reclam, 1987.

Schulz, Walter. "Die problematische Stellung der Kunst in Schopenhauers Philosophie." In Jürgen Brummack et al., eds., *Literaturwissenschaft und Geistesgeschichte: FS für Richard Brinkmann.* Tübingen: Niemeyer, 1981, pp. 403–15.

"Schopenhauer und Nietzsche: Gemeinsamkeiten und Differenzen." In Wolfgang Schirmacher, ed. *Schopenhauer, Nietzsche und die Kunst.* Vienna: Passagen, 1991, pp. 21–34.

Sedlmayr, Hans. *Verlust der Mitte.* Salzburg: Otto Müller, 1998.

Segreff, Klaus-Werner. *Moses Mendelssohn und die Aufklärungsästhetik im 18. Jahrhundert.* Bonn: Bouvier, 1984.

Shapiro, Meyer. *Theory and Philosophy of Art: Style, Artist, and Society.* New York: George Braziller, 1994.

Sheehan, Thomas, ed. *Heidegger: The Man and the Thinker.* Chicago: Precedent Publishing, 1981.

Silk, M. S., and J. P. Stern. *Nietzsche on Tragedy.* Cambridge: Cambridge University Press, 1981.

Sim, Stuart. *Georg Lukács.* Hertfordshire: Harvester Wheatsheaf, 1994.

Solger, K. W. F. *Erwin: Vier Gespräche über das Schöne und die Kunst.* Munich: Fink, 1970.

Steiner, George. *Martin Heidegger.* Chicago: University of Chicago Press, 1991.

Steinkraus, Warre, and Kenneth Schmitz, eds. *Art and Logic in Hegel's Philosophy.* Atlantic Highlands, N.J.: Humanties Press and Sussex: Harvester Press, 1980.

Stepelevich, Lawrence S., ed. *Selected Essays on G. W. F. Hegel.* Atlantic Highlands, N.J.: Humanities Press, 1993.

Stolniz, Jerome. "Ugliness," in *The Encyclopedia of Philosophy.* New York: Macmillan, 1972.

Szondi, Peter. *Poetik und Geschichtsphilosophie I.* Frankfurt am Main: Suhrkamp, 1974.

Taylor, Charles. *Hegel.* Cambridge: Cambridge University Press, 1975.
Vattimo, Gianni. *The End of Modernity.* Baltimore: Johns Hopkins University Press, 1991.
Vischer, Friedrich Theodor. *Über das Erhabene und Komische.* Frankfurt am Main: Suhrkamp, 1967.
Walsh, Sylvia. *Living Poetically: Kierkegaard's Existential Aesthetics.* University Park, Pa.: Penn State University Press, 1994.
Warnke, Georgia. *Gadamer: Hermeneutics, Tradition and Reason.* Stanford, Calif.: Stanford University Press, 1987.
Wellmer, Albrecht. "Wahrheit, Schein, Versöhnung: Adornos ästhetische Rettung der Moderne." In J. Habermas and L. von Friedeburg, eds. *Adorno-Konferenz 1983.* Frankfurt am Main: Suhrkamp, 1983, pp. 138–76.
Wiggershaus, Rolf. *Adorno.* Munich: Beck, 1998.
Winckelmann, Johann Joachim. *Werke in einem Band.* Berlin and Weimar: Aufbau, 1982.
Wischke, Mirko. *Die Schwäche der Schrift: Zur philosophischen Hermenentik Hans-Georg Gadamers.* Cólogne, Weiar, and Vienna: Böhlan, 2001.
Young, Julian. *Nietzsche's Philosophy of Art.* Cambridge: Cambridge University Press, 1992.
Heidegger's Philosophy of Art. Cambridge: Cambridge University Press, 2001.
Zelle, Carsten. "Das Hässliche," in *Historisches Wörterbuch der Rhetorik.* Tübingen: Niemeyer, 1992.
Zuidervaart, Lambert. *Adorno's Aesthetic Philosophy.* Cambridge, Mass.: MIT Press, 1991.
Zuidervaart, Lambert, ed. *The Semblance of Subjectivity.* Cambridge, Mass.: MIT Press, 1997.

Index